KT-526-097

Learning Wireless Java™

PARK LEARNING CENTRE
UNIVERSITY OF GLOUCESTERSHIRE
P.O. Box 220, The Park
Cheltenham GL50 2RH
Tel: 01242 532721

Qusay H. Mahmoud

Beijing · Cambridge · Farnham · Köln · Paris · Sebastopol · Taipei · Tokyo

Learning Wireless Java™
by Qusay H. Mahmoud

Copyright © 2002 O'Reilly & Associates, Inc. All rights reserved.
Printed in the United States of America.

Published by O'Reilly & Associates, Inc., 1005 Gravenstein Highway North, Sebastopol, CA 95472.

O'Reilly & Associates books may be purchased for educational, business, or sales promotional use. Online editions are also available for most titles (*safari.oreilly.com*). For more information, contact our corporate/institutional sales department: (800) 998-9938 or *corporate@oreilly.com*.

Editor:	Robert Eckstein
Production Editor:	Claire Cloutier
Cover Designer:	Ellie Volckhausen
Interior Designer:	Melanie Wang

Printing History:

January 2002:	First Edition.

Nutshell Handbook, the Nutshell Handbook logo, and the O'Reilly logo are registered trademarks of O'Reilly & Associates, Inc. Java™ and all Java-based trademarks and logos are trademarks or registered trademarks of Sun Microsystems, Inc., in the United States and other countries. O'Reilly & Associates, Inc. is independent of Sun Microsystems. Many of the designations used by manufacturers and sellers to distinguish their products are claimed as trademarks. Where those designations appear in this book, and O'Reilly & Associates, Inc. was aware of a trademark claim, the designations have been printed in caps or initial caps. The association between the image of a galago lemur and the topic of wireless Java is a trademark of O'Reilly & Associates, Inc.

While every precaution has been taken in the preparation of this book, the publisher assumes no responsibility for errors or omissions, or for damages resulting from the use of the information contained herein.

ISBN: 0-596-00243-2
[M]

Table of Contents

Part III.   API Quick Reference

Preface

Most Internet technologies are designed for desktop computers or enterprise servers running on reliable networks with relatively high bandwidth. Handheld wireless devices, on the other hand, have a more constrained computing environment. They tend to have less memory, less powerful CPUs, different input devices, and smaller displays.

Since the mid-1990s, various architectures and protocols have been introduced to deal with these constraints. The Wireless Application Protocol (or WAP), which is a specification developed by the WAP Forum (*http://www.wapforum.org*), takes advantage of several data-handling approaches already in use. Developing wireless applications using WAP technologies is similar to developing Web pages with a markup language (e.g., HTML or XML) because WAP technologies are browser-based.

Another approach to developing wireless applications is to use the Java 2 Platform, Micro Edition (J2ME™). The Java™ programming language already plays an important role in modern programming. With WAP, you can use Java servlets and JavaServer Pages™ to generate Wireless Markup Language (WML) pages dynamically. However, with J2ME, you can now write applications in Java and store them directly on a cell phone. This adds a whole new dimension to wireless programming.

Audience

This book is about programming with J2ME on wireless devices. If you're already familiar with the architecture, you probably noticed that the Connected Limited Device Configuration (CLDC) and the Mobile Information Device Profile (MIDP) classes are not large. Therefore, this book is correspondingly compact in size. The book acts as a quick guide for programmers who are familiar with the Java 2 Standard Edition (J2SE™) and want to get up to speed quickly with the J2ME. We assume that you are familiar with Java programming and have worked with the J2SE classes. In addition, we assume that you are familiar with setting up Java to work under various environments (Windows or Unix platforms), as well as compiling and running Java applications.

The book also serves as a quick reference for Java programmers who are interested in developing wireless software applications. The examples presented throughout the book are a good starting point for working with all the MIDP features, including user interface, networking, and databases. However, we should point out that this book is *not* a rehash of the entire J2SE class library. Several of the classes of java.io, java. lang, and java.net are included in the CLDC and MIDP libraries, but are less bulky than their J2SE counterparts. We assume that you already know how to use these classes, although we have included them in the API reference for completeness.

Contents of This Book

This book is divided into three parts. Part I, *Introducing Java 2 Platform, Micro Edition (J2ME)*, gives an overview of the J2ME and includes information about its architectural components: namely, configurations and profiles. Part I also presents detailed coverage of the CLDC and the MIDP.

Chapter 1, *Overview of J2ME*
> This chapter introduces the J2ME environment and also explains configurations and profiles. In addition, it shows you how to set up the J2ME Wireless Toolkit to compile, preverify, and run a simple MIDlet using the command line with the Wireless Toolkit emulator.

Chapter 2, *The Connected Limited Device Configuration (CLDC)*
> This chapter discusses the CLDC, including its requirements, limitations, and the differences between its classes and the classes of the J2SE. In addition, it looks briefly at the standalone CLDC and KVM distribution.

Chapter 3, *The Mobile Information Device Profile (MIDP)*
> This chapter introduces the requirements, limitations, and classes of the MIDP, as well as introducing MIDlets and their associated Java Application Descriptor (JAD) files.

Part II, *Programming with the CLDC and the MIDP*, contains programming details of the MIDP. It shows you how to program the phone interface, handle events, make network connections, and work with databases.

Chapter 4, *Working with MIDlets*
> This chapter picks up where Chapter 3 left off, explaining the MIDlet lifecycle methods, the Java application manager, and showing how to use the KToolbar application inside the J2ME Wireless Toolkit to simplify MIDlet development. We also discuss how to deploy MIDlets and include step-by-step instructions on how to download a MIDlet into a Motorola i85s or i50x J2ME-enabled phone.

Chapter 5, *MIDP GUI Programming*

This chapter introduces the MIDP GUI model and its associated classes. In addition, it gives detailed coverage of both the high-level and low-level MIDP GUI APIs.

Chapter 6, *MIDP Events*

This chapter continues the discussion of the MIDP GUI APIs by describing how various events take place surrounding the graphical components and commands. In addition, we cover the `CommandListener` and `ItemStateListener` interfaces, as well as low-level event handling.

Chapter 7, *Networking*

This chapter discusses the Generic Connection Framework provided by the CLDC and shows how to implement an HTTP connection across the Internet, using a MIDlet. The chapter also includes examples of how to send data to CGI scripts and Java servlets across a network. Finally, the chapter briefly discusses wireless session tracking and security for MIDlet data traveling across the airwaves.

Chapter 8, *Database Programming*

This chapter introduces the concept of data stores, which are simple databases that MIDP applications can use to store persistent data beyond the lifetime of the MIDlet that created them. In addition, the chapter includes a MIDlet that can be used to download stock information from a remote web site.

Chapter 9, *The MIDP for Palm OS*

This chapter gives a quick introduction to the MIDP implementation on the Palm Connected Organizers, including step-by-step instructions on how to deploy MIDlets to a PalmPilot.

Part III, *API Quick Reference*, contains several chapters that are quick references for the J2ME CLDC and MIDP APIs. There is also an appendix that contains bibliographic information and URLs to J2ME specifications, white papers, wireless software development kits, and other information that is important to developers.

Conventions Used in This Book

This book uses the following typographical conventions:

A `Constant Width` font is used for:

- Anything that might appear in a Java program, including keywords, data types, constants, method names, objects, variables, class names, and interface names
- All Java code examples
- Attributes that might appear in a manifest or JAD file

An *italic* font is used for:

- New terms where they are defined
- Pathnames, filenames, directory names, and program names (unless the program name is the name of a Java class; then it appears in constant width, like other class names)
- Internet addresses, such as domain names, URLs, and email addresses

A **boldface** font is used for:

- Example lines of Java code to which we wish to draw attention

Comments and Questions

The information in this book has been tested and verified, but you may find that features or libraries have changed, or you may even find mistakes. You can send any errors you find, as well as suggestions for future editions, to:

O'Reilly and Associates, Inc.
1005 Gravenstein Highway North
Sebastopol, CA 95472
(800) 998-9938 (in the United States or Canada)
(707) 829-0515 (international/local)
(707) 829-0104 (fax)

You can also send electronic messages. To be put on the mailing list or to request a catalog, send email to:

info@oreilly.com

To ask technical questions or comment on the book, send email to:

bookquestions@oreilly.com

I would be pleased to receive feedback on this book. You can contact me by email at:

qmahmoud@javacourses.com

The O'Reilly web site for this book is located at *http://www.oreilly.com/catalog/wirelessjava* and contains all the source examples for this book.

In addition, we have created another web site, *http://www.javacourses.com/wireless*, that includes links to material that supports the use of this book for training and personal study. This web site provides the following supplements:

- Additional source code for new applications
- Links to online J2ME material, and information on other related books
- J2ME tips and tricks

- A set of overhead projector transparencies for instructors interested in using the book in their training courses
- Up-to-date information on topics presented in the book

Acknowledgments

I am deeply grateful to my editor, Robert Eckstein, for all his comments, suggestions, and guidelines throughout the development of this book. I did not know about all the contributions an editor can make to a book until I worked with Bob. Thanks, Bob! Thanks also to the production team at O'Reilly for their hard work on this book.

Special thanks also to Monica Pawlan, Jenny Pratt, Dana Nouri, and Laureen Hudson of the Java Developer Connection (JDC), who either provided comments or edited some of the examples used in this book when they first appeared on the JDC. Also, thanks to the thousands of JDC members who sent in comments and suggestions regarding my articles. Thanks also to the following people who reviewed the contents of this book for accuracy: Ben Griffin, Marc Loy, and Jeff Cunningham.

I would also like to thank my family for their support during my studies, especially my brother, Dr. Mohammad H. Hamdan, for teaching me the value of hard work.

Finally, thanks to my wife, Reema, for her love, support, tolerance, and coffee, and my baby son Yusef, who was born on October 14, 2001, for providing a fun home environment while I finished this book.

Introducing Java 2 Platform, Micro Edition (J2ME)

Part I is an introduction to the Java 2 Micro Edition (J2ME) and J2ME programming. These chapters will give you an overview of the J2ME, and quickly teach you everything you need to know to get started with J2ME programming.

CHAPTER 1

Overview of J2ME

This book is about wireless Java programming with the Java 2 Platform, Micro Edition (J2ME). Sun Microsystems, Inc. introduced J2ME at the JavaOne conference in June 1999 as the younger sibling of both the Java 2 Standard Edition (J2SE) and the Java 2 Enterprise Edition (J2EE). At the time, distributed programming was taking the Java developer community by storm, so most of the participants at the show were more interested in what J2EE had to offer. However, over the next two years, developers also realized that there was tremendous value in having small components running Java. Two years later, at the 2001 JavaOne conference, Sun devoted an entire track for individuals seeking to master the once arcane J2ME. Luckily, you don't need to attend JavaOne to learn about J2ME. Instead, this book will help you through the myriad details of understanding J2ME architecture and programming J2ME applications.

In this chapter, we will present an overview of J2ME's primary components, including virtual machines, configurations, and profiles. We'll then present a few short examples of J2ME-enabled applications to whet your appetite and to show you how easy it is to get started with J2ME.

What Is J2ME?

J2ME is a version of Sun Microsystems' Java that is aimed at the consumer and embedded devices market, which includes electronic commodities such as cellular telephones, pagers, Personal Digital Assistants (PDAs), set-top boxes, and other small devices. Since its release, over 600 companies have joined the development effort, including large corporations such as Palm, Nokia, Motorola, and RIM. However, the direction that J2ME travels is not shrouded in secrecy behind closed corporate doors. Instead, development of J2ME is handled through the Java Community Process (JCP), which allows anyone with an Internet connection to get involved.

J2ME provides a complete set of solutions for creating state-of-the-art networked applications for small devices. It also promises to enable device manufacturers, service providers, and application developers to deploy new applications and services to their customers. However, in doing so, it does not sacrifice some of the founding guidelines of Java, which have become increasingly important these days, namely cross-platform compatibility and security.

A High-Level View

From a high-level view, J2ME defines the following components:

- A series of Java virtual machines, each for use on different types of small devices, each with different requirements
- A group of libraries and APIs that can be run under each of the virtual machines; these are known as *configurations* and *profiles*
- Various tools for deployment and device configuration

The first two components make up the *J2ME runtime environment*. Figure 1-1 provides a relational view of the runtime environment. At its heart is a Java virtual machine, which runs on top of a device's host operating system. Above that is a specific J2ME configuration, which consists of programming libraries that provide basic functionality based on the resource requirements of the device. On top of the configuration are one or more J2ME profiles, which are additional programming libraries that take advantage of kindred functionalities on similar devices.

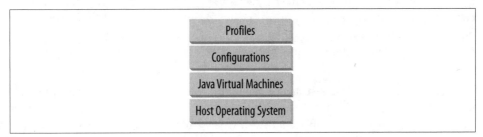

Figure 1-1. The high-level architecture of J2ME runtime environment

If you haven't worked with J2ME before, you're probably wondering about the top two layers. It's important to distinguish between a configuration and a profile in the J2ME world, so let's introduce them now.

Configurations

Cellular telephones, pagers, organizers, and other small devices are diverse in form, functionality, and feature. However, they often use similar processors and have similar amounts of memory. For these reasons, the J2ME designers created *configurations*. Configurations define a horizontal grouping of products based on the available memory budget and processing power of each device. Once this information is known, the configuration then outlines the following:

- The Java programming language features supported
- The Java virtual machine features supported
- The basic Java libraries and APIs supported

Currently, there are two standard configurations in the J2ME world: the *Connected Limited Device Configuration* (CLDC) and the *Connected Device Configuration* (CDC). Let's look at the CDC first.

The CDC

The CDC is targeted toward powerful devices that are intermittently connected to a network, including set-top boxes, Internet TVs, home appliances, and car navigation systems. The CDC contains a full-featured Java virtual machine, similar to that in use today with the J2SE. The difference lies in the respective devices' memory and display capabilities.

Here are the resource requirements for CDC devices, as given by the official J2ME specifications:*

- The device is powered by a 32-bit processor.
- The device has 2 megabytes or more of total memory available for Java. This includes both RAM and flash memory or ROM.
- The device requires the full functionality of the Java 2 "Blue Book" virtual machine.
- The device has connectivity to some kind of network, often with a wireless, intermittent connection and with limited (often 9600 bps or less) bandwidth.
- The device may have a user interface with some degree of sophistication, but a user interface is not mandatory.

The CLDC

The second type of configuration is more prevalent in the J2ME world: the CLDC. This configuration specifies a much smaller footprint for consumer and embedded devices than the CDC. The CLDC was first distributed in October 1999 with the idea of creating a "lowest common denominator" Java platform for embedded devices, specifically in terms of networking, I/O, security, and core libraries. Today, some of the devices that you might find powered by the CLDC include mobile cell phones, two-way pagers, personal digital assistants (PDAs), and personal organizers.

Here are the requirements for the J2ME CLDC, again from the official J2ME specifications:*

---

* The J2ME CDC specifications are located on the Java Community Process web site as JSR-36, which can be found at *http://www.jcp.org/jsr/detail/36.jsp*.

- The device can have between 160 and 512 kilobytes of total memory available for the Java platform, including both RAM and flash memory or ROM.
- The device can have limited power, such as battery-powered operation.
- The device has connectivity to some kind of network, often with a wireless, intermittent connection and with limited (often 9600 bps or less) bandwidth.*
- In addition, the device may have a user interface with some degree of sophistication, but a user interface is not mandatory.

The two products' configurations, along with some of their respective products, are shown in Figure 1-2.

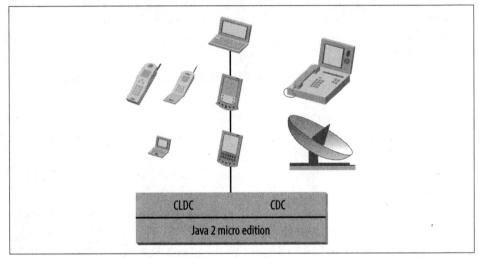

Figure 1-2. J2ME architecture

Note that although the two product groups are supported by different configurations, the line between the two configurations is somewhat blurred. In the future, technological advances will likely make this boundary more and more cloudy. However, for the moment, the important thing to remember is that the boundary between the CLDC and the CDC is defined in terms of the target device's memory budget, battery usage, and the presence or absence of a user interface.

Virtual Machines

As mentioned above, the CLDC and CDC configurations each define their own set of supported features from the Java virtual machine. Consequently, each requires its own Java virtual machine. The CLDC virtual machine is far smaller than the virtual

---

* Note that CLDC stands for *Connected Limited Device Configuration*, not Connectivity-Limited Device Configuration. The difference between the CLDC and the CDC is not in the type or speed of the network connection.

machine required by the CDC, since it supports fewer features. The virtual machine for the CLDC is called the Kilo Virtual Machine (KVM), and the virtual machine for the CDC is called the CVM.

The KVM

The KVM is a complete Java runtime environment for small devices. It's a true Java virtual machine as defined by the Java Virtual Machine Specification, except for some specific deviations that are necessary for proper functioning on small devices. It is specifically designed from the ground up for small, resource-constrained devices with a few hundred kilobytes' total memory.

The KVM was originally created as a research project called "Spotless" at the Sun Microsystems Laboratories. The aim of the virtual machine was to implement a Java virtual machine for the resource-constrained Palm Connected Organizer.*

The CVM

The CVM is designed for larger consumer and embedded devices., such as those found with the CDC. It supports all Java 2 Version 1.3 virtual machine features and libraries for items such as security, weak references, JNI, and Remote Method Invocation (RMI). The reference implementation, currently available from Sun Microsystems, runs on Linux and VxWorks. You can download the reference implementation through the J2ME web site at *http://www.sun.com/j2me*.

Initially, CVM was an acronym for "Compact" Virtual Machine. However, engineers at Sun Microsystems realized that snappy marketers (or poor spellers) may confuse the "compact" in CVM with the K in KVM. So, at present, the C does not stand for anything at all—it is simply known as the CVM.

Profiles

J2ME makes it possible to define Java platforms for vertical product markets by introducing *profiles*. At the implementation level, a profile is a set of APIs that reside on top of a configuration that offers the program access to device-specific capabilities. Following are some examples of profiles that are currently offered through J2ME.

The MIDP

The MIDP is designed to be used with the CLDC, and provides a set of APIs for use by mobile devices, such as cellular phones and two-way pagers. The MIDP contains classes for user interface, persistence storage, and networking. It also includes a standardized runtime environment that allows new applications to be "downloaded" to

---

* In fact, early incarnations of the KVM contained several UI libraries based on the "spotless" graphical toolkit.

end user devices. Small applications that run under the MIDP are called MIDlets. Since this profile is already released, the vast majority of this book is dedicated to the MIDP.

The PDA profile

The PDA profile is based on the CLDC and provides user interface APIs (which are expected to be a subset of the AWT) and data storage APIs for handheld devices. As of this writing, the PDA profile is still in the works and no reference implementation is available yet.

The Foundation profile

The Foundation profile extends the APIs provided by the CDC, but it does not provide any user interface APIs. As the name "foundation" implies, this profile is meant to serve as a foundation for other profiles, such as the Personal profile and the RMI profile.

The Personal profile

The Personal profile extends the Foundation profile to provide a graphical user interface (GUI) capable of running Java Web applets. Since PersonalJava is being redefined as the Personal profile, it will be backward compatible with PersonalJava 1.1 and 1.2 applications. As of this writing, no reference implementation of the Personal profile is available.

The RMI profile

The RMI profile extends the Foundation profile to provide RMI for devices. Since it extends the Foundation profile, the RMI profile is meant to be used with the CDC/Foundation and not the CLDC/MIDP. The RMI profile will be compatible with J2SE RMI API 1.2.x or higher. However, as of this writing, no reference implementation is available yet.

Figure 1-3 shows a global snapshot of current and future J2ME technologies.

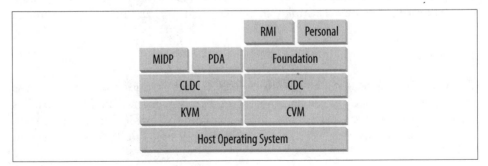

Figure 1-3. J2ME environment

Downloading the J2ME Wireless Toolkit

Now that you know your way around the J2ME landscape, let's get started with J2ME. However, before we can compile and run any J2ME programs, we need to download and install the J2ME Wireless Toolkit. You can obtain the J2ME Wireless Toolkit at the following URL: *http://java.sun.com/products/j2mewtoolkit*.

The version that we use in this book is 1.0.3 beta. It is available for the Microsoft Windows 98/ME and 2000 platforms, as well as Linux and Sun Solaris operating systems. The toolkit requires the presence of at least Version 1.3 of the Java Development Kit (JDK) for the host operating environment.

Once you've downloaded the Wireless Toolkit, double-click on it or execute the resulting binary (depending on your platform) to activate the extraction. This will uncompress the files needed to install the Wireless Toolkit. Note that you may be directed to specify an existing JDK installation on your system. If so, choose the latest stable release of the JDK that you currently have on your system.* In addition, the distribution may also ask you if you would like to install a version of the toolkit that interfaces with Forte™ for Java. If you would like to develop your J2ME applications in the Forte for Java Integrated Development Environment, choose the corresponding option. Be sure that Forte is already installed on your system before doing so.

In this case, we're going to install the Java Wireless Toolkit on a Windows platform into the directory *C:\j2mewtk*. After the installation is completed, this directory will contain all the required classes and tools to run the MIDP applications. (If the installation program asks you to run the ktoolbar program, just ignore it for the moment.) However, we need to do a few more things before we can get started with our examples.

First, we need to add the wireless toolkit binaries to your system path. You can do that on Windows with the following command (again, we've assumed that the Java Wireless Toolkit is installed at *C:\j2mewtk*):

```
SET PATH=%PATH%;C:\j2mewtk\bin
```

If you edit your *C:\AUTOEXEC.BAT* file to add this to the default system path, as shown below, and restart your machine, then you will not have to repeatedly perform this step each time you restart your system.

With Linux and Solaris, the equivalent command is:

```
export PATH=$PATH:install_directory/j2mewtk/bin
```

---

* Try to use a JDK instead of just a Java Runtime Environment (JRE). It's important that you have the javac compiler to create J2ME applications.

Once you've added that directory to your system path, you should be able to run the Java Wireless Toolkit tools from any directory on your system. An easy way to test it is to execute the preverify command, without any arguments. You should see output similar to the following:

```
C:\> preverify
Usage: PREVERIFY.EXE [options] classnames|dirnames ...

where options include:
    -classpath <directories separated by ';'>
                    Directories in which to look for classes
    -d <directory> Directory in which output is written
    @<filename>    Read command line arguments from a text file.
```

In order for the toolkit to work properly, you'll need to have the J2SE tools (notably javac) available on your system executable path as well. Instructions on how to do this are bundled with the JDK, although it really boils down to adding the binary path of the J2SE binaries to your system path.

 If you're familiar with the J2ME Wireless Toolkit already, you're likely wondering why we're not using KToolbar. We'll cover KToolbar in Chapter 4. In the meantime, it helps to see how J2ME works under the hood.

To compile and run J2ME programs from the command line, enter the following commands. Again, feel free to set these system environment variables on the command line, or edit the *AUTOEXEC.BAT* file (or similar) on your system for convenience.

```
SET J2MEWTK_HOME=C:\j2mewtk
SET MIDPAPI=%J2MEWTK_HOME%\lib\midpapi.zip
SET J2MECLASSPATH=%J2MEWTK_HOME%\wtklib\kenv.zip;
    %J2MEWTK_HOME%\wtklib\kvem.jar;%J2MEWTK_HOME%\wtklib\lime.jar
```

On the Linux and Solaris side, the following could be added to your .profile (or equivalent):

```
export J2MEWTK_HOME=/home/qmahmoud/j2mewtk
export MIDPAPI=$J2MEWTK_HOME/lib/midpapi.zip
export J2MECLASSPATH=$J2MEWTK_HOME/wtklib/kenv.zip:
    $J2MEWTK_HOME/wtklib/kvem.jar:$J2MEWTK_HOME/wtklib/lime.jar
```

Note the that final line in either case is really one line; it's been continued here for clarity.

A Simple Example

The examples that we're going to demonstrate here, and throughout the rest of the book, are called MIDlets. If you've programmed with Java applets or servlets before, then you'll likely recognize the similarities in the "fill-in-the-method" program structure. This first example, HelloMidlet.java, shown in Example 1-1, creates a text box and then prints the archetypal "Hello World" in a text box.

Example 1-1. "Hello World"

```java
import javax.microedition.midlet.*;
import javax.microedition.lcdui.*;

public class HelloMidlet extends MIDlet {

    // The display for this MIDlet
    private Display display;
    // TextBox to display text
    TextBox box = null;

    public HelloMidlet() {
    }

    public void startApp() {
        display = Display.getDisplay(this);
        box = new TextBox("Simple Example", "Hello World", 20, 0);
        display.setCurrent(box);
    }

    /**
     * Pause is a no-op since there are no background activities or
     * record stores that need to be closed.
     */
    public void pauseApp() {
    }

    /**
     * Destroy must cleanup everything not handled by the garbage
     * collector. In this case there is nothing to cleanup.
     */
    public void destroyApp(boolean unconditional) {
    }
}
```

This MIDlet consists of a public class definition that extends the MIDlet class found in javax.microedition.midlet. This superclass forms the base of all MIDlets in J2ME. Our HelloMidlet class contains a constructor, as well as the startApp(), pauseApp(), and destroyApp() methods that have been inherited from the MIDlet class. Note that there is no main() method in this program. Instead, the startApp(), pauseApp(), and destroyApp() methods are called by the underlying framework to start up the MIDlet, to pause it, or to destroy it.

Let's start off by compiling our program on the command line. Using the command line is a bit more complex than the KToolbar application that comes with the Wireless Toolkit, so in order to simplify it, be sure that you have entered the additional environment variables shown above. However, there are several steps that we need to perform when compiling J2ME applications, and it's important to see each of the steps as they occur.

As you would expect, the program must be saved in a file called HelloMidlet.java. However, before you compile it, create a directory called *tmpclasses*. Then use the following command to compile the MIDlet from the command line in Windows:

```
C:\midlets> javac -g:none -d tmpclasses -bootclasspath %MIDPAPI% -classpath
    %J2MECLASSPATH% HelloMidlet.java
```

In Linux and Solaris, the command looks like the following:

```
>javac -g:none -d tmpclasses -bootclasspath $MIDPAPI -classpath $J2MECLASSPATH
    HelloMidlet.java
```

This command compiles the Java source file without any debugging info, and sets the appropriate boot and J2ME classpaths to ensure that we don't pick up any J2SE classes. The end result of this command is the creation of the HelloMidlet.class file in the *tmpclasses* directory.

With the J2SE, a class file was all you needed to run the application. However, all MIDlet classes must be *preverified* before they can be run on a target device. Why is this necessary? Remember that one of the tasks of the standard Java virtual machine (the one that comes with the J2SE) is to perform *bytecode verification*. Bytecode verification is one of the most important steps of the Java security model. It performs such tasks as ensuring that the bytecodes of a Java class (and their operands) are all valid; that the code does not overflow or underflow the VM stack; that local variables are not used before they are initialized; that field, method, and class access control modifiers are respected, and other important tasks. However, most of the bytecode verifier is not included with the KVM due to size constraints. The preverifier ensures that the equivalent security checks still take place.

Before you run the preverifier, create another directory called *classes*. Then, use this command to preverify the HelloMidlet class:

```
C:\midlets> preverify -classpath %MIDPAPI%;tmpclasses -d classes tmpclasses
```

Or on Solaris and Linux:

```
> preverify -classpath $MIDPAPI:tmpclasses -d classes tmpclasses
```

The resulting output should look something like this:

```
[Output directory for verified classes: classes]
```

This command takes all the classes inside the *tmpclasses* directory (of which HelloMidlet.class is the only one) and preverifies them, writing the resulting classes to the *classes* directory. Note that the names of the preverified classes remain exactly the same, which is why we created two separate directories to hold them.

If you received an "Illegal constant pool index" class loading error and you're using JDK 1.4, try using JDK 1.3 until this issue is resolved.

The next step is to compress all the classes in the program (again, we have only one) as well as their resources, into a Java Archive (JAR) file. You can use the J2SE jar command to create a JAR file. Make sure you are in the *classes* directory to execute the following command:

```
> jar cvf HelloMidlet.jar HelloMidlet.class
```

The program will compress the HelloMidlet class into a JAR file, creating a manifest for it as well.

Note that with the javac compiler, you can create MIDlets of practically any size. However, that doesn't guarantee that they will fit on the target device for which you're writing the MIDlet. It would nice if there were a way to check if the target device can handle the MIDlet and run it before it is downloaded. Obviously, if a device can't handle the MIDlet, there is no reason to even attempt a download.

To accomplish this, we need a file that manually specifies some pre-download properties, including the size of the MIDlet and its storage requirements. This can be accomplished by creating a Java Application Descriptor (JAD) file with your favorite text editor. Example 1-2 shows a sample JAD file that we can use. Note that you will need to change the MIDlet-Jar-Size entry to correspond to the size of the JAR file that you just created. (In Chapter 3, we will explain the JAD file syntax in more detail.)

Example 1-2. HelloMidlet.jad

```
MIDlet-1: Hello,,HelloMidlet
MIDlet-Name: HelloMidlet
MIDlet-Version: 1.0
MIDlet-Vendor: ORA
MIDlet-Jar-URL: HelloMidlet.jar
MIDlet-Jar-Size: 863
```

Let's save this example JAD file as *HelloMidlet.jad*, again in the *classes* directory that holds the JAR file. Finally, to run this MIDlet, invoke Sun's MIDP emulator to point at the JAD file using the following command:

```
> emulator -Xdescriptor:HelloMidlet.jad
```

If everything worked correctly, you should see a phone similar to Figure 1-4, although the display may be different. Here, the HelloMidlet is running in the default phone that comes with the Java Wireless Toolkit. If you click on the MIDlet on the menu (use the directional arrow pad to move the cursor and the button in the middle to select), and instruct it to "Launch" using the soft button on the lower right, you should see output similar to Figure 1-4. Congratulations! You just created your first Java MIDlet!

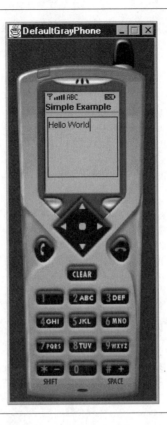

Figure 1-4. HelloMidlet

The gist of this program is in the startApp( ) method. Here, we obtain the current display that the device uses, then create a text box with the words "Hello World" inside of it. Finally, we show the text box on the current display. Don't worry if you don't understand these objects yet; the architecture of MIDlets will become clearer as we move through the book.

A Login MIDlet

Let's move to a more advanced MIDlet. Example 1-3 shows a MIDlet with a hypothetical login screen that prompts the user to log in. If the login is incorrect, the program will repeatedly ask the user to try again.

Example 1-3. A login MIDlet

```
import javax.microedition.midlet.MIDlet;
import javax.microedition.lcdui.*;

public class LoginMidlet extends MIDlet implements CommandListener {
    private Display display;
```

Example 1-3. A login MIDlet (continued)

```java
    private TextField userName;
    private TextField password;
    private Form form;
    private Command cancel;
    private Command login;

    public LoginMidlet() {
        userName = new TextField("LoginID:", "", 10, TextField.ANY);
        password = new TextField("Password:", "", 10, TextField.PASSWORD);
        form = new Form("Sign in");
        cancel = new Command("Cancel", Command.CANCEL, 2);
        login = new Command("Login", Command.OK, 2);
    }

    public void startApp() {
        display = Display.getDisplay(this);
        form.append(userName);
        form.append(password);
        form.addCommand(cancel);
        form.addCommand(login);
        form.setCommandListener(this);
        display.setCurrent(form);
    }

    public void pauseApp() {
    }

    public void destroyApp(boolean unconditional) {
        notifyDestroyed();
    }

    public void validateUser(String name, String password) {
      if (name.equals("qm") && password.equals("j2")) {
        menu();
      } else {
        tryAgain();
      }
    }

    public void menu() {
      List services = new List("Choose one", Choice.EXCLUSIVE);
      services.append("Check Mail", null);
      services.append("Compose", null);
      services.append("Addresses", null);
      services.append("Options", null);
      services.append("Sign Out", null);
      display.setCurrent(services);
    }

    public void tryAgain() {
      Alert error = new Alert("Login Incorrect", "Please try again", null,
          AlertType.ERROR);
```

Example 1-3. A login MIDlet (continued)

```
    error.setTimeout(Alert.FOREVER);
    userName.setString("");
    password.setString("");
    display.setCurrent(error, form);
  }

  public void commandAction(Command c, Displayable d) {
    String label = c.getLabel();
      if(label.equals("Cancel")) {
        destroyApp(true);
      } else if(label.equals("Login")) {
        validateUser(userName.getString(), password.getString());
      }
    }
  }
}
```

Again, don't worry if you can't understand the entire program at this point; this example is just meant to give you a flavor of MIDP programming and some sample applications to compile and run. Chapter 5 and Chapter 6 will explain the GUI classes (such as Display, Form, and TextField), as well as the event-handling classes (such as Command) in much more detail.

That being said, let's present a beginner's overview of how this MIDlet works. As in the previous example, LoginMidlet extends the MIDlet abstract class. It also implements the CommandListener interface by providing an implementation for the commandAction() method. In this method, there are two commands: Login and Cancel. The label of the command is checked: if it is Cancel, the LoginMidlet is destroyed, and if it is Login, then the username and passwords are validated.

In the LoginMidlet's constructor, a Form object, two TextField objects, and two Command objects are created. The TextField and Command objects are added to the form in the startApp() method. In addition, pauseApp() and destroyApp() perform minimal tasks.

Here is how the program operates: if the Login command is given, the application calls the validateUser() method to validate the username and password. If they are valid (in this case, they are hardcoded into the program for simplicity), then the menu() method is called to simulate a list of "useful services." Otherwise, the tryAgain() is called to display an error message and to allow the user to reenter their name and password.

If you are using the command line to compile and execute, save this file named *LoginMidlet.java*, make sure that you have a *classes* and a *tmpclasses* directory, and use javac:

```
C:\midlets> javac -g:none -d tmpclasses -bootclasspath %MIDPAPI% -classpath
    %J2MECLASSPATH% LoginMidlet.java
```

If you are using Solaris or Linux, the command becomes:

```
>javac -g:none -d tmpclasses -bootclasspath $MIDPAPI -classpath $J2MECLASSPATH
    LoginMidlet.java
```

Next, remember that we must preverify the resulting class:

```
C:\midlets> preverify -classpath %MIDPAPI%;tmpclasses -d classes tmpclasses
```

or

```
> preverify -classpath $MIDPAPI:tmpclasses -d classes tmpclasses
```

Again, the preverified class is saved to the *classes* subdirectory in the current directory. Next, compress the resulting class into a JAR file:

```
jar cvf LoginMidlet.jar LoginMidlet.class
```

And finally, create a JAD file that describes the resulting JAR file in detail, as shown in Example 1-4.

Example 1-4. LoginMidlet.jad

```
MIDlet-1: Login,,LoginMidlet
MIDlet-Name: LoginMidlet
MIDlet-Version: 1.0
MIDlet-Vendor: ORA
MIDlet-Jar-URL: LoginMidlet.jar
MIDlet-Jar-Size: 1786
```

Again, don't forget to change the size of the JAR file to match the size of the *LoginMidlet.jar* file after you create it.

At this point, the MIDlet can be run as in the previous example, using the MIDP emulator of the Java Wireless Toolkit, with the following command:

```
emulator -Xdescriptor:LoginMidlet.jad
```

In addition, the MIDlet can be run with any other emulator you may have available. For example, to whet your appetite, Figure 1-5 shows the LoginMidlet running on the Motorola i85s emulator (the i85s is a J2ME-enabled cell phone available from Motorola and Nextel).

Working with the Emulator

Note that the objects represented by the Command class are shown above the two "soft buttons" on the phone (the buttons with the black circles). If a soft button below the command is pressed, the command immediately above it is executed. Here, if the user enters the correct username and matching password and presses the Login button, the menu of services will be displayed. Otherwise, the alert will be displayed and the user can try again.

Figure 1-5. LoginMidlet running in the Motorola i85s emulator (cropped)

Also, you might be caught off guard the first time you try to enter text with your computer keyboard. It doesn't work! That's because you must use the input keys on the phone to enter the text. In this case, to enter the letter "G", press the number "4." To enter the letter "K", press the number "5" twice. Note how each time you press a numeral, the system "cycles" through the letter corresponding to that number. To move down to entering text for the password, use the down arrow.

Well, that's it! You've just created two professional MIDlets using J2ME! In the next two chapters, we're going to take a much closer look at the CLDC and the MIDP, two exciting new areas of wireless Java development.

CHAPTER 2

The Connected Limited Device Configuration (CLDC)

The Connected Limited Device Configuration (CLDC) defines a standard, minimum-footprint Java platform for small, resource-constrained devices. As we mentioned in Chapter 1, the CLDC was designed as a lowest common denominator of Java that can be applicable to a wide variety of devices. However, features specific to a certain vertical market, such as cell phones or pagers, are not found in the CLDC but are instead defined in profiles that sit above it. Configurations primarily target devices with similar amounts of memory and processing power.

This leads to a very important point about the CLDC: there are no optional features. Everything that the CLDC provides is usable on the devices that support it. After all, the primary goal of the CLDC is to ensure portability and interoperability between applications running on various kinds of resource-constrained devices, which is the main objective of programming in Java. In this chapter, we discuss the CLDC and its virtual machine, the KVM, in detail.

Examining the CLDC in Detail

Let's start off with some specifics. According to the specification, the devices targeted by the CLDC have the following characteristics:

160 KB to 512 KB of total memory
 At a minimum, a CLDC device should have 128 KB of non-volatile memory for the Java VM and the CLDC libraries, and at least 32 KB of volatile memory for the VM to use at runtime, independent of any applications.

16-bit or 32-bit processor with at least 25 Mhz speed
 These types of processors are pretty typical in today's handheld devices.

Connectivity to some kind of networking
 With CLDC, this is often a two-way wireless connection with limited bandwidth.

Low power consumption

CLDC devices often operate under battery power. Hence, they have very low power consumption.

Devices that fit these characteristics come in all shapes and sizes. Cell phones and pagers immediately come to mind, but one could also install Java on bar code scanners, video and audio equipment, navigation systems, and other wireless devices yet to come. In fact, as the nature of these devices changes, you can expect that the base specifications for the CLDC will change as well.

Given the constraints listed above, the CLDC currently provides the following functionality to its devices:

- A subset of Java language and virtual machine features
- A subset of core Java libraries (`java.lang` and `java.util`)
- Basic input/output (`java.io`)
- Basic networking support (`javax.microedition.io`)
- Security

Note, however, that the CLDC does not address application life cycle management, user interfaces, event handling, or the interaction between the user and the application. Again, these features fall into the domain of profiles, such as the MIDP, which are implemented on top of the CLDC and add to its functionality.

What's Different About the Java Virtual Machine?

We mentioned that the CLDC does not have any optional features. As you might expect, this means that a number of features have been eliminated from Java virtual machines that support the CLDC, either because they are too expensive (in terms of memory or processing capability) to implement, or because their presence would impose security problems. Therefore, if you're new to programming with the CLDC, you should be aware of the following limitations in CLDC VMs:

No floating point support

The CLDC does not support floating point numbers; therefore, CLDC-based applications cannot use floating point types such as `float` or `double`. This decision was made because most CLDC target devices do not have floating point support in their underlying hardware.

No finalization

The CLDC API currently does not include the `Object.finalize( )` method; you cannot perform final cleanup operations on object data—such as closing resources—before an object is garbage-collected.

Limited error handling

Runtime errors are handled in an implementation-specific manner. The CLDC defines only three error classes: `java.lang.Error`, `java.lang.OutOfMemoryError`, and `java.lang.VirtualMachineError`. Non-runtime errors are handled in a device-dependent manner that often involves terminating the application or even resetting the device.

No Java Native Interface (JNI)

A Java virtual machine supporting the CLDC does not implement the JNI. There are actually two good reasons for this: security, and the fact that implementing JNI is expensive, given the memory constraints of CLDC target devices.

No user-defined class loaders

A Java virtual machine supporting the CLDC must have a built-in class loader that cannot be overridden or replaced by the user. This is for security reasons.

No support for reflection

CLDC applications do not have the ability to use the reflection APIs on their objects or classes. Because reflection is not supported, there is also no support for object serialization or RMI.

No thread groups or daemon threads

While a Java virtual machine that supports the CLDC will implement multi-threading, it cannot support thread groups or daemon threads. If you want to perform thread operations for groups of threads, use the collection objects to store the thread objects at the application level.

No weak references

No application built on a Java virtual machine supporting the CLDC can require weak references.

The KVM

The KVM, which was introduced in the previous chapter, is a complete Java runtime environment for small devices. It is a true Java virtual machine as defined by the Java Virtual Machine Specification, except for some deviations that are necessary for proper functioning on small devices. The KVM was specifically designed for small, resource-constrained devices that have only a few hundred kilobytes total memory.

The J2ME white paper[*] describes the KVM as:

- Designed for both 16-bit and 32-bit CISC or RISC processors and clocked at processors as low as 25 Mhz
- Small, with a static memory footprint of 50 to 80 KB
- Highly portable, modular, and customizable
- As complete and fast as possible, without sacrificing the other design goals listed above

---

[*] See also the KVM white paper, located at *http://java.sun.com/products/cldc/wp/KVMwp.pdf*, for much more detail on the KVM.

The KVM was derived from a research project called Spotless at Sun Microsystems Laboratories. The aim of the project was to implement a Java system for the Palm Connected Organizer.* The KVM is written in the C programming language (using about 24,000 lines of code), so it can be easily ported to various platforms for which a C-language compiler is available. Finally, like a regular JVM, the KVM can load classes from a class path directory as well as from a JAR file.

Class Verification

In the J2SE Java virtual machine, the class verifier is responsible for rejecting invalid class files at runtime. A JVM supporting CLDC must be able to reject invalid class files as well. The class verification process, however, is expensive and time-consuming: it typically takes anywhere from 35 to 110 KB of runtime memory. Since the target size of the KVM is 50 to 80 KB of memory, including a class verifier inside it would violate its size constraints.

The KVM designers decided to move most of the verification work off the device and onto the desktop, where the class files are compiled, or onto the server machine, from which applications are downloaded. This step (off-device class verification) is referred to as *preverification*; that's why we had to run the preverify command on the examples in Chapter 1. Once the preverification is completed, the resulting class files often include extra information to ensure that the runtime verifier can perform its job with only minimal effort and memory. (That's why the preverified version of the LoginMidlet.class in Chapter 1 is slightly larger than the raw class generated by the javac compiler.)

The additional output of the preverification process is the addition of a stack map attribute that maps out critical areas of a class. This additional attribute is used by the runtime verifier to pinpoint critical areas inside the class that must be checked. Also, the preverifier will inline all subroutines in the bytecodes of the class file to prevent any problems at runtime. Don't worry, however. Even with the additional information, the preverified class files can still work with a regular Java runtime verifier.

With the help of the preverification, the CLDC device is only responsible for running a quick scan on the preverified class file to ensure that it was verified and does not contain any illegal instructions. This cuts down significantly on the amount of memory needed for the runtime verifier: only 100 bytes or so.

Security

The CLDC security model is more strict than what you're likely used to with the J2SE. This new security model is primarily concerned with two areas:

---

* If you attended JavaOne 1999, you'll remember that this was a major attraction. They even held a contest to see who could design the best KVM application.

Virtual machine-level security

An application executed by the KVM must not be able to harm the device in which it is running. This is guaranteed by the class verifier, which ensures that the class bytecodes cannot contain references to invalid memory locations. It also ensures that the classes loaded cannot execute in a way that is not allowed by the Java Virtual Machine Specification. As we mentioned, class verification for the CLDC/KVM is a two-step process: off-device preverification in conjunction with a minimal in-device verification. In addition, native methods cannot be invoked at runtime.

Application-level security

Unlike the J2SE, the CLDC/KVM combination does not allow the customization of a security manager. A JVM supporting CLDC provides a simple sandbox security model that enforces security by ensuring that applications run in a closed environment, and that applications may only call classes supported by the device.

What's Different About the Core Java Libraries?

The first thing that you'll probably notice when working with the CLDC is that only a bare minimum of Java APIs have been included. The reason for this is obvious if you download the Java 2 SDK: the standard edition APIs require close to 20 megabytes of memory! This is memory that most small devices simply do not have. Hence, one of the primary goals in designing the core CLDC libraries was to boil the J2SE APIs off into a minimum set of libraries that could still be used for meaningful application and profile development.

With that in mind, it's helpful to think of the CLDC library APIs as divided into two categories: classes that are a subset of the J2SE APIs and new classes that are specific to the CLDC. Let's look at the former group first.

Classes inherited from J2SE

The CLDC uses only thirty-seven classes from the J2SE platform. These classes come from the java.lang, java.io, and java.util packages, which are derived from JDK 1.2 APIs. Note that according to the J2ME specification, "Each class that has the same name and package name as a J2SE class must be identical to, or a subset of, the corresponding J2SE class. The semantics of the classes and methods cannot be changed, and the classes cannot add any public or protected methods or fields that are not available in the corresponding J2SE class libraries." In other words, you cannot add, but you can take away. And many classes have functionality taken away.

The inherited classes and interfaces (not including exceptions) from the J2SE platform are shown in Table 2-1.

Table 2-1. Inherited, non-exceptional classes

Package	Classes
java.lang	Boolean, Byte, Character, Class, Integer, Long, Math, Object, Runnable, Runtime, Short, String, StringBuffer, System, Thread, Throwable
java.io	ByteArrayInputStream, ByteArrayOutputStream, DataInput, DataOutput, DataInputStream, DataOutputStream, InputStream, OutputStream, InputStreamReader, OutputStreamWriter, PrintStream, Reader, Writer
java.util	Calendar, Date, Enumeration, Hashtable, Random, Stack, TimeZone, Vector

Because all inherited classes must throw precisely the same exceptions as regular J2SE classes, the following 29 exception and error classes shown in Table 2-2 also derive from the J2SE APIs.

Table 2-2 . Inherited exception and error classes

Package	Class
java.lang	ArithmeticException, ArrayIndexOutOfBoundsException, ArrayStoreException, ClassCastException, ClassNotFoundException, Error, Exception, IllegalAccessException, IllegalArgumentException, IllegalMonitorStateException, IllegalThreadStateException, IndexOutOfBoundsException, InstantiationException, InterruptedException, OutOfMemoryException, NegativeArraySizeException, NumberFormatException, NullPointerException, RuntimeException, SecurityException, StringIndexOutOfBoundsException, VirtualMachineError
java.io	EOFException, IOException, InterruptedIOException, UnsupportedEncodingException, UTFDataFormatException
java.util	EmptyStackException, NoSuchElementException

When programming with the CLDC, there are many internal modifications to the J2SE classes you're used to. Here are some of the more common classes that may cause problems.

String and StringBuffer

The following methods have been removed from the ubiquitous java.lang.String class, either because they refer to floating-point data types or because their presence is redundant:

```
public void valueOf(float f)
public void valueOf(double d)
public int compareToIgnoreCase(String str)
public boolean equalsIgnoreCase(String anotherStr)
public static copyValueOf(char[] data)
public static String copyValueOf(char[] data, int offset,
    int count)
public String intern()
public int lastIndexOf(String str)
public int lastIndexOf(String str, int fromIndex)
public boolean regionMatches(int toffset, String other,
    int ooffset, int len)
public String toLowerCase(java.util.Locale locale)
public String toUpperCase(java.util.Locale locale)
```

For the same reasons, the following methods have been eliminated from the java.lang.StringBuffer class.

```
public StringBuffer append(float f)
public StringBuffer append(double d)
public StringBuffer insert(int offset, float f)
public StringBuffer insert(int offset, double d)
public StringBuffer insert(int index, char[] str,
      int offset, int len)
public StringBuffer replace(int start, int end, String str)
public String substring(int start)
public String substring(int start, int end)
```

Runtime

The java.lang.Runtime class has eliminated most of its methods for the CLDC. Here, only the following subset of methods is now available:

```
public void exit(int status);
public native long freeMemory( );
public native void gc( );
public static Runtime getRuntime( );
public native long totalMemory( );
```

System

In addition, the java.lang.System class only has the following fields and methods available to it:

```
public static final PrintStream err;
public static final PrintStream out;
public static native void arraycopy(Object src,
   int src_position, Object dst, int dst_position, int length);
public static native long currentTimeMillis( );
public static void exit(int status);
public static void gc( );
public static String getProperty(String key);
public static native int identityHashCode(Object x);
```

Math

Finally, as you might expect, the java.lang.Math class has eliminated all methods dealing with complex floating-point operations (which was the vast majority of methods in that class), and now only has the following methods:

```
public static int abs(int a);
public static long abs(long a);
public static int max(int a, int b);
public static long max(long a, long b);
public static int min(int a, int b);
public static long min(long a, long b);
```

In many cases, the absence of these methods are only a minor inconvenience and suitable workarounds can be used. J2ME functionalities that require the use of floating-point values, however, may have to expand their floating-point values to integers with an implied decimal point and improvise with the more limited set of integer operations.

What's Different About I/O and Networking?

Recall that the J2SE provides the java.io and java.net packages for I/O and network connectivity. The CLDC inherits some of the classes in the java.io package. However, the major difference is that it does not inherit classes related to *file* I/O. For example, the popular FileInputStream and FileOutputStream classes are not present. In addition, the FileReader and FileWriter classes are not offered for reading and writing text data. This is because not all CLDC devices support the concept of a filesystem.

As for the java.net package, the J2SE provides several classes for network connectivity. However, none of these classes have been inherited because not all devices require TCP/IP or UDP/IP. (Some devices may not even have an IP stack.) Instead, the CLDC expert group decided to define a more generic set of classes for J2ME I/O and network connectivity. These classes are known as the *Generic Connection Framework,* and are found in the javax.microedition.io package.

The Generic Connection Framework

The Generic Connection Framework is a platform-independent framework that provides its functionality without any dependence on the specific features of a device. In fact, this framework is so generic that it doesn't implement any of the I/O or network connectivity interfaces; rather, the profile above it provides such implementation.

Here's a quick rundown of how the Generic Connection Framework works: all connections are created using the static open() method from the factory Connector class. If successful, this method returns an object that implements one of the generic connection interfaces for the host device. If you're a J2SE programmer, this will be much different than what you're used to. However, it will also be much easier. To give you a taste of what this is like, here are some example connections from the J2ME specification that you might request from a CLDC application and the appropriate syntax to implement them:

HTTP connection
```
Connector.open("http://www.ora.com:port");
```
Socket connection
```
Connector.open("socket://www.ora.com:port");
```
Communication with a port
```
Connector.open("comm:0;baudrate=9600");
```

The goal of the above syntax is to isolate any differences in the protocol that you're attempting to connect with into a simple string. This way, most of the application's code remains the same, regardless of the protocol you use. The Generic Connection Framework is discussed in more detail in Chapter 7.

Differences with Property Support in the CLDC

Virtual machines that support the CLDC, such as the KVM, do not implement the `java.util.Properties` class, which follows from the lack of filesystem functionality that we mentioned above. However, four system properties are supported for each J2ME/CLDC device, and can be accessed by using the method `System. getProperty(String key)`. The four properties available are described in Table 2-3.

Table 2-3. System properties

System property	Description	Default value
`microedition.platform`	Name of the host platform or device	`null`
`microedition.encoding`	Default character encoding	`"ISO8859_1"`
`microedition.configuration`	Name and version of the support configuration	`"CLDC-1.0"`
`microedition.profiles`	Name of the supported profiles	`null`

There's very little to say here, except that you can use these properties to ensure that you're indeed on a CLDC device that supports the proper encoding and profiles for your application. The MIDP profile defines some additional properties, which we will discuss in Chapter 3.

Using the Standalone CLDC and KVM

If you want to experiment with the raw KVM and CLDC classes, you can download the standalone CLDC and KVM. As of this writing, the latest edition of the CLDC itself is version 1.0.2. The CLDC 1.0.2 contains an updated version of the KVM. The KVM code has been rewritten to improve performance and includes a faster byte-code interpreter, better garbage collection, Java-level debugging APIs, preverifier improvements, and several bug fixes. If you wish to download the standalone CLDC and KVM, you can find it at the following address: *http://java.sun.com/products/kvm*.

Note that this is different than the J2ME Wireless Toolkit that we used in Chapter 1. This distribution does not contain any MIDP classes, nor does it contain a MIDP emulator. Hence, it will only execute programs that adhere to the base CLDC specification and not any MIDP functionality. If you are solely interested in writing applications for the MIDP, you can just read through this section without taking any action.

This distribution contains KVM implementations for Windows, Solaris, and Linux operating systems, as well as the CLDC classes that can be used to compile and run applications. After downloading and uncompressing the distribution, you should have a series of directories, as shown in Table 2-4.

Table 2-4. CLDC/KVM directories

Directory	Description
api	The Java classes and source code for the CLDC
bin	Binaries for each of the target platforms
build	Utility that builds directories and makefiles for each target platform
docs	PDF documentation, as well as compressed javadocs
jam	Java Application Manager, which can be used to dynamically download classes into the KVM
kvm	Source and build files pertaining to the KVM
samples	Sample code that can be used with the CLDC
tools	Source for the various tools used with the CLDC

Feel free to look through the *api* directory to see what you have. It's not much, compared to the J2SE. In any case, there are some interesting things that we can show you with the KVM and the CLDC in this distribution. First, create a simple program that can be run with the CLDC as follows:

```java
public class CLDCTest {
    public static void main(String[] args) {
        System.out.println("Hello CLDC!");
    }
}
```

Then, try compiling the program with the standard javac compiler. In the example below, we use a command line, similar to that in the first chapter, in order to ensure that only the CLDC classes are used. Note that the subsequent series of commands assumes that you are in the base directory of the CLDC/KVM distribution:

```
javac -bootclasspath api/classes.zip CLDCTest.java
```

Remember that we must preverify our resulting class before running it with the KVM, like we did in Chapter 1. You can do so with the following command:

```
bin/[targetOS]/preverify -classpath api/classes.zip:. CLDCTest
```

As before, this should create a separate directory, here called *output*, where the preverified class has been stored. You can now run this class with the KVM, using the following command:

```
bin/[targetOS]/kvm -classpath api/classes.zip:output CLDCTest
Hello CLDC!
```

Next, try modifying the source code so that it adds a declaration of the float variable:

```
public class CLDCTest {

    float f;

    public static void main(String[] args) {
        System.out.println("Hello CLDC!");
    }
}
```

And again, try recompiling it and preverifying it with the above commands. If you try running the resulting program, the KVM will flag the inclusion of a floating-point field in the class as an error:

```
ALERT: Bad field signature
```

Why didn't the compiler flag the use of the floating-point variable as an error? Remember that you're using the javac compiler from J2SE to compile your J2ME programs, and that compiler is all too familiar with the use of floating-point variables. Hence, it will assume that the primitive data types that it knows about are fine for use with whatever JVM is on the other side of the compilation. In addition, the preverifier will not search for floating-point variables because its job (at least, on the desktop side) is to look for security issues within classes, not to hunt down invalid primitive data types. (Remember we mentioned earlier that preverified class files must work under the regular J2SE.) Hence, the KVM itself has to tell us that one of our fields is not supported in the virtual machine, which it does by scanning through the class files before executing them. There's an important lesson here: just because the compiler and preverifier successfully translated a source file to a class with only the CLDC classes on its bootclasspath doesn't mean that it will still run. You should always test it with the KVM as well, to see if the code has any VM issues.

That's not to say that if we used a method that is no longer in the CLDC classes, the compiler wouldn't notice. For example, assume that we modified our code to be the following:

```
public class CLDCTest {

    static String s = "Hello CLDC!";
    static int r = s.compareToIgnoreCase("HELLO CLDC!");

    public static void main(String[] args) {
        System.out.println(s + ":" + r);
    }
}
```

This yields the following compiler error:

```
CLDCTest.java:4: cannot resolve symbol
symbol:   method compareToIgnoreCase(java.lang.String)
location: class java.lang.String
```

Here, the compiler flagged an error because the String class that was located on its bootclasspath does not contain the method in question, compareToIgnoreCase( ). As we mentioned earlier in the chapter, this method has been omitted in the CLDC subset of java.lang.String.

CLDC Next Generation

Finally, let's briefly mention the CLDC Next Generation (NG). The CLDC NG is a specification that is currently in development and that aims to define a revised version of the CLDC. The goal of the CLDC NG is to make the CLDC more compliant with the Java language and virtual machine specifications by reintroducing features such as floating-point support and improved error-handling capabilities.

Some other goals of the CLDC NG will be to:

- Maintain backward compatibility with CLDC 1.0.
- Maintain small footprint (limit API growth).
- Continue focus on small, resource-constrained, connected devices.
- Investigate the possibility of adding a minimal security manager.

Note, however, that not many new APIs will be reintroduced to the CLDC with this revision. Devices that require significantly more complete Java libraries should use the Connected Device Configuration (CDC) instead. You can follow the progress of the CLDC NG at the Java Community Process web site at: *http://www.jcp.org/*.

CHAPTER 3

The Mobile Information
Device Profile (MIDP)

The Mobile Information Device Profile (MIDP) is built on top of the CLDC, and defines an open application development environment for what Sun calls *Mobile Information Devices* (MIDs). In simpler terms, MIDP is the J2ME profile that is used for wireless devices, such as mobile phones and pagers. This chapter expands on the previous chapter by introducing some of the fundamental concepts of MIDP and offering programming guidelines that are used throughout the remainder of this book.

As we mentioned in Chapter 1, the MIDP is governed by the Java Community Process. The MIDP is JSR 37, which is part of the Java Community Process. Like the CLDC, the MIDP is an ever-changing standard that actively solicits input from corporations and the general programming community. You can find more information on the MIDP at the following URL: *http://java.sun.com/products/midp*.

Mobile Information Devices

Again, let's start off with some specifics. The MIDP standard defines a MID as a device with the following minimum characteristics:

Display
    A screen size of at least 96 × 54 pixels with at least a 1-bit display depth

Input
    A one-handed keyboard, two-handed keyboard, or touch screen

Memory
    32 KB of volatile memory for the Java runtime (heap); 128 KB of non-volatile memory for the MIDP components; and 8 KB of non-volatile memory for application-created persistent data

Networking
    A two-way intermittent connection, usually wireless, with limited bandwidth

Because the MIDP is built on top of the CLDC, it addresses the following areas that are omitted by the CLDC:

Application Life Cycle Management
> The MIDP includes the javax.microedition.midlet package, which contains classes and methods for starting, pausing, and destroying applications in the host environment.

User Interface and Events
> The MIDP also provides the javax.microedition.lcdui packages, which include classes and interfaces for creating GUI components for applications.

Network Connectivity
> The MIDP extends the ContentConnection interface of the Generic Connection Framework by providing the HttpConnection interface, as well as a subset implementation of the HTTP protocol.

Storing Data on Device
> The MIDP also provides the javax.microedition.rms package, which implements a record-based database management system. This provides applications with the capability to store data on the device.

The MIDP has received wide corporate backing, from companies such as AOL, DDI, Ericsson, Fujitsu, Hitachi, Matsushita, Mitsubishi, Motorola, NEC, Nokia, NTT DoCoMo, Palm, Research in Motion (RIM), Samsung, Sharp, Siemens, Sony, Sprint, and Symbian. In the second quarter of 2001, Motorola released the first MIDP-enabled cellular phones, the i50x and the i85s.* Over the next year or two, you'll likely see an impressive amount of MIDP-enabled devices reach the market.

Class Additions

The MIDP adds the following packages to those available through the CLDC, as shown in Table 3-1.

Table 3-1. New packages in the MIDP

Package	Description
javax.microedition.lcdui	Graphical interface components and events
javax.microedition.midlet	Application life cycle
javax.microedition.rms	Record storage

Here are the classes that are included with each of the new packages. The first package, javax.microedition.lcdui, contains interfaces and classes, listed in Table 3-2, that are used to build graphical interfaces on the limited displays of CLDC devices. These classes are discussed in detail in Chapter 5 and Chapter 6.

---

* The service for the i50x and i85s phones is provided in the United States and Canada by Nextel, Inc.

Table 3-2. Classes and interfaces in the javax.microedition.lcdui package

Name	Type
Choice	Interface
CommandListener	Interface
ItemStateListener	Interface
Alert	Class
AlertType	Class
Canvas	Class
ChoiceGroup	Class
Command	Class
DateField	Class
Display	Class
Displayable	Class
Font	Class
Form	Class
Gauge	Class
Graphics	Class
Image	Class
ImageItem	Class
Item	Class
List	Class
Screen	Class
StringItem	Class
TextBox	Class
TextField	Class
Ticker	Class

The next package, javax.microedition.midlet (see Table 3-3), adds only one class that serves as the base class for all MIDlets. This class can only throw one exception as well, which notifies listeners of a state change in the MIDlet. This class is discussed in detail in Chapter 4.

Table 3-3. Class and exception in the javax.microedition.midlet package

Name	Type
MIDlet	Class
MIDletStateChangeException	Exception

Finally, the javax.microedition.rms package provides four interfaces, one class, and five exceptions (see Table 3-4) for performing persistent data storage on MIDP devices. The four interfaces allow you to create implementing classes that customize how the record store compares, enumerates through, filters, and handles events that occur with data records. These classes are discussed in detail in Chapter 8.

Table 3-4. The classes, interfaces, and exceptions in the javax.microedition.rms package

Name	Type
RecordComparator	Interface
RecordEnumeration	Interface
RecordFilter	Interface
RecordListener	Interface
RecordStore	Class
InvalidRecordIDException	Exception
RecordStoreException	Exception
RecordStoreFullException	Exception
RecordStoreNotFoundException	Exception
RecordStoreNotOpenException	Exception

In addition to these packages, the MIDP also adds two classes and one exception to those classes in the java.lang and java.util packages of the CLDC. These classes are similar to those found in the Java SDK 1.3.

- java.lang.IllegalStateException (exception)
- java.util.Timer (class)
- java.util.TimerTask (class)

As you can see, there aren't many classes in the MIDP. However, that's not unexpected, given that we need to fit MIDP programs in such a limited space. But don't worry. We'll discuss each of the new classes, interfaces, and exceptions of the MIDP as we progress through the remainder of the book.

System Properties

The MIDP defines two additional property values (in addition to the eight in the previous chapter) that can be retrieved using the java.lang.System.getProperty( ) method. These are shown in Table 3-5:

Table 3-5. System properties defined by the MIDP

System property	Description
microedition.local	The current locale of the device (default: null)
microedition.profiles	Must contain at least "MIDP-1.0"

The microedition.local property consists of the language and country code separated by a dash "-". For example, "en-CA" for English Canada and "en-US" for English USA. Note that the language code must be lowercase, and the country code must be uppercase.

More About MIDlets

In Chapter 1, we introduced you to MIDlets, applications that run on MIDP devices. MIDlets are written as one or more Java classes whose objects are compressed into a JAR file. Like Java applets, MIDP applications have an application life cycle while running on a mobile device. Specifically, a MIDlet can be in one of three states:

- Paused
- Active
- Destroyed

Figure 3-1 shows the rules for transitioning between states.

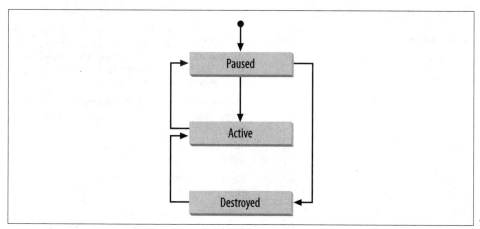

Figure 3-1. MIDlet transition states

Here is a quick rundown of how MIDP applications change state: when a MIDlet is first started, it is placed in the paused state. After it's ready, the controlling software will then place the MIDlet in the active state. At this point, the MIDlet is running and the user can interact with it. The application can be placed back in the paused state by either the MIDP system or the program itself. In addition, the MIDP can be moved to the destroyed state from either the paused or the active state, again by either the MIDP system or the programmer. In the destroyed state, the MIDlet should release all of the resources it currently has back to the MIDP system.

We'll cover this in more detail in the following chapter, where we create and execute a MIDlet with multiple states. In the meantime, this quick introduction brings us to the point where we must first introduce some important concepts.

What Is a MIDlet Suite?

A *MIDlet suite* is simply two or more MIDlets that are packaged in a JAR file. MIDlets within the same suite can use the classes and resources contained in the JAR file, much like any standard Java application, the classes of which are loaded by the same class loader.

The JAR Manifest

The JAR file of a MIDlet suite often contains a manifest file with MIDlet attributes defined. These attributes describe the contents of the JAR file, which is in turn used by the application management software to identify and install the MIDlet suite. The attributes defined by the MIDP specification are listed in Table 3-6.

Table 3-6. JAR manifest attributes

Attribute name	Required	Description
MicroEdition-Configuration	Yes	The name and version of the J2ME configuration required. This uses the same format as the `MicroEdition.configuration` system property (for example, "CLDC-1.0").
MicroEdition-Profile	Yes	The name and version of the J2ME profile required. This uses the same format as the `microedition.profiles` system property (for example, "MIDP-1.0").
MIDlet-*n*	Yes	The name, icon, and class, separated by commas, of the *n*th MIDlet in the MIDlet suite.
MIDlet-Data-Size	No	The minimum number of bytes of persistent storage that the MIDlet requires. The default is zero.
MIDlet-Description	No	A description of the `MIDlet` suite.
MIDlet-Icon	No	The pathname of a PNG file within the JAR file to identify the MIDlet suite (not the individual MIDlets). It is used by the application management software to display an icon to identify the suite.
MIDlet-Info-URL	Yes	A pointer to a URL containing a detailed description of the MIDlet suite.
MIDlet-Name	Yes	The name of the MIDlet suite.
MIDlet-Vendor	Yes	The name of the organization (or vendor) providing the suite.
MIDlet-Version	Yes	The version number of the MIDlet suite presented in the format XX.YY.ZZ, where XX is the major, YY is the minor, and ZZ is the micro. If the micro is omitted, the default is zero. Therefore, the micro is optional. This information is used by the application management software for install and upgrade uses.

Example 3-1 shows a sample manifest for a MIDlet suite (in this case, only two MIDlets) for a shopping MIDlet.

Example 3-1. A sample manifest

```
MIDlet-Name: ShopOnLine
MIDlet-Version: 1.0
MIDlet-Vendor: SELKOM
MIDlet-Description: a shopping MIDlet
MIDlet-Info-URL: http://www.selkom.com/shop
MIDlet-Data-Size: 500
MIDlet-1: BuyMIDlet, /icons/buy.png, com.selkom.BuyMIDlet
MIDlet-2: PayMIDlet, /icons/sell.png, com.selkom.SellMIDlet
MicroEdition-Profile: MIDP-1.0
MicroEdition-Configuration: CLDC-1.0
```

Java Application Descriptor (JAD)

Using a manifest to describe the MIDlets in the suite is a bit problematic. In Chapter 1, we mentioned that before downloading a MIDlet or a MIDlet suite to a device, the Java Application Manager should check to make sure there is enough space for it. Using a manifest, however, means that the Java Application Manager should download the JAR file in order to read the manifest. Imagine downloading a MIDlet suite only to discover it cannot be installed on your device because it requires the next generation MIDP. To avoid these problems, the MIDP specification also defines the Java Application Descriptor (JAD).

A JAD file is a text file that is similar to a manifest. Unlike a manifest, however, it is not packaged in the JAR file. Similar to a manifest, it consists of a series of attributes used to describe a MIDlet suite. The possible attributes are shown in Table 3-7.

Table 3-7. JAD attributes

Attribute name	Required	Description
MIDlet-Name	Yes	The name of the MIDlet suite.
MIDlet-Version	Yes	The version number of the MIDlet suite. The format is XX.YY or XX.YY.ZZ, where XX is the major, YY is the minor, and ZZ is the micro that is optional. If the micro is omitted, the default is zero.
MIDlet-Vendor	Yes	The vendor of the MIDlet suite.
MIDlet-Jar-URL	Yes	The URL from which to download the MIDlet suite.
MIDlet-Jar-Size	Yes	The size of the MIDlet suite in bytes.
MIDlet-Description	No	A description of the MIDlet suite.
MIDlet-Icon	No	The pathname of a PNG file for the suite. The icon is used to identify the suite.
MIDlet-Info-URL	No	A URL that describes the MIDlet suite in greater detail.
MIDlet-Data-Size	No	The minimum number of bytes of persistent storage the MIDlet suite requires. If not specified, the default is zero.

As you can see from Table 3-5 and Table 3-6, there are some common attributes between the manifest and the JAD file. The mandatory attributes that must be duplicated in both the manifest and the JAD file are: MIDlet-Name, MIDlet-Version, and MIDlet-Vendor.

Example 3-2 shows a JAD file for the same hypothetical MIDlet suite.

Example 3-2. A sample JAD file

```
MIDlet-Name: ShopOnLine
MIDlet-Version: 1.0
MIDlet-Vendor: SELKOM
MIDlet-Jar-URL: http://www.selkom.com/shop/mid.jar
MIDlet-Jar-Size: 3544
MIDlet-Data-Size: 500
```

And that's the difference between a JAR manifest file and a JAD file in a MIDlet suite.

Programming Guidelines

Before we start programming with MIDlets, let's briefly discuss some guidelines that are useful when developing applications for mobile information devices such as cell phones and PDAs that you likely haven't considered before.

Performance

When programming for mobile devices with a small memory footprint, it is crucial to make your applications run faster. The less time your application takes to run, the happier your customers will be. For the J2SE programmer, here are some ways to help you achieve the best performance:

- Use local variables instead of fields. Accessing local variables is quicker than accessing class members.
- Minimize method calls. Remember that the Java virtual machine uses the stack to load and store a stack frame for every method it executes. For example, instead of doing something like:

```
for (int i=0; i<obj.getLength(); i++) {
    // do something with array elements
}
```

where the length of the array is evaluated every time through the loop, it is much more efficient to do this:

```
int len = obj.getLength();
for (int i=0; i<len; i++) {
    // do something with array elements
}
```

- Avoid string concatenation. This may cause a lot of object creation and subsequent garbage collection, and therefore decreases performance and increases the application's memory usage. It's often more efficient to use `StringBuffer` instead.

- Minimize object creation. Object creation leads to object destruction and reduces performance. Instead, design objects that can be recycled. Instead of creating return objects inside of methods, consider passing in a reference to the return object and modifying its values.

- Avoid synchronization. If an operation takes longer than a fraction of a second to run, consider placing it in a separate thread.

Programming with the CLDC and the MIDP

Part II starts by elaborating on some of the concepts introduced in Chapter 3. Later chapters show how to program with the CLDC/MIDP APIs, including GUI, event handling, networking, and databases. Chapter 9 shows how to convert MIDlets into executable Palm applications for handheld devices running Palm OS v3.5 or higher.

CHAPTER 4

Working with MIDlets

MIDlets are very simple to implement. All MIDlets must extend the javax. microedition.midlet.MIDlet abstract class and implement certain methods in that class. The MIDlet abstract class provides the basic functionality required in all MIDlets. A MIDlet runs in a controlled environment and therefore must implement certain methods that allow the *application manager* (which installs and runs the MIDlet) to control the behavior of the MIDlet. These methods are known as *life cycle methods*, since they reflect various states in which a MIDlet can be.

You'll recall from the previous chapter that a MIDlet can be in one of three states: paused, active, or destroyed. The state chart in Figure 4-1 shows the possible state transitions of a MIDlet, this time with the addition of the methods that the Java Manager will call inside the MIDlet code during those transitions.

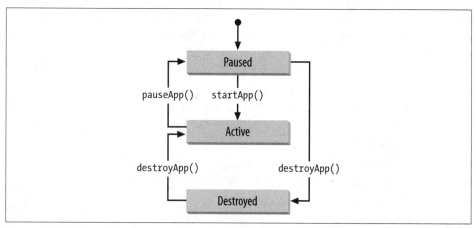

Figure 4-1. MIDlet state transitions

Here, the javax.microedition.midlet.MIDlet abstract class defines three life cycle methods that are called during the state transitions: pauseApp(), startApp(), and destroyApp(). These three methods were present in the example we developed in Chapter 1. The responsibilities for these three life cycle methods are as follows.

```
public void startApp( )
```
This method indicates that the MIDlet is moving from a paused state to an active state. Here, the MIDlet will typically initialize any objects that are required while the MIDlet is active, and set the current display.

```
public void pauseApp( )
```
This method is called when the MIDlet is moving from an active state to a paused state. This means that it will pause any threads that are currently active, as well as optionally setting the next display to be shown when the MIDlet is re-activated. Data can be persisted, if necessary, and retrieved later when the MIDlet is activated again.

```
public void destroyApp(boolean unconditional)
```
This method indicates that the MIDlet is moving to the destroyed state. It should free or close all resources that have been acquired during the life of the MIDlet. In addition, the method should persist any data that it wishes to save for future use.

It is important to note that startApp( ) can be called more than once. In addition to being called when the MIDlet is first activated to move the MIDlet from the paused state to the active state, it can also be called if the MIDlet has been paused during execution and wishes to again return to the active state.

The Application Manager

The application manager, sometimes called the Application Management System (AMS) or MIDlet management software, is software that is preinstalled on a MIDP device and that functions as an operating environment. For example, on a Motorola i85s, the Java Apps menu item will start the application manager, which immediately shows the Java logo and the words "Mobile Information Device Profile Compatible" and then displays a menu of the MIDlet suites that have been installed on the phone.

However, the application manager must do more than simply show a menu of the MIDlet suites that are installed. According to the MIDP specification, the application manager must be able to:

- Retrieve a MIDlet suite from somewhere, possibly through a serial connection, infrared connection, or across a wireless connection to the Internet
- Install a MIDlet suite on the MIDP device
- Perform version management on MIDlet suites that are installed
- Launch a MIDlet from a MIDlet suite and provide an operating environment for the KVM, as well as any system, MIDP, and CLDC classes
- Delete a previously installed MIDlet suite

As a MIDlet programmer, you typically won't need to be concerned with the internals of the application manager running on the device—it's unique to each device. However, some insight into its responsibilities is important when designing MIDP applications. In this case, the MIDlet life cycle methods can be called by the application manager to control the MIDlet state:

- When the user launches a MIDlet, the application manager creates a new instance of the MIDlet class by calling its zero-argument constructor. This typically performs the one-time initialization. Once this is done, the MIDlet will be placed in a paused state. However, if any exception occurs during the instantiation of the MIDlet class, the application manager will move the class to the destroyed state.

- After the MIDlet has been placed in the paused state, the application manager calls startApp( ) to transition it to the active state.

- The application manager can then call pauseApp( ) to move it from the active state to the paused state, either via a request from the program itself or from the operating environment.

- destroyApp( ) can be called by the application manager to transition the MIDlet to the destroyed state. The destroyApp() method takes a boolean argument to indicate if the MIDlet should clean up or not.

Example 4-1 shows a MIDlet skeleton class that implements the life cycle methods of the javax.microedition.midlet.MIDlet class.

Example 4-1. MIDlet skeleton

```
import javax.microedition.midlet.*;

public class MyMIDlet extends MIDlet {

    public MyMIDlet( ) {
        // constructor
    }

    public void startApp( ) {
        // entering active state
    }

    public void pauseApp( ) {
        // entering paused state
    }

    public void destroyApp(boolean unconditional) {
        // entering destroyed state
    }
}
```

Believe it or not, this class is all you need to create a MIDlet. The only thing we should reiterate is our earlier warning that startApp( ) can be called more than once.

Hence, if you have any one-time initialization that you wish to perform for your MIDlet, be sure that it is placed in the constructor of the MIDlet object and not in the startApp( ) method.

Earlier, we mentioned that a MIDlet could change its own state if needed. The javax.microedition.midlet.MIDlet abstract class provides three methods that can be called by a MIDlet to control its own state transitions:

public void notifyPause( )
> A MIDlet may call this method to pause itself. It can be called while in the active state, to inform the Java Application Manager that the MIDlet has entered the paused state.

public void resumeRequest( )
> A MIDlet may call this method to express interest in entering the active state. The application manager also calls this method to determine which MIDlet to activate, then it calls its startApp( ) method.

public void notifyDestroyed( )
> A MIDlet calls this method to destroy itself. It can be called while in the active state or the paused state, to indicate to the application manager that it has entered the destroyed state. Note that the application manager will not call destroyApp( ). Consequently, the MIDlet manages the release of its resources.

Creating MIDlets

Now that you're familiar with MIDlet states and the application manager, let's create another MIDlet. As you've probably guessed by now, this involves the following five steps:

1. Write the MIDlet.
2. Compile the MIDlet's source code.
3. Preverify the MIDlet's class file.
4. Package the application in a JAR file.
5. Create a JAD file.

Let's review each of these steps. First, we'll look at the command-line technique that was shown in Chapter 1. Then, we'll introduce the KToolbar application, which comes with the J2ME Wireless Toolkit and which can make our lives much easier.

Write the MIDlet

The first step in the development life cycle is to write the MIDlet. Example 4-2 shows a simple MIDlet, PaymentMIDlet. This MIDlet creates a List object of type EXCLUSIVE (that is, only one option can be selected at a time), and adds three methods of payments to it. It displays a list of options for the user to select a method of payment.

Example 4-2. Sample MIDlet

```java
import javax.microedition.midlet.*;
import javax.microedition.lcdui.*;

public class PaymentMIDlet extends MIDlet {

    // The display for this MIDlet
    private Display display;

    // List to display payment methods
    List method = null;

    public PaymentMIDlet() {
        method = new List("Method of Payment",
            Choice.EXCLUSIVE);
    }

    public void startApp() {
        display = Display.getDisplay(this);
        method.append("Visa", null);
        method.append("MasterCard", null);
        method.append("Amex", null);
        display.setCurrent(method);
    }

    /**
     * Pause is a no-op since there are no background
     * activities or record stores that need to be closed.
     */

    public void pauseApp() {
    }

    /**
     * Destroy must cleanup everything not handled by the
     * garbage collector. In this case there is nothing to
     * cleanup.
     */

    public void destroyApp(boolean unconditional) {
    }
}
```

Compile the Source Code

To compile the source code with the command-line tools of the Java Wireless Toolkit, use the javac command. Remember that you should use the -bootclasspath option to make sure the source code is compiled against the correct CLDC and MIDP classes.

```
C:\midlets> javac -bootclasspath C:\j2mewtk\lib\midpapi.zip PaymentMIDlet.java
```

This command produces the `PaymentMidlet.class` file in the current directory. This is a slightly simplified version of the command we used in Chapter 1, which puts the resulting class file in a temporary directory.

Preverify the Class File

The next step is to preverify the class file using the preverify command:

```
C:j2mewtk\bin> preverify -classpath C:\midlets;C:\j2mewtk\lib\midpapi.zip
    PaymentMIDlet
```

Again, a slightly different approach. This command creates an *output* subdirectory in the current directory and writes a new file `PaymentMIDlet.class`. This is the preverified class that the KVM can run with its modified class verifier.

Package the Application in a JAR File

In order to enable dynamic downloading of MIDP applications, the application must be packaged in a JAR file. To create a JAR file, use the jar command:

```
C:\midlets> jar cvf payment.jar PaymentMidlet.class
```

Create a JAD File

A JAD file is necessary if you want to run a CLDC-compliant application. Example 4-3 shows a sample JAD file for the payment MIDlet.

Example 4-3. A sample JAD file

```
MIDlet-1: payment,,PaymentMIDlet
MIDlet-Name: Payment
MIDlet-Version: 1.0
MIDlet-Vendor: ORA
MIDlet-Jar-URL: payment.jar
MIDlet-Jar-Size: 961
```

Once you have the JAD file, you can test your application using the MIDP emulator using the emulator command of the Java Wireless Toolkit, as shown here:

```
C:\j2mewtk\bin> emulator -Xdescriptor:C;\midlets\payment.jad
```

If all goes well, activate the MIDlet and you will see output similar to Figure 4-2.

If your MIDP application consists of multiple MIDlets, they can all be in one JAR file as a MIDlet suite. However, you would need to specify them in the JAD file using the MIDlet-*n* entry, where *n* is the number of the MIDlet. Consider the JAD file in Example 4-4, with three hypothetical MIDlets.

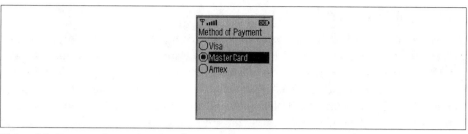

Figure 4-2. Running the payment MIDlet

Example 4-4. Three hypothetical MIDlets

```
MIDlet-1: Buy, , BuyMidlet
MIDlet-2: Sell, , SellMidlet
MIDlet-3: Trade, , TradeMidlet
MIDlet-Name: Trading
MIDlet-Version: 1.0
MIDlet-Vendor: ORA
MIDlet-Jar-URL: trade.jar
MIDlet-Jar-Size: 2961
```

If you run this JAD file, you would see something similar to Figure 4-3.

Figure 4-3. MIDlet suite

A MIDP application may consist of multiple MIDlets, as shown in Figure 4-3. Similarly, a desktop application consists of menus and options, as shown in Figure 4-4.

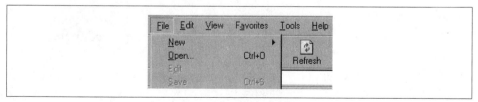

Figure 4-4. Desktop application

Simplifying the Development

You have now seen how to compile, preverify, create JAR and JAD files, and run MIDlets from the command line. This is fine if you want to understand what's happening behind the scenes. However, there is an alternative. An integrated development environment, such as the J2ME Wireless Toolkit, can be used to simplify the development and deployment of MIDlets. The J2ME Wireless Toolkit comes with an application called KToolbar. The following steps show how to use the KToolbar to set up a simple MIDlet, develop the application, package it, and run it.

1. In Microsoft Windows, choose Start → Programs → J2ME Wireless Toolkit → KToolbar to start the development environment. Figure 4-5 shows the resulting KToolbar screen.

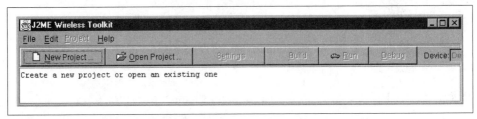

Figure 4-5. KToolbar screen

2. Click on the New Project button to create a new project called payment, and call the MIDlet class `PaymentMIDlet`, as shown in Figure 4-6.

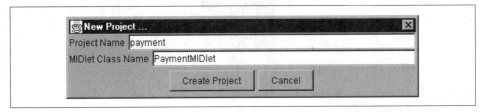

Figure 4-6. New project

3. Once you click on Create Project in Figure 4-6, you will get a setting project window, as shown in Figure 4-7. This window allows you to modify the MIDlet attributes. All the required attributes are shown in Figure 4-7.

4. If you click on the Optional tab, you will get a window with all the optional attributes, which are shown in Figure 4-8.

5. Once you click OK, you will get the original KToolbar screen with information to indicate where to save your source and resource files. Assuming the Wireless Toolkit is installed in the directory *C:\J2MEWTK*, then you will be told to save your Java source files in *C:\J2MEWTK\apps\payment\src* and your resource files (e.g., icons) in *C:\J2MEWTK\apps\payment\res*.

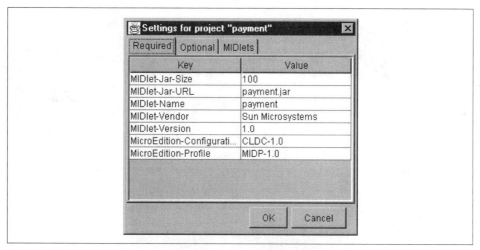

Figure 4-7. Required attributes

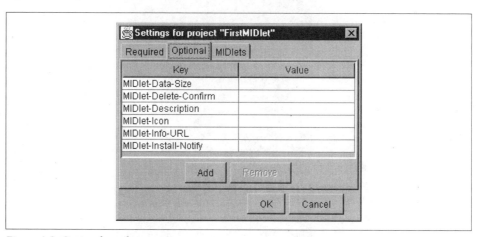

Figure 4-8. Optional attributes

Now, use your favorite text editor and write PaymentMIDlet, or simply copy the source from Example 4-2. Then, save it in the required location and click on the Build button to compile it. Note that the KToolbar application performs all the steps of compiling the application, preverifying the classes, compressing them into a JAR file, and creating a corresponding JAD file for you. All you have to do is to click the Run button to run it. Then you can test your MIDlet using a default phone, Motorola's i85s, or a Palm OS, as shown in Figure 4-9.

Choose your favorite testing device to test the MIDlet. For example, Figure 4-10 shows the PaymentMIDlet running in a default gray phone device.

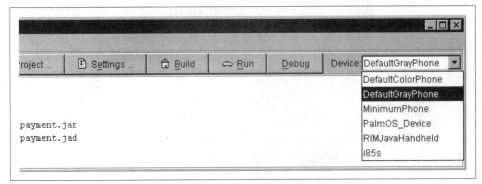

Figure 4-9. Select a testing device (upper right corner of KToolbar)

Figure 4-10. PaymentMIDlet on the default phone

Figure 4-11 shows the PaymentMIDlet running on Motorola's i85s device.

Figure 4-11. PaymentMIDlet on the Motorola i85s

Figure 4-12 shows the same application running on a Palm Pilot and Figure 4-13 shows the `PaymentMIDlet` application running on RIM's BlackBerry. Chapter 9 discusses how to install the Java Application Manager on a real Palm OS device and how to convert existing MIDlets into PRC executable files for handheld devices running Palm OS 3.5 or higher.

Deploying MIDlets

As of this writing, deploying MIDlets is still an experimental process. However, the Java application manager that comes with the MIDP reference implementation now provides some clues about how we can deploy MIDlets to various devices. Specifically, MIDlets can be installed in two ways:

- Using a data cable or other dedicated physical connection from a local host computer
- Using a network to which the device is intermittently connected

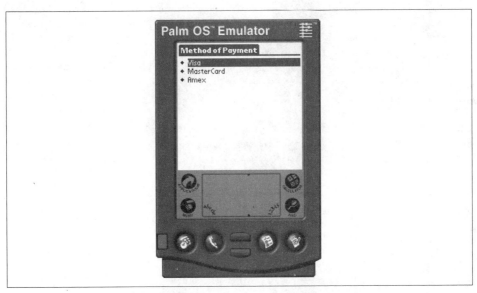

Figure 4-12. PaymentMIDlet on Palm OS

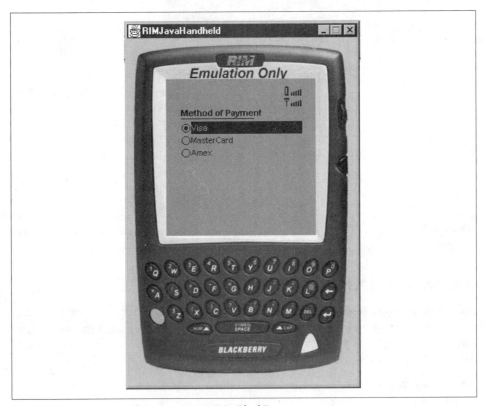

Figure 4-13. PaymentMIDlet running on RIM's BlackBerry

The first method works well with PDAs, which are often used with a host computer, with which the PDAs frequently synchronize their data. For example, the MIDP for Palm implementation, which is discussed in Chapter 9, is a good example of this; its application manager allows MIDlet suites to be installed from a host PC during the synchronization process.

The second method is more popular when installing MIDlets on cell phones and other wireless devices. With these devices, the most likely delivery transport is the wireless network itself. The process of deploying MIDlet suites over a network is referred to as *over-the-air (OTA) provisioning*. OTA provisioning is not yet part of the MIDP specification, but it is likely to become the dominant mechanism for distributing MIDlets and will probably be included in the formal specification soon.

Deploying OTA

As of this writing, OTA provisioning is just starting to be used with J2ME devices such as the Motorola i85s/i50x series of cell phones. OTA provisioning allows MIDlet providers to install their MIDlet suites via web servers that provide hypertext links. This allows you to download MIDlet suites to a cell phone via a WAP or Internet microbrowser. Here is a brief description of how this process works.

First, to deploy a MIDlet from a web server, you need to reconfigure your web server by adding a new MIME type:

```
text/vnd.sun.j2me.app-descriptor jad
```

How to add the MIME type depends on what server you are running. For example, if you're running Apache Tomcat, you would add a new MIME type by adding a new entry in the *web.xml* server configuration file, as follows:

```
<mime-mapping>
    <extension>jad</extension>
    <mime-type>text/vnd.sun.j2me.app-descriptor</mime-type>
</mime-mapping>
```

You would then use the following type of procedure to install a MIDlet suite from a web page:

1. Click on a link, which will probably request a file with a JAD extension, such as the following:

   ```
   <A HREF='MyApp.jad'>Click here to install the MIDlet suite</A>
   ```

2. The server will then send the *MyApp.jad* file to the phone with the MIME type set to text/vnd.sun.j2me.app-descriptor, as described earlier. Recall that the JAD file must contain the MIDlet-Jar-URL and MIDlet-Jar-Size properties, which tell the device where to download the MIDlet suite, as well as the suite's size in bytes.

3. The Java application manager on the phone will then ask if you want to install the MIDlet into the phone, assuming that the phone has the resources to run the MIDlet (i.e., that there's enough space on the device to hold the MIDlet suite).

4. If you answer yes, the entire JAR file will be downloaded from the server, using the properties specified in the JAD file.

Once the MIDlet is downloaded, it will be installed the first time you try to use it. A downloaded MIDlet stays on the device until you remove it (unlike Java applets).

Deploying to the Motorola i50x/i85s

You can also download J2ME applications to a Motorola/Nextel i50x or i85s device from your desktop through a data cable. This cable does not come with the phone itself, but can be ordered online from Nextel. The iDEN update software can then be downloaded from the iDEN development site (*http://www.motorola.com/idendev*).

In addition, you can also purchase a data cable that comes with a CD-ROM containing the iDEN update software from Nextel from this site. Obtaining the software may involve authorization from your carrier, which can take between one and five days. Once you are granted authorization, however, you can install applications on up to five individual phones. The following paragraphs describe how to use the Motorola iDEN update software to download a J2ME MIDlet to your phone.

After you have obtained the update software, start it up and choose the J2ME Developers tab on the far left. This will result in a screen similar to that in Figure 4-14. From here, you can choose a JAD file to download the application into your phone through the data cable. Note that the JAD file and the JAR file must reside in the same directory and must have the same filename (excluding the extension).

For the most part, downloading an application to the phone is easy. However, the Motorola i85s and i50x phones will perform a number of checks to ensure the integrity of the application while installing it. You should observe the following rules to ensure that the phone will install the application.

The JAD file downloaded to the i85s or i50x must contain at least the following entries, which are case-sensitive:

```
MIDlet-Name:
MIDlet-Version:
MIDlet-Vendor:
MIDlet-Jar-Size:
MIDlet-Jar-URL:
```

It can also contain the following optional entries:

```
MIDlet-Description:
MIDlet-Info-URL:
MIDlet-Data-Size:
```

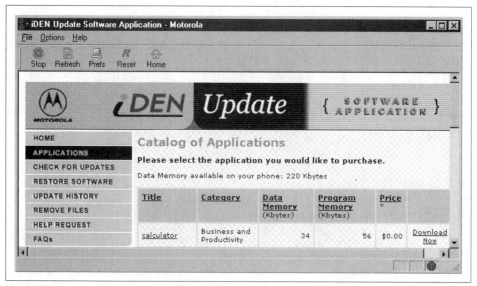

Figure 4-14. Motorola iDEN update software

In addition, the JAD file can contain any other MIDlet-specific information that does not begin with the letters "MIDlet-".

Remember from Chapter 3 that the JAR file *must* contain a manifest with at least the following information, which must be identical to the data in the JAD file:

```
MIDlet-Name:
MIDlet-Version:
MIDlet-Vendor:
```

If you do not include this information in the manifest, the phone will respond with a "Descriptor Error" when it is attempting to install the application. If this happens, simply press the Menu button while the MIDlet is selected and remove it from the system.

Here are some other things to note when downloading to the Motorola i85s or i50x:

- The JAD file is case-sensitive.
- The maximum file length for both the JAD and the JAR file is 16 characters, which includes the four characters for the extension (e.g., *.JAD* or *.JAR*).
- The byte size of the JAR file must be accurately stated in the JAD file.
- Each of the attributes in the JAD and JAR file manifests must have a value associated with it. You cannot leave an attribute value blank.
- Classes which are instantiated using the `Class.forName()` method must be identified in the JAD file using the attribute: `iDEN-Install-Class-n:`, where n is a positive integer. The class name is listed afterward without the `.class` extension.

Example 4-5 shows the manifest information that we would be using if we wanted to download the HelloMidlet application from Chapter 1 to the Motorola i85s. Remember that the manifest must contain the three specified attributes (MIDlet-Name, MIDlet-Version, and MIDlet-Vendor) and that they must be identical to the values in the JAD file. If they differ, the phone will not install the MIDlet. We have also included the MIDlet class identification information and the profile and configuration version numbers, which we recommend that you include in your MIDlet manifests as well.

Example 4-5. Manifest.mf

```
MIDlet-Name: HelloMidlet
MIDlet-Vendor: ORA
MIDlet-Version: 1.0.0
MIDlet-1: HelloMidlet,,HelloMidlet
MicroEdition-Profile: MIDP-1.0
MicroEdition-Configuration: CLDC-1.0
```

At this point, let's create a compressed JAR file of the classes that make up the MIDlet. With the manifest and the preverified class in the same directory, enter the following command:

```
>jar cvfm HelloMidlet.jar manifest.mf HelloMidlet.class
```

Once that is completed, you'll need to create the JAD file. Example 4-6 shows the JAD file for our HelloMidlet application. Note that we had to change the value of the MIDlet-Jar-Size attribute to match the size, in bytes, of the JAR file that we just created. In this case, it turned out to be 954 bytes with the additional manifest information.

Example 4-6. HelloMidlet.jad

```
MIDlet-1: HelloMidlet,,HelloMidlet
MIDlet-Jar-Size: 954
MIDlet-Jar-URL: http://www.oreilly.com/
MIDlet-Name: HelloMidlet
MIDlet-Vendor: ORA
MIDlet-Version: 1.0.0
MIDlet-Description: A sample application
```

Now we're ready to go. Again, be sure that the JAD file and the JAR file have the same name and reside in the same directory. Then use the iDEN software tools to download the application to your phone. It should only take a few seconds once you've chosen the target JAD file. After the download has completed, start the Java Application Manager on the phone (Java Apps under the Main Menu) and select the HelloMidlet application. Press the soft button to install it. You are now installing your first Java MIDlet on a real device. If everything goes okay, you can run your program after it completes the installation and verification steps.

CHAPTER 5

MIDP GUI Programming

User interface requirements for handheld devices are different from those for desktop computers. For example, the display size of handheld devices is smaller, and input devices do not always include pointing tools such as a mouse or pen input. For these reasons, you cannot follow the same user-interface programming guidelines for applications running on handheld devices that you can on desktop computers.

The CLDC itself does not define any GUI functionality. Instead, the official GUI classes for the J2ME are included in profiles such as the MIDP and are defined by the Java Community Process (JCP). You'll note that the GUI classes included in the MIDP are not based on the Abstract Window Toolkit (AWT). That seems like a major issue, which brings us to the following question.

Why Not Reuse the AWT?

After a great deal of consideration, the MIDP Expert Group decided not to subset the existing AWT and Project Swing classes for the following reasons:

- AWT is designed for desktop computers and optimized for these machines.
- AWT assumes certain user interaction models. The component set of the AWT is designed to work with a pointing device such as a mouse; however, many handheld devices, such as cell phones, have only a keypad for user input.
- AWT has a rich feature set, and includes support for functionality that is not found or is impractical to implement on handheld devices. For example, the AWT has extensive support for window management, such as resizing overlapping windows. However, the limited display size of handheld devices makes resizing a window impractical. Therefore, the window and layout managers within the AWT are not required for handheld devices.

- When a user interacts with an AWT-based application, event objects are created dynamically. These objects exist only until each associated event is processed by the application or system, at which time the object becomes eligible for garbage collection. The limited CPU and memory of handheld devices, however, cannot handle the burden.

The MIDP GUI APIs

Because of the issues outlined earlier, the MIDP contains its own abbreviated GUI, which is much different from AWT. The MIDP GUI consists of both high-level and low-level APIs, each with their own set of events. This chapter discusses and shows examples of using objects from both the high-level and low-level APIs. Handling events from APIs, however, is deferred to the next chapter.

The high-level API is designed for applications where portability between mobile information devices is important. To achieve portability, the API employs a high-level abstraction and gives you little control over its look and feel. For example, you cannot define the visual appearance (shape, color, or font) of the high-level components. Most interactions with the components are encapsulated by the implementation; the application will not be aware of them. Consequently, the underlying implementation does the necessary adaptation to the device's hardware and native user interface style. Classes that implement the high-level API all inherit the javax.microedition.lcdui.Screen class.

The low-level API provides little abstraction. It is designed for applications that need precise placement and control of graphic elements, as well as access to low-level input events. This API gives the application full control over what is being drawn on the display. The javax.microedition.lcdui.Canvas and javax.microedition.lcdui.Graphics classes implement the low-level API. However, we should point out that MIDlets that access the low-level API are not guaranteed to be portable, because this API provides mechanisms to access details that are specific to a particular device.

The MIDP GUI Model

Here's how the MIDP GUI model works, in a nutshell. In order to show something on a MIDP device, you'll need to obtain the device's *display,* which is represented by the javax.microedition.lcdui.Display class. The Display class is the one and only display manager that is instantiated for each active MIDlet and provides methods to retrieve information about the device's display capabilities.

Obtaining the device's display is easy. However, this object by itself isn't very interesting. Instead, the more interesting abstraction is the *screen*, which encapsulates and organizes graphics objects and coordinates user input through the device. Screens are represented by the javax.microedition.lcdui.Screen object and are shown by the Display object by calling its setCurrent( ) method. There can be several screens in an application, but only one screen at a time can be visible (or *current*) in a display, and the user can traverse only through the items on that screen. Figure 5-1 shows the one-to-many relationship between the display and its screens.

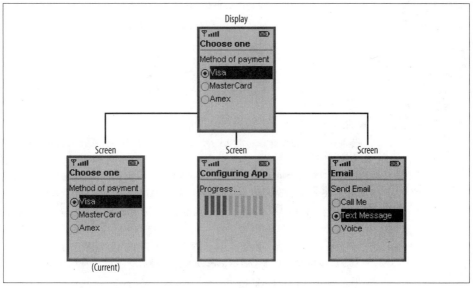

Figure 5-1. Relationship between display and screens

There are three types of screens in the MIDP GUI:

- Screens that entirely encapsulate a complex user interface component, such as a List or TextBox component (the List component is shown in Figure 5-8 and the TextBox component is shown in Figure 5-5). The structure of these screens is predefined, and the application cannot add other components to these screens.

- Generic screens that use a Form component. The application can add text, images, and a simple set of related UI components to the form, which acts as a container.

- Screens used within the context of the low-level API, such as a subclass of the Canvas or Graphics class.

The lcdui Package

All MIDP GUI classes are contained in the javax.microedition.lcdui package. This package contains three interfaces and twenty-one classes, as shown in Table 5-1 and Table 5-2.

Table 5-1. lcdui interfaces

Interface	Description
Choice	Defines an API for a user interface component that implements a selection from a pre-defined number of choices
CommandListener	Used by applications that need to receive high-level events from implementations
ItemStateListener	Used by applications that need to receive events that indicate changes in the internal state of the interactive items

Table 5-2. lcdui classes

Class	Description
Alert	A screen that shows data to the user and waits for a certain period of time before proceeding to the next screen.
AlertType	A utility class that indicates the nature of the alert.
Canvas	The base class for writing applications that need to handle low-level events and to issue graphics calls for drawing to the display.
ChoiceGroup	A group of selectable elements intended to be placed within a Form.
Command	A construct that encapsulates the semantic information of an action.
DateField	An editable component for presenting calendar data and time information that may be placed into a Form.
Display	A utility that represents the manager of the display and input devices of the system.
Displayable	An object that has the capability of being placed on the display.
Font	A utility that represents font and font metrics.
Form	A screen that contains an arbitrary mixture of items (images, text, text fields, or choice groups, for instance).
Gauge	A utility that implements a bar graph display of a value intended for use in a form.
Graphics	A utility that provides a simple two-dimensional geometric rendering capability.
Image	A utility that holds graphical image data.
ImageItem	A utility that provides layout control when Image objects are added to a form or alert.
Item	A superclass for all components that can be added to a Form or Alert.
List	A screen containing a list of choices.
Screen	The superclass of all high-level user interface classes.
StringItem	An item that can contain a String.
TextBox	A screen that allows the user to enter and edit text.
TextField	An editable text component that can be placed into a Form.
Ticker	A ticker-type piece of text that runs continuously across the display. It can be attached to all screen types except Canvas.

The class diagram in Figure 5-2 shows the major classes and the relationships between them.

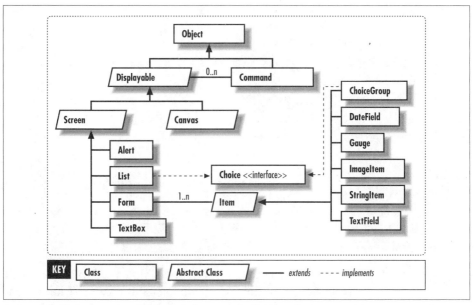

Figure 5-2. Class diagram of the major classes in the lcdui package

The High-Level MIDP APIs

Now, let's see how the various classes in the high-level API can be used to create GUI components. We will cover two parts of this process: working with screens and the components that subclass them, and working with forms and the components that can be arranged in them.

Working with Screens

Having seen an example of a screen, a few questions immediately come to mind: how do you manage screens, how do you navigate through them, and how do you manage the display and the input devices? The answer is that all this functionality is implemented by the Display class, which includes methods for requesting that objects be displayed on the device, and for retrieving properties of the device.

Display

A reference to the device's display can be obtained by providing a MIDlet reference to the static getDisplay( ) method.

```
public static Display getDisplay(MIDlet c);
```

This is typically done in the startApp( ) method of a MIDlet, as follows:

```
public class MyMIDlet extends MIDlet {

    Display display = null;

    public MyMIDlet( ) { // constructor
    }

    public void startApp( ) {
        display = Display.getDisplay(this);
    }

    // other methods
}
```

 The getDisplay( ) method should be called after the beginning of the MIDlet's startApp( ) method, as shown earlier. It should *never* be called from the MIDlet's constructor, as per the MIDP specification, as it may not be properly initialized by the application manager at that time.

After you obtain a reference to the device's display, you simply need to create a GUI component to show. Note that all of the GUI components in Figure 5-2 implement the Displayable abstract class. You can pass the GUI component you create to one of Display's two setCurrent( ) methods:

```
public void setCurrent(Displayable d);
public void setCurrent(Alert alert, Displayable d);
```

The second method is used when you want to show a temporary alert message followed by the displayable GUI element. We'll discuss alerts later on in this chapter.

To find out what is currently being displayed on the device, use the getCurrent( ) method, which returns a reference to the Displayable object that is currently being displayed.

```
public Displayable getCurrent( );
```

In addition, the Display class (which is really the manager of the device) provides two methods for querying the display to determine the types of colors it supports:

```
public void boolean inColor( );
public int numColors( );
```

The first method, isColor( ), returns a boolean: true if the device supports color and false if it only supports grayscale. The numColors( ) method returns an integer number of distinct colors supported by the device.

Screen

As we mentioned before, the basic unit of interaction between the user and the device is the screen, which is an object that encapsulates device-specific graphics user input. As you can see from the class diagram in Figure 5-2, there are four types of high-level screens, shown by the subclasses: TextBox, List, Alert, and Form.

However, Screen is an abstract class with some functionality of its own. Every Screen can have two additional characteristics: a title and a ticker. The screen title is simply a String that appears above the screen contents. The ticker is a graphical component that appears above the title and can be used to scroll information across to the user. Both are optional, although the title will default to a standard string. If the ticker is omitted, it is not shown at all and the space is given instead to the screen. We'll discuss the Ticker component shortly. However, Figure 5-3 shows the relative positions of the title and the ticker properties in a Screen object.

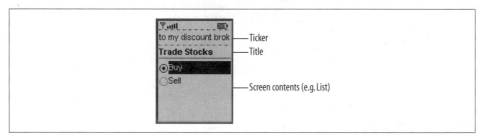

Figure 5-3. Titles and tickers on a screen

The following methods of the Screen class can be used to set and retrieve the title and the ticker, respectively.

```
public void setTitle(String title);
public String getTitle( );
public void setTicker(Ticker ticker);
public Ticker getTicker( );
```

Ticker

The Ticker class implements a tickertape, or a piece of text that runs continuously across the display. A ticker can be attached to one or more of the four screens discussed earlier, namely: Alert, TextBox, List, and Form. To create a ticker object, use the Ticker constructor:

```
public Ticker(String str);
```

You can access the string used in the ticker with the following methods:

```
public String getString( );
public void setString(String s);
```

Once a ticker is created, it can be attached to a screen using the screen's setTicker( ) method. For example, the following snippet of code creates a List screen and attaches a ticker to it:

```
Display display = Display.getDisplay();
List list = new List("Trade Stocks", Choice.EXCLUSIVE);
list.append("Buy", null);
list.append("Sell", null);
list.setTicker(new Ticker("Welcome to my discount broker"));
display.setCurrent(list);
```

Figure 5-4 shows what a ticker looks like. It is located above the List component in the display.

Figure 5-4. An example of a ticker

There are a few points to note about a ticker:

- No method calls are provided for starting and stopping the ticker.
- The ticker string scrolls continuously. In other words, when the string finishes scrolling off the display, the ticker starts over at the beginning of the string. It may help to add some spaces at the end of the ticker string so the message ends do not appear tied together.
- The direction and the speed of the scrolling are determined by the MIDP implementation.

TextBox

A TextBox object is a screen that allows the user to enter and edit text. You can use a TextBox if your MIDlet needs some kind of input such as a name, a phone number, an email address, or a password. To create a TextBox object, you need to specify four parameters, as shown in the TextBox's constructor:

```
public TextBox(String title, String text, int maxSize, int constraints);
```

The title is reused as the screen title, while the text and maxSize are used to determine the initial (or default) text and maximum size of the text box. Finally, constraints can be used to limit the user's input. The constraints used are static constant integers of the TextField class, which are shared between TextField and TextBox, and are as follows:

TextField.ANY

The user is allowed to enter any character.

TextField.EMAILADDR

Input must be an email address.

TextField.NUMBER

Input must be an integer value.

TextField.PASSWD

The text entered will be masked (replaced by asterisks), so the characters typed are not visible.

TextField.PHONENUMBER

Input must be a phone number.

TextField.URL

Input must be a URL.

If you use a constraint other than TextField.ANY, the implementation will perform validation to make sure that the characters that are input conform to the requested type. (For example, TextField.NUMBER will not allow letters to be entered.) This is the only validation that is performed.

Note that the TextField.PASSWD constraint can be combined with any of the other constraints using the bitwise OR "|" operator. For example, if you wanted to create a TextBox that constrained input to a phone number but also wanted to keep the entered data hidden, you would create the object as follows:

```
TextBox t = new TextBox("Tel", "", 12, TextField.PHONENUMBER |
    TextField.PASSWD);
```

If you wish to set or retrieve the current constraints that are active for the TextBox, use the following methods:

```
public int getConstraints();
public void setConstrants(int c);
```

Another thing that we should point out is that a text box has a *capacity*, or a maximum size, which is the number of characters of text that it can hold. However, each MIDP implementation may place a boundary on the maximum size, which could be smaller than the size the application requested. The maximum size imposed by the implementation can be retrieved using the getMaxSize() method and (potentially) reset using the setMaxSize() method.

```
public int getMaxSize();
public void setMaxSize(int size);
```

A well-written MIDP application should always compare the requested size against the current maximum size.

In the current MIDP reference implementation from Sun Microsystems, getMaxSize( ) always returns the requested size by the MIDlet. But don't let that get you out of the habit of checking.

You can set or retrieve the entire text in the TextBox with the setString( ) and getString( ) methods:

```
public String getString( );
public void setString(String s);
```

In addition, if you would like to see the number of characters in the text that has been entered, use the size( ) method, which returns an integer:

```
public int size( );
```

You can also manipulate the text in the TextBox quite easily by deleting, inserting, or replacing the current text using the following methods:

```
public void delete(int offset, int length);
public void insert(char[] data, int offset, int length, int position);
public void insert(String src, int position);
public void setChars(char[] data, int offset, int length);
```

Finally, if you want to find out which position the caret, also known as the insertion beam, is currently in front of, TextBox includes the following method:

```
public int getCaretPosition( );
```

Here's a simple example. The following snippet of code creates a TextBox object with the label "TextBox" and initial text set to "This is a text box". The maximum size is 20 characters, which can be any type of characters.

```
TextBox tb = new TextBox("TextBox", "This is a textbox", 20, TextField.ANY);
Display display = Display.getDisplay(this);
display.setCurrent(tb);
```

If you write a complete MIDlet and run it in an emulator, you will see something similar to Figure 5-5. Note that if the text to be displayed is larger than the size of one screen, the implementation will let the user scroll to view and edit any part of the text. How this is done is implementation-dependent.

Figure 5-5. A TextBox example

Alert

An alert is an ordinary screen that can contain text and an image. It informs the user about errors and other exceptional conditions. An alert can either be *modal* or *timed.*

A modal alert remains on the screen until the user dismisses it, at which point it returns to either the screen that was displayed before it, or a screen specifically chosen by the application. This is useful if you require the user to make a choice. For example, you might display a message such as "Are you sure?" and offer "Yes" and "No" options. Note that a MIDP implementation will automatically provide a way to dismiss a modal alert. Sun's reference implementation, for example, provides a Done command mapped to a soft button.

A timed alert, on the other hand, is displayed for a certain amount of time (typically a few seconds). It is useful for displaying an informative message that does not need to be acknowledged by the user. For example, you might want to display a message that says "Your message has been sent". However, note that if you specify a timed alert that has too much content to be displayed all at once, it automatically becomes a modal alert!

An alert can be created as an instance of the Alert class, which has the following two constructors:

```
public Alert(String title);
public Alert(String title, String alertText, Image alertImage,
    AlertType alertType);
```

The first constructor creates a timed alert. However, as you probably noticed, the timeout value is not specified in the constructor. Instead, the alert will use the default timeout value, which can be obtained for each device using the immutable getDefaultTimeout() method. If you want to change the alert's timeout, use the setTimeout() method with an integer that specifies the timeout in milliseconds. To obtain the current timeout for the alert, use the getTimeout() method.

```
public int getDefaultTimeout();
public int getTimeout();
public void setTimeout(int t);
```

For example, the following snippet of code creates a timed alert with a timeout value set to four seconds:

```
Alert alert = new Alert("title");
alert.setTimeout(4000);
```

You can also pass in the constant value Alert.FOREVER. This will keep the alert up indefinitely, which has the side effect of turning a timed dialog into a modal dialog.

```
alert.setTimeout(Alert.FOREVER);
```

You can create a more specialized alert using the second constructor. This constructor allows you to associate an icon with the alert, using an Image object. Also, an alert may have a type associated with it to provide an indication of the nature of the alert.

The MIDP implementation may use this type to play an appropriate sound when the alert is presented to the user. The AlertType class provides five types of alerts: AlertType.ALARM, AlertType.CONFIRMATION, AlertType.ERROR, AlertType.INFO, and AlertType.WARNING. As an example, the following snippet of code creates an alert of type AlertType.CONFIRMATION, and it does not have an icon associated with it:

```
public Alert(String title, String messageString, Image alertImage,
    AlertType alertType);
```

Note that any or all of the parameters in the second constructor may be null if you wish to omit the image, the title, the text, or the alert type. The additional properties set in the constructor each has its own set of accessors within the Alert class:

```
public Image getImage();
public String getString();
public AlertType getType();
public void setImage(Image img);
public void setString(String str);
public void setType(AlertType type);
```

Now, let's see examples of both timed and modal alerts. The following snippets of code create a TextBox object and a timed alert. When the MIDlet is activated, the alert will be displayed, and after five seconds the text box will be displayed automatically, courtesy of the Display.setCurrent() method.

```
TextBox tb = new TextBox("text box",
    "Welcome to MIDP GUI Programming", 40, TextField.ANY);
Alert timedAlert = new Alert("Confirmation",
    "Your message has been sent!", null, AlertType.CONFIRMATION);
TimedAlert.setTimeout(5000);
Display display = Display.getDisplay(this);
Display.setCurrent(timedAlert, tb);
```

Figure 5-6 shows how the code above is displayed. The alert, which says "Your message has been sent!" is displayed first. After five seconds, the current display returns to the text box that says "Welcome to MIDP GUI Programming."

Figure 5-6. An example of a timed alert

As you can see from the previous example, timed alerts do not need user intervention. On the other hand, modal alerts stay up until the user dismisses them, as shown in the following example.

```
TextBox tb = new TextBox("text box", "Welcome to MIDP Programming",
        40, Textfield.ANY);
Alert modalAert = new Alert("Error",
        "Network error. Please try again later.",
        null, AlertType.ERROR);
modalAlert.setTimeout(Alert.FOREVER);
Display display = Display.getDisplay(this);
display.setCurrent(modalAlert, tb);
```

In this case, the network error screen stays up until the user dismisses it, using the soft button that corresponds to the Done command, as shown in Figure 5-7. The Done command, for modal alerts, is provided automatically by Sun's MIDP reference implementation. In this example, the text box screen becomes the current screen only after the user dismisses the alert.

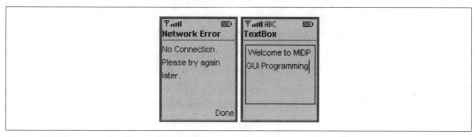

Figure 5-7. An example of a modal alert

List

A list is a screen containing selectable choices. Both List and ChoiceGroup have common behavior defined by the Choice interface. The user can interact with a list by moving from element to element. Note that this high-level API interaction does not cause any programming events to be fired back to the application. That only occurs when a selection has been made.

A list can be created as an instance of the List class, which has the following two constructors:

```
public List(String title, int listType);
public List(String title, int listType, String[] stringElements,
            Image[] imageElements);
```

The first constructor is used to create an empty list, specifying the title and the type of the list. There are three types of list choices that can be passed in for the second parameter: IMPLICIT, EXCLUSIVE, and MULTIPLE. These options can be specified using the constants provided in the Choice interface, which is implemented by the List class.

- An EXCLUSIVE type of list has no more than one choice selected at a time, which is similar to a group of radio buttons in the AWT world.
- An IMPLICIT type is an EXCLUSIVE choice where the focused choice is implicitly selected, much like a drop-down menu.
- The MULTIPLE type is a list that can have arbitrary number of choices selected at a time, and presents itself as a series of checkboxes.

As an example, the following snippet of code creates a list of type EXCLUSIVE, the title of which is "Choose one".

```
List list = new List("Choose one", Choice.EXCLUSIVE);
```

Once you have created an empty list, you can insert, append, or replace choices in the list. Each choice has an integer index that represents its position in the list. The first choice starts at 0 and extends to the current size of the list minus one. The List class provides the following methods for these operations.

```
public int append(String stringElement, Image imageElement);
public void insert(int index, String stringElement, Image imageElement);
public void set(int index, String stringElement, Image imageElement);
```

Note that a choice is composed of a text string and an optional image. For example, here is how to add a couple of choices to the earlier list. Note that the append( ) method returns the index that was assigned to the choice that was passed in, in case we might need it later.

```
int saveIndex = list.append("save", null);
int deleteIndex = list.append("delete", null);
```

You can delete any index in the list using the following method:

```
public void delete(int index);
```

If you want to retrieve the string element or the image element for any index, the following methods will do the trick:

```
public String getString(int index);
public Image getImage(int index);
```

If you want to set, unset, or retrieve the currently selected index in the list, or query any index to see if it is currently selected, use the following methods:

```
public int getSelectedIndex( )
public boolean isSelected(int index);
public setSelectedIndex(int index, boolean selected);
```

Finally, you can use a boolean array to set the selection state of the entire list. This is known as the selection flag, and can be accessed using the following methods. Note that the getSelectedFlags( ) method does not return a boolean array, but instead modifies one that has been passed in (and returns the number of elements that are selected as an integer); this is a common optimization technique that prevents the creation of a new array each time the method is called. The array must be at least as long as the number of elements in the list. If it is longer, then the array elements beyond it are set to false.

```
public int getSelectedFlags(boolean[] selectedArray);
public void setSelectedFlags(boolean[] selectedArray);
```

For a list of type MULTIPLE, the setSelectedFlags( ) method sets the selected state of every element in the list. For a list of type EXCLUSIVE or IMPLICIT, exactly one element in the boolean array must be set to true; if no element is true, then the first element will be selected. If two or more elements are true, the implementation chooses the first true element and selects it.

Let's look at some examples of the List component. The following snippet of code shows an example where a list of type EXCLUSIVE is created and displayed:

```
Display display = Display.getDisplay(this);
List menu = new List("Edit", Choice.EXCLUSIVE);
menu.append("Save");
menu.append("Move to");
menu.append("delete");
display.setCurrent(menu);
```

In this list, only one choice can be selected, as shown in Figure 5-8.

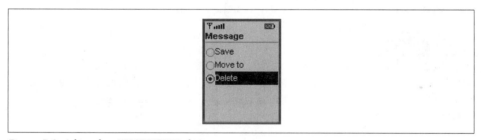

Figure 5-8. A list of an EXCLUSIVE choice

If you change the type of the list to IMPLICIT, then the result would be similar to Figure 5-9. Note that the radio buttons have disappeared.

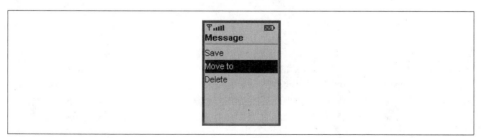

Figure 5-9. A list of an IMPLICIT choice

Similar to an EXCLUSIVE type, only one choice can be selected at a time in this list; however, the focused choice will be implicitly selected, instead of having to select it to color in a circle on the left. The third type of list is MULTIPLE, where multiple selections can be made, as shown in Figure 5-10.

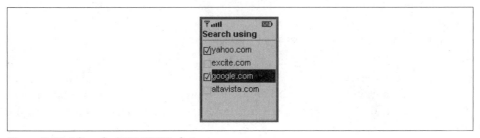

Figure 5-10. A list of a MULTIPLE choice

As we mentioned before, choices in a list are referred to by indices, which are consecutive integers in the range zero to the size of the list, minus 1 (e.g., size( ) - 1). Zero (0) refers to the first choice and size( ) - 1 refers to the last choice. For example, to delete the "Move To" choice in Figure 5-9:

```
list.delete(1);
```

Here, we use the second List constructor to create a list, specifying its title, the type of the list, and an array of strings and images to be used as its initial contents. The following code creates a list with two initial choices and no images:

```
List list2 = new List("Make a selection", Choice.EXCLUSIVE,
    {"Add", "Delete"}, null);
```

The number of elements in the list is determined by the length of the stringElements array passed into the constructor, which cannot be null. The imageElements array, however, can be null. However, if it is non-null, it must be the same length as the stringElements array.

Working with Forms

In addition to screen-based components, you also have the ability to use forms to combine multiple components into one screen. This section discusses the Form class as well as the components that can be placed on a form.

Form

A Form object is a screen that contains an arbitrary mixture of items, including read-only and editable text fields, images, date fields, gauges, and choice groups. As we mentioned before, any subclass of the Item class (which we'll discuss shortly) can be placed on a Form object. The Form class has the following two constructors:

```
public Form(String title);
public Form(String title, Item[] items);
```

The first constructor is used to create a new empty form, specifying only its title. The second constructor is used to create a new form with a title and initial contents. As an example, the following line of code creates an empty form that has the title "Choose an Item", as shown in Figure 5-11. This is basically a regular screen.

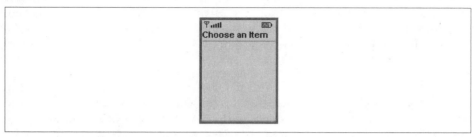

Figure 5-11. An empty form

```
Form form = new Form("Choose an Item");
```

The Form object does not use any sort of layout manager. Instead, the Form object will arrange its components much like a list, usually top to bottom. And like the choices within a list, items within a form can be edited using appropriate operations such as insert, append, and delete. The methods of the Form class, along with their signatures, are listed below.

First, to append an image to the end of the form, you can use the following method:

```
public int append(Image img);
```

This method appends an object that subclasses the Item object:

```
public int append(Item item);
```

You can also append a generic string, using the following method:

```
public int append(String str);
```

This method deletes the item at the given position in the form, shrinking the size of the form by one.

```
public void delete(int itemNum):
```

You can access any item in the form at its given position using the following method. The contents of the form will be left unchanged.

```
public Item get(int itemNum);
```

This method inserts an item in the form just prior to the index specified:

```
public void insert(int itemNum, Item item);
```

The following method replaces the previous item by setting the item referenced by itemNum to the specified Item given:

```
public int set(int itemNum, Item item);
```

Finally, in order to find the current number of items that are in the form, use the size( ) method:

```
public int size( );
```

The GUI components that can be placed on a form are the following: ChoiceGroup, DateField, Gauge, ImageItem, StringItem, and TextField. All of these items are sub-classes of the Item abstract class. We will see how to place these items on a form shortly. But first, let's introduce each one in turn.

Item

The Item abstract class acts as the base class for all components that can be placed either on a form or an alert. All Item objects have a label (i.e., a string attached to the item), which can be accessed using the following methods:

```
public String getLabel( );
public void setLabel(String s);
```

These are the only two methods in this abstract class.

ChoiceGroup

A ChoiceGroup object represents a group of selectable choices to be placed on a Form object. Similar to the List class, it implements the Choice interface. It also extends the Item abstract class. This object may mandate that a single choice be made, or it may allow multiple choices. The ChoiceGroup class has the following two constructors:

```
public ChoiceGroup(String label, int choiceType);
public ChoiceGroup(String label, int choiceType,
    String[] stringElements, Image[] imageElements);
```

The first constructor is used to create an empty choice group, specifying its label and type. Since this class implements the Choice interface, you might think that there are three types of choices you can use. However, when using a choice group, only two choices are available: EXCLUSIVE and MULTIPLE. The IMPLICIT type is not available for use with a choice group, like it was with the List component. There is no need to have a "menu" like choice field inside of a form. (Remember that EXCLUSIVE is a choice having exactly one choice selected at a time; and MULTIPLE is a choice that can have an arbitrary number of choices selected at a time.)

The second ChoiceGroup constructor can be used to create a new choice group, specifying its title and type, as well as an array of strings and images to be used as its initial contents.

Once you have created an empty choice, you can insert, append, or replace choices in it, exactly as in a List component. Again, each choice has an integer index that represents its position in the list. The first choice starts at 0 and extends to the current size of the list, minus one. The ChoiceGroup class provides the following methods for these operations.

```
public int append(String stringElement, Image imageElement);
public void insert(int index, String stringElement, Image imageElement);
public void set(int index, String stringElement, Image imageElement);
```

Note that a choice is composed of a text string and an optional image. For example, here is how to add a couple of choices to the earlier list. Note that the append() method returns the index that was assigned to the choice that was passed in, in case we might need it later.

```
int saveIndex = list.append("save", null);
int deleteIndex = list.append("delete", null);
```

In addition, you can delete any index in the choice group using the following method:

```
public void delete(int index);
```

If you want to retrieve the string element or the image element for any index, the following methods are useful:

```
public String getString(int index);
public Image getImage(int index);
```

If you want to set, unset, or retrieve the currently selected index in the choice group, or query any index to see if it is currently selected, use the following:

```
public int getSelectedIndex()
public boolean isSelected(int index);
public setSelectedIndex(int index, boolean selected);
```

Finally, just as with the List component, you can use a boolean selection flags array to set the selection state of the entire choice group. Again, the getSelectedFlags() method does not return a boolean array, but instead modifies one that has been passed in (and returns the number of elements that are selected as an integer as an optimization technique). The array must be at least as long as the number of elements in the list. If it is longer, then the array elements beyond it are set to false.

```
public int getSelectedFlags(boolean[] selectedArray);
public void setSelectedFlags(boolean[] selectedArray);
```

For a list of type MULTIPLE, the setSelectedFlags() method sets the selected state of every element in the list. For a list of type EXCLUSIVE, exactly one element in the boolean array must be set to true; if no element is true, then the first element will be selected. If two or more elements are true, the implementation chooses the first true element and selects it.

The following snippet of code creates a new empty ChoiceGroup object whose title is "Selection", and whose type is EXCLUSIVE:

```
ChoiceGroup choices = new ChoiceGroup("Method of payment",
    Choice.EXCLUSIVE);
```

The following code adds several new choices to the choice group.

```
choices.append("Visa", null);
choices.append("Master Card", null);
choices.append("Amex", null);
```

Similar to choices within a list, choices within a choice group can be edited using the familiar insert, append, and delete methods. In addition, choices are referred to by their indexes. For example, to delete the last choice:

```
choices.delete(2);
```

It is important to note that once a choice group has been created and populated, it cannot be displayed using setCurrent( ), as a list can. A choice group is a subclass of item and has to be placed on a form, which can in turn be displayed using setCurrent( ).

```
Form form = new Form("Choose one");
form.append(choices);
Display.setCurrent(form);
```

Figure 5-12 shows an example of an EXCLUSIVE choice group, and Figure 5-13 shows an example of a MULTIPLE choice group. Again, the IMPLICIT choice is not available for use with the ChoiceGroup class; if you attempt to use it, an IllegalArgumentException will be thrown.

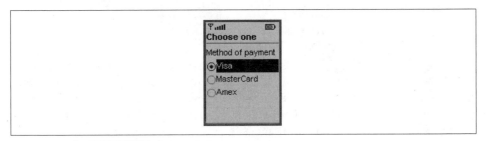

Figure 5-12. An EXCLUSIVE choice group

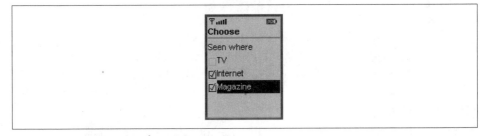

Figure 5-13. A MULTIPLE choice group

DateField

A DateField object is an editable component for representing calendar date and time information that can be placed on a Form object. It can be configured to accept date or time information, or both. A DateField object can be created using one of the following two constructors:

```
public DateField(String label, int mode);
public DateField(String label, int mode, TimeZone timeZone);
```

The first constructor is used to create a DateField object with the specified label and mode. This mode can be specified providing one of the static fields: DateField.DATE, DateField.TIME, or DateField.DATE_TIME. The DateField.DATE input mode allows you to set date information, DateField.TIME allows for clock time information (hours and minutes), and DateField.DATE_TIME allows for setting both.

The DateField object has the following methods to access the properties added onto the Form object (remember that the label property is defined in the Item abstract class):

```
public Date getDate()
public int getInputMode()
public void setDate(Date date);
public void setInputMode(int mode);
```

In addition, you can use the toString() method to output a string-based copy of the date or time data.

```
public String toString();
```

As an example, the following code creates a DateField object with the label as "Today's date" and the mode as DateField.DATE:

```
DateField date = new DateField("Today's date", DateField.DATE);
```

To display a date field, first create a Form object, and then use the append() method of the form to add the date field.

```
Form form = new Form("Date Info");
form.append(date);
Display.setCurrent(form);
```

In this example, since the DATE input mode is selected, the MIDlet would display a <date> item for the user to select, as shown in Figure 5-14. Once selected, it will display the current calendar date, and you should be able to set a new date.

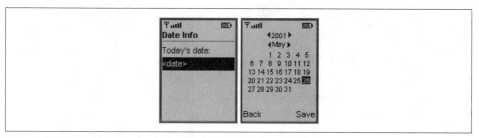

Figure 5-14. A date field representing the calendar date

If the DateField.TIME input mode is used, the MIDlet would display a <time> item for the user to select, as shown in Figure 5-15. Once selected, the current clock time information will be displayed, and you can likewise set a new time.

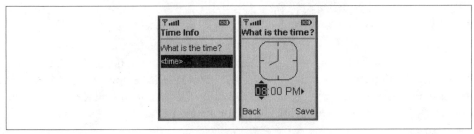

Figure 5-15. A date field representing clock time information

Finally, if the DateField.DATE_TIME input mode is used, the MIDlet would display the items <date> and <time> and you would be allowed to choose one at a time.

Note that you can initialize the date and time before displaying the component. You can do so using the following snippet of code:

```
d = new DateField("Today: ", DateField.DATE);
d.setDate(new Date());
form = new Form("Date & Time");
form.append(d);    display.setCurrent(form);
```

At this point, the date field displays the current date and time, as shown in Figure 5-16.

Figure 5-16. A date field represented with the DATE_TIME constant

The second DateField constructor is used to create a date field specifying its label, input mode, and time zone information. For example, the following snippet of code creates a DateField object where the time zone is GMT:

```
DateField date = new DateField("date", DateField.DATE,
                        TimeZone.getTimeZone("GMT"));
```

If the TimeZone field is null, the default time zone (based on the time zone where the program is running) is used. Hence, the following two lines of code do exactly the same thing:

```
DateField date1 = new DateField("date", DateField.DATE);
DateField date2 = new DateField("date", DateField.DATE, TimeZone.getDefault());
```

The TimeZone class is part of the java.util package, which has been inherited from the J2SE.

Gauge

A Gauge object represents a bar graph display that can be used within a form. The Gauge class has the following constructor:

```
public Gauge(String label, boolean interactive, int maxValue,
    int initialValue);
```

This constructor is used to create a new Gauge object with the given label, in interactive or non-interactive mode, with the given maximum and initial values. In interactive mode, the user is allowed to modify the gauge's current value; in non-interactive mode, the user is not allowed to change the value at all (e.g., what you might see in a progress bar). You can query whether the gauge is currently in interactive mode with the following method:

```
public boolean isInteractive();
```

The Gauge object also provides the following methods to access the current value and maximum value properties that we saw in the constructor:

```
public int getMaxValue();
public int getValue();
public void setMaxValue(int maxValue);
public void setValue(int value);
```

A gauge will always maintain a current value between zero and the maximum value specified. For example, the following snippet of code creates an interactive gauge where the maximum value is 20 and the initial value is 0:

```
Gauge gauge = new Gauge("graph", true, 20, 0);
```

Once a Gauge object is created, it can be placed on a Form component, like the other components that we've seen:

```
Form form = new Form("item");
form.append(gauge);
```

This interactive gauge is shown in Figure 5-17. Note that the style of the gauge is of an ascending arc from right to left, as you might see on a LED volume control.

Figure 5-17. An example of an interactive gauge

If the gauge is used to reflect progress, the application will need to keep updating it. In this case, it will need to keep a reference to it handy and repeatedly call setValue( ) to reflect the current progress.

The following snippet of code shows an example of a non-interactive gauge that reflects a progress bar:

```
Display display = Display.getDisplay(this);
Gauge progressbar = new Gauge("Progress", false, 20, 9);
Form form = new Form("Configuring App);
form.append(progressbar);
```

This progress bar is shown in Figure 5-18. Note here that the non-interactive form of a gauge is level from right to left.

Figure 5-18. A non-interactive gauge representing a progress bar

Image and ImageItem

An ImageItem object is an image component that contains a reference to an Image object. First, let's briefly introduce the Image class. We will revisit it again later when we talk about low-level APIs.

The Image class is used as a graphical image data holder. Depending on how they are created, images can either be *immutable* or *mutable*. Immutable images are generally created by loading image data from resource bundles, from files, or across a network. Once they are created, they may not be modified. Mutable images, on the other hand, are created in off-screen memory and can be modified.

Images that are to be placed within an Alert, Form, or ImageItem must be immutable, since the implementation will use them to update the display without notifying the application. Otherwise, the containing Alert or Form would have to be updated on every graphics call.

A mutable image can be created using one of the static createImage( ) methods of the Image class.

```
public static Image createImage(int width, int height);
```

The other three static createImage( ) methods are used to create immutable images:

```
public static Image createImage(Image image);
public static Image createImage(String name);
public static Image createImage(byte[] imageData, int imageOffset,
    int imageLength);
```

Here is an example of creating an immutable image from a graphics file:

```
Image image = Image.createImage("/Duke.png");
```

This image can then be placed on a Form object in the typical fashion:

```
Form form = new Form("Duke");
form.append(image);
```

Note that the graphics file has the extension *png*. This acronym stands for Portable Network Graphics. All MIDP implementations are required to support images stored in at least Version 1.0 of PNG. As of this writing, no other graphics formats are accepted. Also, if you're using the emulator within J2ME Wireless Toolkit's KToolbar application, note that the reference to Duke using */duke.png* means that the Duke is in the *res* directory, *c:\j2mewtk\apps\Myproject\res*. Figure 5-19 depicts the screen shown with this example.

Figure 5-19. Placing an Image object on a form

The Image class has a few methods that can come in handy to discover the height, width, and mutable status of any image:

```
public int getHeight();
public int getWidth();
public boolean isMutable();
```

In addition, if the image is mutable, you can obtain a Graphics object of the image using the following method. (We'll cover this in much more detail when we discuss the low-level graphics API.)

```
public Graphics getGraphics();
```

Now, let's see how to use the ImageItem class, which provides control and layout when Image objects are added to a form or an alert. To create an ImageItem object, use the ImageItem constructor:

```
public ImageItem(String label, Image img, int layout,
    String altText);
```

This constructor is used to create a new immutable ImageItem object with a given label, image, layout directive, and alternative text string. The altText parameter specifies a string to be displayed in place of the image if it exceeds the capacity of the display. The layout parameter is a combination of the following values, which are static field members of the ImageItem class:

ImageItem.LAYOUT_CENTER
> The image should be horizontally centered.

ImageItem.LAYOUT_DEFAULT
> You should use the default formatting of the container of the image.

ImageItem.LAYOUT_LEFT
> The image should be close to the left edge of the drawing area.

ImageItem.LAYOUT_NEWLINE_AFTER
> A new line should be started after the image is drawn.

ImageItem.LAYOUT_NEWLINE_BEFORE
> A new line should be started before the image is drawn.

ImageItem.LAYOUT_RIGHT
> The image should be close to the right edge of the drawing area.

There are some rules on how the above layout values can be combined:

- ImageItem.LAYOUT_DEFAULT cannot be combined with any other directive.
- ImageItem.LAYOUT_LEFT, ImageItem.LAYOUT_RIGHT, and ImageItem.LAYOUT_CENTER are mutually exclusive.
- You can combine ImageItem.LAYOUT_LEFT, ImageItem.LAYOUT_RIGHT, and ImageItem.LAYOUT_CENTER with ImageItem.LAYOUT_NEWLINE_AFTER and ImageItem. LAYOUT_NEWLINE_BEFORE.

 The layout directives serve merely as a hint, but it may be ignored by the implementation. Such is the case with Sun's MIDP reference implementation.

The ImageItem class also contains the following methods to access the properties that we just saw in the constructor:

```
public String getAltText();
public Image getImage();
public int getLayout();
public void setAltText(String altText);
public void setImage(Image img);
public void setLayout(int layout);
```

So, to create an ImageItem object, use the above ImageItem constructor:

```
Image img = Image.createImage("/Duke.png");
ImageItem imageItem = new ImageItem("Image", img,
    ImageItem.LAYOUT_CENTER, "img");

Form form = new Form("Duke");
form.append(imageItem);
```

This example would produce a screen similar to that in Figure 5-19, except that this one would have a title for the ImageItem object.

StringItem

A StringItem object is a text component item that may contain a string that cannot be edited by the user. A StringItem has a label that can be modified by the application. The contents of StringItem can be modified by the application as well. Here is the constructor:

```
public StringItem(String label, String contents);
```

Creating a StringItem object is easy:

```
StringItem si = new StringItem("label", "contents");
```

The setText() and getText( ) methods are used to set and get the StringItem contents; the setLabel() and getLabel( ) methods, which are defined in the Item abstract class, are used to set and get the label of the StringItem:

```
public void setText(String s);
public void setLabel(String l);
public String getText( );
public String getLabel( );
```

The following snippet of code creates a StringItem object and places it within a Form object. The form is then set to be the current screen, as shown in Figure 5-20.

Figure 5-20. The user cannot edit the contents of a StringItem object

```
Display display = display.getDisplay(this);
StringItem si = new StringItem("String item:\n", "Hello World!");
Form form = new Form("Greetings");
form.append(si);
display.setCurrent(form);
```

TextField

Unlike StringItem, a TextField object is an editable text component that may be placed on a Form. Similar to a TextBox, however, a TextField has a capacity (or a maximum size), which is the number of characters that can be stored in the object. Again, the MIDP implementation may place a boundary on the maximum size, which could be smaller than the size the application requested. The maximum size imposed by the implementation can be retrieved using getMaxSize( ). But, as mentioned earlier, in Sun's MIDP reference implementation, the getMaxSize( ) method returns the size requested by the application.

Use a TextField object if your MIDlet requires input from the user. A TextField object can be created as an instance of the TextField class, which has the following constructor:

```
public TextField(String label, String text, int maxSize, int
    constraints);
```

This constructor is used to create a new TextField object with the given label, initial contents, maximum size in characters, and constraints. The constraints field is used to limit the user's input. The constraints are the TextField's static constants, which are shared with TextBox as discussed earlier, and they are: TextField.ANY, TextField. EMAILADDR, TextField.NUMBER, TextField.PASSWD, TextField.PHONENUMBER, and TextField.URL. Again, if you use a constraint other than TextField.ANY, the TextField will perform a simple validation to make sure that the characters that are input are of the requested type.

If you wish to set or retrieve the current constraints that are active for the TextField, use the following methods:

```
public int getConstraints( );
public void setConstrants(int c);
```

The maximum size imposed by the implementation can be retrieved using the getMaxSize( ) method, and (potentially) reset using the setMaxSize( ) method.

```
public int getMaxSize( );
public void setMaxSize(int size);
```

You can set or retrieve the entire text in the TextField with the setString( ) and getString( ) methods:

```
public String getString( );
public void setString(String s);
```

In addition, if you would like to see the number of characters in the text that has been entered, use the size( ) method, which returns an integer:

```
public int size( );
```

The methods to delete, insert, or replace the current text are identical to TextBox:

```
public void delete(int offset, int length);
public void insert(char[] data, int offset, int length, int position);
public void insert(String src, int position);
public void setChars(char[] data, int offset, int length);
```

Finally, if you want to find out which position the *caret*, also known as the insertion beam, is currently in front of, TextField includes the following method:

```
public int getCaretPosition();
```

The following code shows this component in action. It creates a login form with two text fields, one for loginID and the other for the password. Once started, you can enter your username and a password, as shown in Figure 5-21.

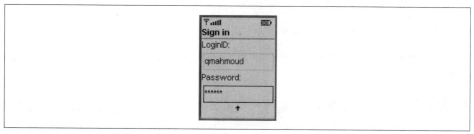

Figure 5-21. Example of TextField

```
Display display = Display.getDisplay(this);
TextField userName = new TextField("LoginID:", "", 10,
    TextField.ANY);
TextField password = new TextField("Password:", "", 10,
    TextField.PASSWORD);
Form form = new Form("Sign in");
form.append(userName);
form.append(password);
display.setCurrent(form);
```

Creating Low-Level GUI Components

In the high-level API, you have no control of what is displayed on the screen and very little freedom to "play" with the components programmatically. The implementation is responsible for selecting the best approach for the device. Some applications, however, such as games, may need more control over what is drawn on the screen. The MIDP javax.microedition.lcdui package also provides a low-level API for handling such cases.

In order to directly draw lines, text, and shapes on the screen, you must use the Canvas class. The Canvas class provides a blank screen on which a MIDlet can draw. For example, let's draw the string "HelloWorld" on the screen. There's a simple way to do this: subclass the Canvas class, which is an abstract class that extends Displayable, and override the paint() method. The resulting class, MyCanvas, is shown in Example 5-1.

The implementation of the paint( ) method uses the drawing capabilities of the javax.microedition.lcdui.Graphics class. In the paint( ) method, the drawing color is set to red, then a rectangle is drawn in the current color. The methods getWidth( ) and getHeight( ) return the width and height of the Canvas, respectively. The next call to setColor( ) sets the drawing color to white; then the string "Hello World!" is drawn in the top left corner of the screen.

Example 5-1. Subclassing Canvas

```
import javax.microedition.lcdui.*;

public class MyCanvas extends Canvas {
    public void paint(Graphics g) {
        g.setColor(255, 0, 0);
        g.fillRect(0, 0, getWidth(), getHeight());
        g.setColor(255, 255, 255);
        g.drawString("Hello World!", 0, 0, g.TOP | g.LEFT);
    }
}
```

Now, in order to view the MyCanvas, it must be instantiated and displayed. Since Canvas is a subclass of Displayable, it can be displayed the same way any other screen using the setCurrent( ) method. Example 5-2 shows the resulting MIDlet.

Example 5-2. Instantiating and displaying MyCanvas

```
import javax.microedition.midlet.*;
import javax.microedition.lcdui.*;

public class MyMidlet extends MIDlet {
    public MyMidlet() { // constructor
    }

    public void startApp() {
        Canvas canvas = new MyCanvas();
        Display display = Display.getDisplay(this);
        display.setCurrent(canvas);
    }

    public void pauseApp() {
    }

    public void destroyApp(boolean unconditional) {
    }
}
```

If you run this in the Wireless Toolkit emulator, you will see something similar to Figure 5-22. Note from Example 5-1 that the colors are set to red and white, but since a grayscale display is being used, the colors are mapped to appropriate shades of black and white. Try switching displays to see which devices give a better feel for the colors.

Figure 5-22. Drawing "Hello World!" on a Canvas

Drawing Graphics

The (0,0) coordinate represents the upper left corner of the display. The numeric value of the x-coordinate increases from left to right, and the numeric value of the y-coordinate increases from top to bottom. Applications should always check the dimensions of the drawing area by using the following methods of the Canvas class:

```
public int getHeight();
public int getWidth();
```

These two methods return the height and width of the displayable area in pixels, respectively.

The drawing model used is called *pixel replacement*. It works by replacing the destination pixel value with the current pixel value specified in the graphics objects being used for rendering. A 24-bit color model is provided with 8 bits each for Red, Green, and Blue (RGB). However, since not all devices support color, colors requested by applications will be mapped into colors available on the devices. A well-written application, however, may check if a device supports color. This can be done using the isColor() and numColors() methods of the Display class, which we covered earlier in the chapter.

The Graphics class provides the setColor() and getColor() methods for setting and getting the color. Unlike the AWT/Swing, however, there is no setBackground() and setForeground(), so you need to explicitly call fillRect(), as shown in Example 5-1. Most of the other methods in the Graphics class are self-explanatory and similar to methods in the AWT version of this class. However, let's go over a few of them here to see how they work in the J2ME environment.

Double Buffering

The double buffering technique is often used to perform smooth effect animation. In this technique, you do not draw to the display, but instead to a copy of the display (an off-screen buffer) that is maintained in memory. When you are done drawing to the buffer, you then copy the contents of the buffer to the display. The rationale here is that copying the contents of memory to the display is faster than drawing by using primitives.

To implement double buffering, first create a mutable image with the size of the screen:

```
int width = getWidth();
int height = getHeight();
Image buffer = Image.createImage(width, height);
```

Next, obtain a graphics context for the buffer:

```
Graphics gc = buffer.getGraphics();
```

Now, you can draw to the buffer:

```
// animate
// ..
gc.drawRect(20, 20, 25, 30);
```

When you need to copy the buffer to the screen, you can override the paint() method to draw the buffer to the device display:

```
public void paint(Graphics g) {
    g.drawImage(buffer, 0, 0, 0);
}
```

 Note that some MIDP implementations are already double-buffered, and therefore this work may not be necessary. To check if the graphics are double-buffered by an implementation, use the Canvas. isDoubleBuffered() method.

Threading Issues

The MIDP GUI APIs are thread-safe. In other words, the methods can be called at any time from any thread. The only exception is the serviceRepaints() method of the Canvas class, which immediately calls the paint() method to force immediate repainting of the display. This means that if paint() tries to synchronize on any object that is already locked by the application when serviceRepaints() is called, the application will deadlock. To avoid deadlocks, do not lock an object that will be used by the paint() method if serviceRepaints() is involved.

In addition, you can use the callSerially() method of the Display class to execute code after all pending repaints are served, as shown in the following segment of code:

```
class TestCanvas extends Canvas implements Runnable {
    void doSomething() {
        // code fragment 1
        callSerially(this);
    }

    public void run() {
        // code fragment 2
    }
}
```

Here, the object's run() method will be called after the initial call.

Fonts

Fonts cannot be created by applications. Instead, an application requests a font based on attributes (i.e., size, face, style) and the underlying implementation will attempt to return a font that closely resembles the requested font. The Font class represents various fonts and metrics. There are three font attributes defined in the Font class, and each may have different values, as follows:

Face
> MONOSPACE, PROPORTIONAL, SYSTEM

Size
> SMALL, MEDIUM, LARGE

Style
> BOLD, ITALIC, PLAIN, UNDERLINED

For example, to specify a medium size font, use Font.SIZE_MEDIUM, and to specify an italic style, use Font.STYLE_ITALIC, and so on. Values for the style attributes may be combined using the OR (|) operator; values for the other attributes may not be combined. For example, the value of this style attribute specifies a plain, underlined font:

> STYLE_PLAIN | STYLE_UNDERLINED

However, the following is illegal:

> SIZE_SMALL | SIZE_MEDIUM

This is also illegal:

> FACE_SYSTEM | FACE_MONOSPACE

Each font in the system is actually implemented individually, so in order to obtain an object representing a font, use the getFont( ) method. This method takes three arguments for the font face, size, and style, respectively. For example, the following snippet of code obtains a Font object with the specified face, style, and size attributes:

> Font font = Font.getFont(FACE_SYSTEM, STYLE_PLAIN, SIZE_MEDIUM);

If a matching font does not exist, the implementation will attempt to provide the closest match, which is always a valid Font object.

Once a font is obtained, you can use methods from the Font class to retrieve information about that font. For example, you can use the methods getFace(), getSize( ), and getStyle( ) to retrieve information about the face, size, and style of the font, respectively.

Let's look at an example. The code in Example 5-3 subclasses the Canvas class. In this example, the drawing color is set to white, a rectangle is drawn in the current color, then the drawing color is set to black. The rest of the code draws the system fonts on the device screen, as shown in Figure 5-23.

Figure 5-23. Drawing system fonts on the device screen

Example 5-3. Using fonts

```
import javax.microedition.lcdui.*;

public class FontCanvas extends Canvas {
    public void paint(Graphics g) {
        g.setColor(0xffffff);
        g.fillRect(0, 0, getWidth(), getHeight());
        g.setColor(0x000000);

        g.setFont(Font.getFont(Font.FACE_SYSTEM, Font.STYLE_PLAIN,
            Font.SIZE_LARGE));
        g.drawString("System Font", 0, 0, g.LEFT | g.TOP);
        g.setFont(Font.getFont(Font.FACE_SYSTEM, Font.STYLE_PLAIN,
            Font.SIZE_MEDIUM));
        g.drawString("Medium Size", 0, 15, g.LEFT | g.TOP);
        g.setFont(Font.getFont(Font.FACE_SYSTEM, Font.STYLE_BOLD,
            Font.SIZE_MEDIUM));
        g.drawString("Bold Style", 0, 30, g.LEFT | g.TOP);
        g.setFont(Font.getFont(Font.FACE_SYSTEM, Font.STYLE_ITALIC,
            Font.SIZE_MEDIUM));
        g.drawString("Italic Style", 0, 45, g.LEFT | g.TOP);
        g.setFont(Font.getFont(Font.FACE_SYSTEM,
            Font.STYLE_UNDERLINED, Font.SIZE_MEDIUM));
        g.drawString("Underlined Style", 0, 60, g.LEFT | g.TOP);
    }
}
```

Now, we instantiate the FontCanvas class and display it, as shown in Example 5-4.

Example 5-4. Instantiating and displaying the FontCanvas class

```
import javax.microedition.midlet.*;
import javax.microedition.lcdui.*;

public class FontMidlet extends MIDlet {
    public FontMidlet() { // constructor
    }

    public void startApp() {
        Canvas canvas = new FontCanvas();
        Display display = Display.getDisplay(this);
```

Example 5-4. Instantiating and displaying the FontCanvas class (continued)

```
        display.setCurrent(canvas);
    }

    public void pauseApp( ) {
    }

    public void destroyApp(boolean unconditional) {
    }
}
```

Guidelines for GUI Programming for MIDP Devices

As we close this chapter, keep in mind some important guidelines when designing MIDlets with graphical API functionality:

- Be sure to make the MIDlet user interface simple and easy to use. Remember that your applications will likely be used by novice users who probably haven't used a J2ME-enabled phone and may not be familiar with its interface.

- Use the high-level API as much as possible, so that your MIDlets are portable across different handheld devices.

- If your application requires you to use the low-level API, keep to the platform-independent part of the low-level API. This means that your MIDlets should not assume any other keys than those defined in the Canvas class. We'll discuss this in more detail in the next chapter.

- MIDlets should never assume any specific screen size; instead, they should query the size of the display and adjust accordingly.

- Entering alphanumeric data through a handheld device can be tedious. If possible, provide a list of choices from which the user can select.

CHAPTER 6

MIDP Events

In AWT and Swing, events are generated when a user interacts with an application. For example, if the user selects Save from the File menu, the application is notified of this action and responds to the generated event. The same model holds true for the MIDP. However, as mentioned in the previous chapter, there are two MIDP user interface APIs: high-level and low-level. Therefore, there are two kinds of events: high-level (such as selecting an item from a list) and low-level (such as pressing a key on the device).

This chapter discusses event handling in the MIDP and shows, through examples, how to handle high-level and low-level MIDP events generated by the components of the previous chapter. We start with an explanation of a simple application of events: navigating between screens.

Screen Navigation

A MIDlet developer needs to provide ways for the user to navigate through the different screens that make up the MIDlet. Because we can only show one screen at a time, however, we need to tie a mechanism to each screen that indicates to the MIDlet that the user has completed working with the current Displayable screen. We can do this by using the Command class, which is part of the javax.microedition.lcdui package. Let's take a closer look at the Command class now.

Commands

Just like a design pattern with the same name, the Command class encapsulates the semantic information of an action. Note that it only contains information about a command, not the actual functionality that is executed when a command is activated. Here is the constructor of the Command class:

```
public Command(String label, int commandType, int priority);
```

This is the only constructor for the Command class. Hence, creating a Command object is extremely simple:

```
Command infoCommand = new Command("Info", Command.SCREEN, 2);
```

The Command class constructor takes three parameters, and therefore contains the following three lightweight pieces of information: *label*, *command type*, and *priority*.

- The *label* is a string used for the visual representation of the command. For example, the label may appear next to a soft button on the device or as an element in a menu.

- The *command type* element specifies the command's intent. The predefined types are actually static integers in the Command class: BACK, CANCEL, EXIT, HELP, ITEM, OK, SCREEN, and STOP.

- The *priority* value describes the importance of this command relative to other commands on the screen. A priority value of 1 indicates the most important command; higher priority values indicate commands of lesser importance.

Each component that extends Displayable (such as Screen or Canvas) has the following methods available to it:

```
public void addCommand(Command c);
public void removeCommand(Command c);
```

These methods allow you to bind a command to a Displayable object. (That's pretty much all of them; recall Figure 5-2.) When the MIDlet executes, the device assigns a visual representation of the command (typically a soft button or menu item) and chooses its placement based on the command type, placing similar commands based on their priority values. Consider the following example, where a TextBox object is created along with three commands. The commands are added to the TextBox object, and the current screen is then set to be the TextBox object:

```
Display display = Display.getDisplay(this);
TextBox tb = new TextBox("MIDP", "Welcome to MIDP", 40,
    TextField.ANY);
Command exitCommand = new Command("Exit", Command.SCREEN, 1);
Command infoCommand = new Command("Info", Command.SCREEN, 2);
Command buyCommand = new Command("Buy", Command.SCREEN, 2);
tb.addCommand(exitCommand);
tb.addComment(infoCommand);
tb.addCommand(buyCommand);
display.setCurrent(tb);
```

Look carefully at what this code displays in Figure 6-1. Here, the application manager maps the Exit command to the screen using the soft button on the lower left, but then creates a Menu command to hold the Info and Buy commands. Clicking the right soft button under Menu takes you to a screen with a two-button menu: Info and Buy. This is because the Info and Buy commands are of lesser priority than the Exit command.

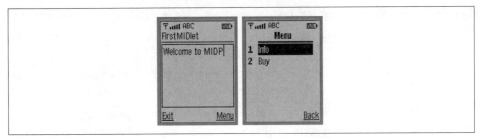

Figure 6-1. Exit, Info, and Buy commands

The general strategy that the application manager will follow is to assign as many commands with a high priority to as many soft buttons as are available. If there are not enough soft buttons, the implementation will likely group the remaining in a secondary menu that can be selected using a Menu soft button, as shown above. However, the exact rules for how each device handles this type of situation are implementation-dependent.

The Command class provides only the following three methods for retrieving the type, label, and priority values:

```
public int getCommandType( );
public String getLabel( );
public int getPriority( );
```

Note that there is no way to reset these object properties once they are set in the constructor.

> The MIDP UI API lets you set up a screen with no commands, but this is generally not useful because the user cannot move to another screen. It is important to note that the Command class can be used with both the high-level and the low-level APIs. Hence, commands can be placed on Screen objects as well as Canvas objects.

As we mentioned before, the command itself only contains information about a command, not the actual action that happens when a command is activated. The action is defined in a CommandListener, which is a *callback* object that is associated with the screen.

The CommandListener Interface

When a user interacts with a MIDlet, such as by selecting an item in a list or interacting with a Gauge, events are generated. Your application is then notified to handle these events through the use of callbacks. Callbacks are actually invocations of programmer-defined methods performed by the underlying application in response to actions taken by a user at runtime.

Callbacks are used in many programming environments, especially in GUI construction kits. For example, the AWT API makes heavy use of callbacks. When a user interacts with a component, for example, the interface code calls back the computational code to respond to the user's action. In some languages such as C/C++, callbacks are implemented by passing a function pointer to another function. The receiving function uses the function pointer to invoke another function when a particular event occurs. Because the Java programming language does not have pointers, however, callbacks are implemented with interfaces. An interface defines a set of methods, but unlike a class, it does not implement their behavior. Instead, you provide interface method implementations for the class that implements the interface.

There are four kinds of user interface callbacks in the MIDP:

- Abstract commands that are part of the high-level API
- Low-level events that represent single-key presses and releases
- Calls to the paint( ) method of a Canvas class
- Calls to a Runnable object's run() method, requested by a call to the callSerially( ) method of the Display class

Note that all user-interface callbacks are serialized by the application manager. In other words, they all occur one after another in a single thread of execution, and never at the same time. User interface callbacks are called as soon as the previous callback returns. In addition, the MIDP user interface API is thread-safe and includes a mechanism for event synchronization. An application can use the callSerially( ) method of the Display class to execute an operation serially with events.

Both Screen and Canvas objects can have listeners for commands that are sent when user interaction occurs. For an object to be a listener, it must implement the CommandListener interface. You can register a listener by using the setCommandListener( ) method, which is part of the Displayable class and is inherited by both Screen and Canvas. Note that there can only be one CommandListener object for each Displayable that the MIDlet has created.

```
public void setCommandListener(CommandListener c);
```

The CommandListener interface is for MIDlets that need to receive high-level events from the implementation. This interface has one method that a listener must implement, which is the commandAction( ) method.

```
public void commandAction(Command c, Displayable d);
```

The first parameter is a command object that identifies the command (if any) that has been added to Displayable with the addCommand( ) method and invoked. The second parameter is the Displayable object where the event occurred.

Handling simple events

Let's look at a simple example. In Example 6-1, a List component is created and filled with the strings "Item1", "Item2", "Item3", and "Item4". The prepare( ) method is called whenever an item is selected. The testItem#( ) methods (where # is a number between 1 and 4) each call the prepare( ) method and set the name of the menu.

Example 6-1. Handling high-level events

```
import javax.microedition.lcdui.*;
import javax.microedition.midlet.*;

public class EventEx1 extends MIDlet implements CommandListener {

    // display manager
    Display display = null;

    // a menu with items
    List menu = null; // main menu

    // textbox
    TextBox input = null;

    // command
    static final Command backCommand = new Command("Back",
        Command.BACK, 0);
    static final Command mainMenuCommand = new Command("Main",
        Command.SCREEN, 1);
    static final Command exitCommand = new Command("Exit",
        Command.STOP, 2);

    String currentMenu = null;

    // constructor
    public EventEx1( ) {
    }

    /**
     * Start the MIDlet by creating a list of items and associating
     * the exit command with it.
     */

    public void startApp( ) throws MIDletStateChangeException {
        display = Display.getDisplay(this);
        menu = new List("Menu Items", Choice.IMPLICIT);
        menu.append("Item1", null);
        menu.append("Item2", null);
        menu.append("Item3", null);
        menu.append("Item4", null);
        menu.addCommand(exitCommand);
        menu.setCommandListener(this);

        mainMenu( );
    }
```

Example 6-1. Handling high-level events (continued)

```java
public void pauseApp( ) {
    display = null;
    menu = null;
    input = null;
}

public void destroyApp(boolean unconditional) {
    notifyDestroyed( );
}


// main menu
void mainMenu( ) {
    display.setCurrent(menu);
    currentMenu = "Main";
}

/**
 * a generic method that will be called when any of
 * the items on the list are selected.
 */

public void prepare( ) {
    input = new TextBox("Enter some text: ", "", 5,
        TextField.ANY);
    input.addCommand(backCommand);
    input.setCommandListener(this);
    input.setString("");
    display.setCurrent(input);
}

/**
 * Test item1.
 */
public void testItem1( ) {
    prepare( );
    currentMenu = "item1";
}

/**
 * Test item2.
 */
public void testItem2( ) {
    prepare( );
    currentMenu = "item2";
}

/**
 * Test item3.
 */
public void testItem3( ) {
    prepare( );
```

Example 6-1. Handling high-level events (continued)

```
        currentMenu = "item3";
    }

    /**
     * Test item4.
     */
    public void testItem4( ) {
        prepare( );
        currentMenu = "item4";
    }

    /**
     * Handle events.
     */
    public void commandAction(Command c, Displayable d) {

        String label = c.getLabel( );

        if (label.equals("Exit")) {
            destroyApp(true);
        } else if (label.equals("Back")) {
            if(currentMenu.equals("item1") ||
                currentMenu.equals("item2") ||
                currentMenu.equals("item3") ||
                currentMenu.equals("item4"))  {
                // go back to menu
                mainMenu( );
            }

        } else {
            List down = (List)display.getCurrent( );
            switch(down.getSelectedIndex( )) {
                case 0: testItem1( );break;
                case 1: testItem2( );break;
                case 2: testItem3( );break;
                case 3: testItem4( );break;
            }
        }
    }
}
```

The EventEx1 class implements the CommandListener interface by providing an implementation for the commandAction( ) method. In this implementation, the label of the command passed into the callback method is checked. If the label equals Exit, the MIDlet is destroyed. If the label equals Back and the current menu is "Item1", "Item2", "Item3", or "Item4", the program goes back to the main menu. Otherwise, the selected item is found and the appropriate method is called. Note that when you have an item list, you can use the Display.getCurrent( ) method to return the list, and then switch between the items to determine which item is selected. If you run the EventEx1 MIDlet, you should see output similar to Figure 6-2.

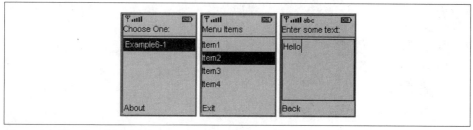

Figure 6-2. Handling high-level events

Creating GUI components and handling events

Now let's look at another example that demonstrates how to create various GUI components and to handle their events. The MIDlet in this example allows you to test lists, forms, choices, gauges, text fields, and text boxes. The EventEx2 MIDlet shown in Example 6-2 makes use of the following classes, listed in alphabetical order, from the javax.microedition.lcdui package: Alert, AlertType, Command, DateField, Display, Displayable, Form, Gauge, List, TextBox, TextField, and Ticker, as well as the CommandListener interface.

Example 6-2. Constructing and testing GUI components

```
import javax.microedition.lcdui.*;
import javax.microedition.midlet.*;

public class EventEx2 extends MIDlet implements CommandListener {
    // display manager
    Display display = null;

    // a menu with items
    List menu = null; // main menu

    // list of choices
    List choose = null;

    // textbox
    TextBox input = null;

    // ticker
    Ticker ticker = new Ticker("Test GUI Components");

    // alerts
    final Alert soundAlert = new Alert("sound Alert");

    // date
    DateField date = new DateField("Today's date: ",
        DateField.DATE);

    // form
    Form form = new Form("Form for Stuff");
```

Example 6-2. Constructing and testing GUI components (continued)

```java
// gauge
Gauge gauge = new Gauge("Gauge Label", true, 10, 0);

// text field
TextField textfield = new TextField("TextField Label", "abc",
    50, 0);

// command
static final Command backCommand = new Command("Back",
    Command.BACK, 0);
static final Command mainMenuCommand = new Command("Main",
    Command.SCREEN, 1);
static final Command exitCommand = new Command("Exit",
    Command.STOP, 2);
String currentMenu = null;

// constructor.
public EventEx2( ) {
}

/**
 * Start the MIDlet by creating a list of items and associating
 * the exit command with it.
 */

public void startApp( ) throws MIDletStateChangeException {
    display = Display.getDisplay(this);
    menu = new List("Test Components", Choice.IMPLICIT);
    menu.append("Test TextBox", null);
    menu.append("Test List", null);
    menu.append("Test Alert", null);
    menu.append("Test Date", null);
    menu.append("Test Form", null);
    menu.addCommand(exitCommand);
    menu.setCommandListener(this);
    menu.setTicker(ticker);

    mainMenu( );
}

public void pauseApp( ) {
    display = null;
    choose = null;
    menu = null;
    ticker = null;
    form = null;
    input = null;
    gauge = null;
    textfield = null;
}

public void destroyApp(boolean unconditional) {
    notifyDestroyed( );
}
```

Example 6-2. Constructing and testing GUI components (continued)

```java
// main menu
void mainMenu( ) {
   display.setCurrent(menu);
   currentMenu = "Main";
}

/**
 * Test the TextBox component.
 */
public void testTextBox( ) {
   input = new TextBox("Enter Some Text:", "", 5,
      TextField.ANY);
   input.setTicker(new Ticker("testTextBox"));
   input.addCommand(backCommand);
   input.setCommandListener(this);
   input.setString("");
   display.setCurrent(input);
   currentMenu = "input";
}

/**
 * Test the List component.
 */
public void testList( ) {
   choose = new List("Choose Items", Choice.MULTIPLE);
   choose.setTicker(new Ticker("listTest"));
   choose.addCommand(backCommand);
   choose.setCommandListener(this);
   choose.append("Item 1", null);
   choose.append("Item 2", null);
   choose.append("Item 3", null);
   display.setCurrent(choose);
   currentMenu = "list";
}

/**
 * Test the Alert component.
 */
public void testAlert( ) {
   soundAlert.setType(AlertType.ERROR);
   soundAlert.setString("** ERROR **");
   display.setCurrent(soundAlert);
}

/**
 * Test the DateField component.
 */
public void testDate( ) {
   java.util.Date now = new java.util.Date( );
   date.setDate(now);
   Form f = new Form("Today's date");
   f.append(date);
```

Example 6-2. Constructing and testing GUI components (continued)

```
        f.addCommand(backCommand);
        f.setCommandListener(this);
        display.setCurrent(f);
        currentMenu = "date";
    }

    /**
     * Test the Form component.
     */
    public void testForm( ) {
        form.append(gauge);
        form.append(textfield);
        form.addCommand(backCommand);
        form.setCommandListener(this);
        display.setCurrent(form);
        currentMenu = "form";
    }

    /**
     * Handle events.
     */
    public void commandAction(Command c, Displayable d) {
        String label = c.getLabel( );
        if (label.equals("Exit")) {
            destroyApp(true);
        } else if (label.equals("Back")) {
            if(currentMenu.equals("list") ||
                currentMenu.equals("input") ||
                currentMenu.equals("date") ||
                currentMenu.equals("form")) {
                // go back to menu
                mainMenu( );
            }
        } else {
            List down = (List)display.getCurrent( );
            switch(down.getSelectedIndex( )) {
                case 0: testTextBox( );break;
                case 1: testList( );break;
                case 2: testAlert( );break;
                case 3: testDate( );break;
                case 4: testForm( );break;
            }
        }
    }
}
```

To test the EventEx2 MIDlet using the J2ME Wireless Toolkit, do the following:

1. Create a new project (call it Example 6-2) and a MIDlet class (call it EventEx2), copy the code to the appropriate location, and compile it.

2. Run the EventEx2 MIDlet in the emulator.

3. You should see the name of the project (Example 6-2) in the application manager, as shown in Figure 6-3.

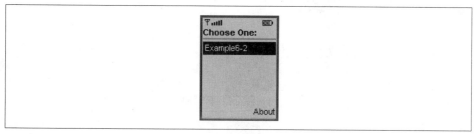

Figure 6-3. Project Example 6-2 MIDlet

4. Activate the MIDlet.

5. As the MIDlet runs, you see a menu with the following options: Test TextBox, Test List, Test Alert, Test Date, and Test Form, as shown in Figure 6-4.

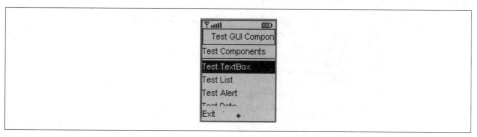

Figure 6-4. EventEx2 MIDlet

6. Choose a test to perform.

Tests from the EventEx2 MIDlet are shown in Figure 6-5.

If you have a soundcard, you will hear a warning sound with the alert. The remaining tests from the EventEx2 MIDlet are shown in Figure 6-6.

The ItemStateListener Interface

Applications use the ItemStateListener interface to receive events that indicate changes in the internal state of items within a Form screen. Items within a Form screen may be changed when the user performs any of the following actions:

- Adjusts the value of an interactive Gauge.
- Enters or modifies the values of a TextField.
- Enters a new date or time in a DateField.
- Changes the set of selected values in a ChoiceGroup.

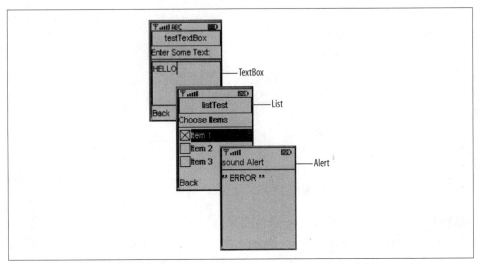

Figure 6-5. The TextBox, List, and Alert tests

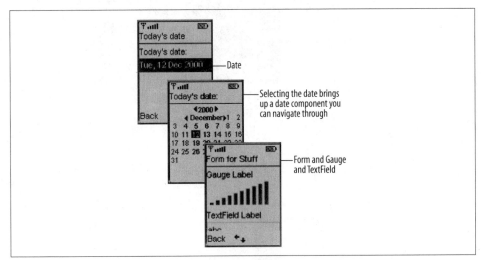

Figure 6-6. DateField, Calendar, and Form, with Gauge and TextField tests

This interface has only one method that a listener must implement:

```
public void itemStateChanged(Item item);
```

You can use the setItemStateListener( ) method of the Form class to register a listener for these conditions, as shown in the next section.

Changing the date

In Example 6-3, a DateField object is created and added to a form. When you click on the date, you can change it by navigating through the calendar. When the date is changed, a message appears.

Example 6-3. Implementing the ItemStateListener interface

```
import javax.microedition.midlet.*;
import javax.microedition.lcdui.*;

public class EventEx3 extends MIDlet {
   Display display;

   public EventEx3( ) {
      display = Display.getDisplay(this);
   }

   public void destroyApp (boolean unconditional) {
      notifyDestroyed( );
      System.out.println("App destroyed ");
   }

   public void pauseApp ( ) {
      display = null;
      System.out.println("App paused.");
   }

   public void startApp ( ) {
      Form form = new Form("Change Date");

      ItemStateListener listener = new ItemStateListener( ) {
         java.util.Calendar cal = java.util.Calendar.
             getInstance(java.util.TimeZone.getDefault( ));

         public void itemStateChanged(Item item) {
            cal.setTime(((DateField)item).getDate( ));
            System.out.println("\nDate has changed");
         }
      };

      // register for events
      form.setItemStateListener(listener);

      // get today's date
      java.util.Date now = new java.util.Date( );
      DateField dateItem = new DateField("Today's date:",
          DateField.DATE);
      dateItem.setDate(now);

      // add date to the Form screen
      form.append(dateItem);
      display.setCurrent(form);
   }
}
```

Here, the ItemStateListener interface is implemented as an anonymous inner class by providing an implementation to the itemStateChanged( ) method. If you run the EventEx3 MIDlet, you should see output similar to Figure 6-7.

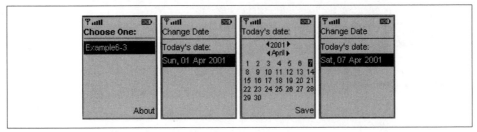

Figure 6-7. Implementing the ItemStateListener interface

Handling Low-Level Events

If you use the Canvas class to write applications to access low-level input events or to issue graphics calls for drawing to the display, you must handle low-level events. Game applications are likely to use the Canvas class because it provides methods to handle game actions and key events. The key events are reported with respect to key-codes that are directly bound to concrete keys on the device.

The Canvas class, which is a subclass of Displayable, allows the application to register a listener for commands, but it requires applications to subclass the listener first. Also, while screens allow the application to define a listener and register it with an instance of the Screen class, the Canvas class does not allow this, because several listener interfaces need to be created, one for each kind of event.

Key Events

Every key for which events are reported is assigned a keycode. The MIDP defines the following keycodes in the Canvas class:

KEY_NUM0
    The keycode for key 0

KEY_NUM1
    The keycode for key 1

KEY_NUM2
    The keycode for key 2

KEY_NUM3
    The keycode for key 3

KEY_NUM4
    The keycode for key 4

KEY_NUM5
    The keycode for key 5

KEY_NUM6
    The keycode for key 6

KEY_NUM7
>   The keycode for key 7

KEY_NUM8
>   The keycode for key 8

KEY_NUM9
>   The keycode for key 9

KEY_STAR
>   The keycode for the star key "*"

KEY_POUND
>   The keycode for the pound key "#"

As you probably guessed, these are the keys 0..9, *, and #. Other keys might exist on some devices, but for portability, applications should use only the standard key-codes. The getKeyName( ) method is used to retrieve an informative string for a key.

Game Actions

If your application needs arrow keys and gaming-related events, use game actions instead of keycodes. Canvas defines the following constants as well:

UP
>   A constant for the UP game action

DOWN
>   A constant for the DOWN game action

LEFT
>   A constant for the LEFT game action

RIGHT
>   A constant for the RIGHT game action

FIRE
>   A constant for the FIRE game action

GAME_A
>   A constant for the general purpose "A" game action

GAME_B
>   A constant for the general purpose "B" game action

GAME_C
>   A constant for the general purpose "C" game action

GAME_D
>   A constant for the general purpose "D" game action

While each keycode is mapped to one game action, a game action can be associated with more than one keycode. The translation between the two is done with the getKeyCode( ) and getGameAction( ) methods.

If your application uses game actions and you want the application to be portable, you should translate key events into game actions with the getGameAction( ) method and test the result. For example, the game actions UP, DOWN, LEFT, and RIGHT can be mapped differently on different devices. The getGameAction( ) method returns the RIGHT game action, for example, when the user presses the key that is a natural right on the device.

Event Delivery Methods

The following methods of the Canvas class are available for handling low-level events:

```
protected void keyPressed(int keyCode);
protected void keyReleased(int keyCode);
protected void keyRepeated(int keyCode);
protected void pointerPressed(int x, int y);
protected void pointerDragged(int x, int y);
protected void pointerReleased(int x, int y);
```

These methods are callbacks that you should override in a class that extends the Canvas class. There are a couple of important things to note here:

- The keyRepeated( ) method might not be available on all devices. Your application should check the availability of repeat actions by calling the hasRepeatEvents( ) method.

- The pointer events may not be present on all devices, so before using the pointerPressed(), pointerDragged(), and pointerReleased( ) methods, your application should check if a pointer mechanism is available by calling the hasPointerEvents() and hasPointerMotionEvents( ) methods first.

Handling low-level events

Example 6-4 shows how to handle low-level events. In this example, the Canvas class is subclassed to use an anonymous inner class, an implementation is provided for the keyPressed() and keyReleased( ) methods, and an empty implementation is provided for the paint( ) method. When a key is pressed or released, the application prints the value of that key.

Example 6-4. Handling low-level events

```
import javax.microedition.midlet.*;
import javax.microedition.lcdui.*;

public class EventEx4 extends MIDlet {
   Display display;
   Command exit;
```

Example 6-4. Handling low-level events (continued)

```
    public EventEx4( ) {
        display = Display.getDisplay(this);
    }

    public void destroyApp (boolean unconditional) {
    }

    public void pauseApp ( ) {
        System.out.println("App paused.");
    }

    public void startApp ( ) {
        display = Display.getDisplay(this);

        Canvas canvas = new Canvas( ) { // anonymous class
            public void paint(Graphics g) {
            }

            protected void keyPressed(int keyCode) {
                if (keyCode > 0) {
                    System.out.println("keyPressed " +((char)keyCode));
                } else {
                    System.out.println("keyPressed action "
                        +getGameAction(keyCode));
                }
            }

            protected void keyReleased(int keyCode) {
                if (keyCode > 0) {
                    System.out.println("keyReleased " +((char)keyCode));
                } else {
                    System.out.println("keyReleased action "
                        +getGameAction(keyCode));
                }
            }
        }; // end of anonymous class

        exit = new Command("Exit", Command.STOP, 1);
        canvas.addCommand(exit);
        canvas.setCommandListener(new CommandListener( ) {
            public void commandAction(Command c, Displayable d) {
                if(c == exit) {
                    notifyDestroyed( );
                } else {
                    System.out.println("Saw the command: "+c);
                }
            }
        });
        display.setCurrent(canvas);
    }
}
```

If you run the EventEx3 MIDlet and activate it, you should see output similar to that in Figure 6-8.

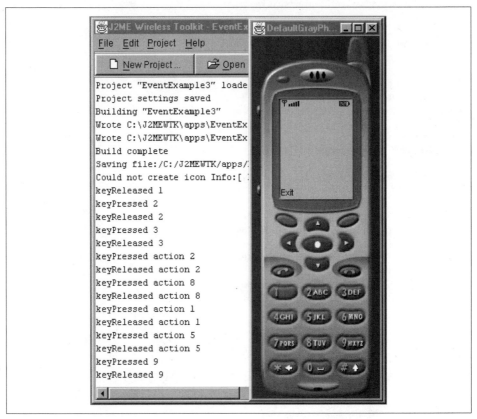

Figure 6-8. Handling low-level events

An alternative implementation for the keyPressed( ) method is to interpret the keys at runtime, as shown in the following segment of code:

```
public void keyPressed(int keyCode) {
    int action = getGameAction(keyCode);
    switch(action) {
        case LEFT: System.out.println("MOVE TO THE LEFT");break;
        case RIGHT: System.out.println("MOVE TO THE RIGHT");break;
        // and so on....
    }
}
```

CHAPTER 7

Networking

Way back in Chapter 1, we briefly introduced the CLDC Generic Connection Framework. Let's quickly review why it was necessary to create an entirely new networking library for the CLDC.

The java.io and java.net packages of the J2SE are not suitable for handheld devices with a small memory footprint, for the following reasons:

- Device manufacturers who work with circuit-switched networks require stream-based connections such as the Transport Control Protocol (TCP), which is a connection-oriented protocol.

- Device manufacturers working with packet-switched networks require datagram-based connections such as the User Datagram Protocol (UDP), which is a connectionless protocol.

- Other handheld devices have specific mechanisms for communications.

All this variation makes designing networking facilities for the CLDC quite a challenge. This challenge has led to the design of a set of related abstractions that can be used at the programming level instead of using different abstractions for different forms of communications. For example, the J2SE java.net package provides a set of related abstractions in the form of over 20 networking classes, including Socket, ServerSocket, and DatagramSocket. With the CLDC, however, we need to go a step further to save space.

Generic Connections

In the Generic Connection Framework, all connections are created using the static open() methods from a single class: javax.microedition.io.Connector. If successful, these methods return an object that implements one of the generic connection interfaces. Figure 7-1 shows how these interfaces form an inheritance hierarchy. The Connection interface (don't confuse Connection with Connector) is the base interface.

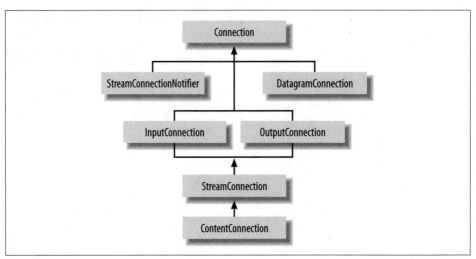

Figure 7-1. Connection interface hierarchy

- The Connection interface represents the most basic connection type. It can only be opened and closed.
- The InputConnection interface represents a device from which data can be read. Its openInputStream( ) method returns an input stream for the connection.
- The OutputConnection interface represents a device to which data can be written. Likewise, its openOutputStream( ) method returns an output stream for the connection.
- The StreamConnection interface combines the input and output connections.
- The ContentConnection interface extends the StreamConnection interface. It provides access to some of the basic metadata information provided by HTTP connections.
- The StreamConnectionNotifier interface waits for a connection to be established. It returns an object that implements the StreamConnection interface, on which a communication link has been established.
- The DatagramConnection interface is used to represent a datagram endpoint.

The simplest open( ) method of the Connector class has the following syntax:

```
public Connection open(String name) throws java.io.IOException;
```

The String parameter has the format "scheme:targetaddress;parameters" and conforms to the URL syntax in RFC 2396. Here are a few examples:

Establish an HTTP connection
```
Connector.open("http://www.ora.com");
```

Start a socket connection
```
Connector.open("socket://www.ora.com:80");
```

Establish a datagram connection
```
Connector.open("datagram://192.168.2.101:2345");
```

Communicate with a port
```
Connector.open("comm:0;baudrate=9600");
```

Open files
```
Connector.open("file:/myfile.txt");
```

The goal of the above syntax is to isolate the differences between the setup of one protocol and another protocol into a simple string that characterizes the type of connection. Most of the application's code remains the same, regardless of the protocol you use. You will see the benefits of this in the examples later in this chapter.

 The connection examples above are for illustration only. The CLDC itself does not provide any protocol implementations, because no implementations should be provided at the configuration level. In addition, a J2ME profile such as the MIDP does not have to provide implementations for all of the protocols mentioned earlier. The MIDP implementation from Sun Microsystems, for example, provides an implementation for the HTTP protocol, but it does not provide implementations for socket or datagram connections.

The Connector class provides two other static open( ) methods that can be used to open connections, which have the following signatures:
```
public static Connection open(String url, int mode)
    throws java.io.IOException;
public static Connection open(String url, int mode, boolean timeouts)
    throws java.io.IOException;
```

The first method takes two parameters: the URL for the connection and the access mode. The access mode is used to indicate to the protocol handler the intentions of the calling code. The access mode can be one of the following constants, which are defined in the Connector class:
```
public static final int READ;
public static final int WRITE;
public static final int READ_WRITE;
```

You can use these constants to specify if the connection is going to be exclusively read from (READ), exclusively written to (WRITE), or both (READ_WRITE). If the access mode parameter is omitted, the READ_WRITE default will be used. It is important, however, to note that these flags are protocol-dependent. For example, a connection to a printer would not allow READ access.

The other open( ) method takes an additional third parameter, which is a boolean flag to indicate that the calling code wants to receive a timeout exception in the form of a java.io.InterruptedIOException. The timeout value is not given, as it is protocol-dependent, and there is no guarantee that the underlying protocol implementation will throw the timeout exception. If this parameter is omitted, then no timeout exceptions will be thrown.

MIDP Connectivity

The MIDP extends the CLDC Generic Connection Framework to provide support for the HTTP protocol. Why HTTP? Well, HTTP can be implemented using both IP protocols (such as TCP/IP) or non-IP protocols (such as WAP and I-mode). In the latter case, the device would have to utilize a gateway that could perform URL naming resolution to access the Internet, as shown in Figure 7-2.

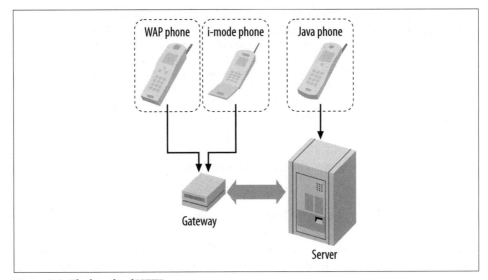

Figure 7-2. The benefit of HTTP support

 All of the MIDP 1.0 implementations must provide support for the HTTP protocol. Therefore, we encourage you to only use protocols supported by the MIDP (i.e., HTTP), as this will allow the application to be portable across all mobile information devices.

The idea of having the MIDP support the HTTP protocol is very clever. For network programming, you can revert to the HTTP programming model, and your applications will run on any MIDP device, whether it is a GSM phone with a WAP stack, a phone with I-mode, a Palm VII wireless, or a handheld device with Bluetooth.

The HttpConnection Interface

The HttpConnection interface is part of the javax.microedition.io package. This interface defines the necessary methods and constants to exchange data through an HTTP connection. It has the following methods (the constants, which have been omitted here to save space, are documented in Appendix D):

```
public interface HttpConnection extends ContentConnection {
      // public instance methods
   public long getDate() throws IOException;
   public long getExpiration() throws IOException;
   public String getFile();
   public String getHeaderField(int n) throws IOException;
   public String getHeaderField(String name) throws IOException;
   public long getHeaderFieldDate(String name, long def) throws IOException;
   public int getHeaderFieldInt(String name, int def) throws IOException;
   public String getHeaderFieldKey(int n) throws IOException;
   public String getHost();
   public long getLastModified() throws IOException;
   public int getPort();
   public String getProtocol();
   public String getQuery();
   public String getRef();
   public String getRequestMethod();
   public String getRequestProperty(String key);
   public int getResponseCode() throws IOException;
   public String getResponseMessage() throws IOException;
   public String getURL();
   public void setRequestMethod(String method) throws IOException;
   public void setRequestProperty(String key, String value) throws IOException;
}
```

The HTTP protocol is a request-response application protocol in which the parameters of the request must be set before the request is sent. The connection could be in one of the three following states:

Setup

No connection has been established yet.

Connected

A connection has been made and the request has been sent; a response is expected soon.

Closed

The connection has been closed. Some methods will throw an IOException if called.

Only in the setup state can the methods setRequestMethod() and setRequestProperty() be invoked. These can be used to cover the HTTP headers that are typically seen in an HTTP request. For example, suppose you have the following connection:

```
HttpConnection c = (HttpConnection)
    Connector.open("http://www.ora.com");
```

You can set the request method to be of type POST as follows:

```
c.setRequestMethod(HttpConnection.POST);
```

You can also use the setRequestProperty( ) method to set some of the HTTP header information. For example, you can set the User-Agent property as follows:

```
c.setRequestProperty("User-Agent",
    "Profile/MIDP-1.0 Configuration/CLDC-1.0");
```

The following methods of HttpConnection (or its sub-interfaces), which cause data to be transmitted or received, will cause a state transition from the setup state to the connected state:

```
public long getDate( ) throws java.io.IOException
public String getEncoding( )
public long getExpiration( ) throws java.io.IOException
public String getHeaderField(String name) throws java.io.IOException
public long getHeaderFieldDate(String name, long def) throws
    java.io.IOException
public int getHeaderFieldInt(String name, int def) throws
    java.io.IOException
public String getHeaderFieldKey(int n) throws java.io.IOException
public long getLastModified( ) throws java.io.IOException
public long getLength( )
public int getResponseCode( ) throws java.io.IOException
public String getResponseMessage( ) throws java.io.IOException
public String getType( )
public DataInputStream openDataInputStream(String name) throws
    java.io.IOException
public DataOutputStream openDataOutputStream(String name) throws
    java.io.IOException
public InputStream openInputStream(String name) throws
    java.io.IOException
public OutputStream openOutputStream(String name) throws
    java.io.IOException
```

While the connection is open (i.e., in the connected state), the following methods can be safely invoked:

```
public void close( ) throws java.io.IOException
public String getFile( )
public String getHost( )
public int getPort( )
```

```
public String getProtocol( )
public String getQuery( )
public String getRequestMethod( )
public String getRequestProperty(String key)
public String getURL( )
```

Before we look at sample applications, let's briefly review some of the concepts that our examples will be using: the HTTP programming model, CGI, and Java servlets.

The HTTP Programming Model

HTTP is a request-response application protocol. When programming with Java HTTP libraries, such as the Generic Connection Framework, the parameters of the request must always be set before the request is sent. This allows the entire request, including parameters, to be sent at the same time.

Request Methods

There are two commands to send data from a form on a web page to a CGI script or a servlet hosted by the HTTP server. These commands are GET and POST. Each of these has a different way of sending data to the server.

- For the GET method, the input values are sent as part of the URL in the QUERY_STRING environment variable.

- For the POST method, data is sent as an input stream and its length is saved in the CONTENT_LENGTH environment variable.

The POST method is more secure, and you can send more data using it. As an example, consider the following HTML code for the form shown in Figure 7-3.

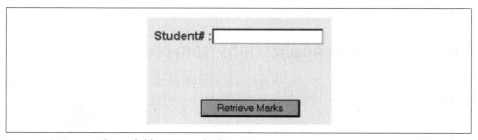

Figure 7-3. Form with one field (GET method)

```
<form action=http://www.somesite.com/cgi-bin/getgrade.cgi method="GET">
Student#:
<input type="text" name="idnum" size=30>
<input name="RetrieveMarks" value="Retrieve Marks" type="submit">
</form>
```

This form is handled by the script at *http://www.somesite.com/cgi-bin/getgrade.cgi*. Note that the form uses the GET method to transmit the information. When the user enters a student number, such as 112233, and clicks the Retrieve Marks button, the form data is sent to the CGI script as part of the URL. Hence, the encoded URL is: *http://www.somesite.com/cgi-bin/getgrade.cgi?idnum=112233*.

In the case of POST, however, input values are not sent as part of the URL. They are sent as an input stream in a separate message.

If the user enters a string with spaces, all spaces are replaced by the pluses (+). Also, if the form requires multiple input values for different fields, the fields are separated by an ampersand (&). For example, if the above form has two input fields—one for the student name and the other for the student number—the names of the fields are name and idnum, respectively. Suppose the input values are "Sam Lee" for name and "112233" for idnum. Then the encoded URL would be: *http://www.somesite.com/cgi-bin/getgrade.cgi?name=Sam+Lee&idnum=112233*.

Servlets

Java servlets also support a request and response programming model. When a client sends a request to the server, the server relays the request to the servlet. The servlet then constructs a response that the server relays back to the client. Unlike CGI scripts, however, servlets are written in Java and run within the same process as the HTTP server.

When a client request is made, the server first calls upon the service( ) method of the servlet and passes it a request and response object. The servlet then determines whether this request is a GET or POST operation, and calls either the HttpServlet. doGet( ) or HttpServlet.doPost( ) methods as needed. Both the doGet( ) and doPost( ) methods take a request object, HttpServletRequest, and a response object, HttpServletResponse, as parameters.[*]

Invoking Remote Applications from MIDlets

Now let's look at some examples of fetching HTTP pages and invoking CGI scripts and servlets from MIDlets using the connection framework.

Fetching a Page

Example 7-1 shows how to read the contents of a file referenced by a URL, using a StreamConnection. An HttpConnection can also be used, but since no HTTP-specific behavior is needed here, the StreamConnection is used. The application is very simple.

---

[*] This is just enough information to get you through this chapter. If you'd like to learn more about Java servlets, we recommend *Java Servlet Programming* by Jason Hunter (O'Reilly).

The `Connector.open()` method opens a connection to the URL and returns a `StreamConnection` object. Then an `InputStream` is opened through which to read the contents of the file, one character at a time, until the end of the file (signaled by a character value of -1) is reached. In the event that an exception is thrown, both the stream and connection are closed.

Example 7-1. Fetching a page referenced by a URL

```java
import java.io.*;
import javax.microedition.io.*;
import javax.microedition.lcdui.*;
import javax.microedition.midlet.*;

public class FetchPageMidlet extends MIDlet {

    private Display display;

    String url = "http://www.javacourses.com/hello.txt";

    public FetchPageMidlet() {
        display = Display.getDisplay(this);
    }

    /**
     * This will be invoked when we start the MIDlet
     */
    public void startApp() {
        try {
            getViaStreamConnection(url);
        } catch (IOException e) {
            //Handle Exceptions any other way you like.
            System.out.println("IOException " + e);
            e.printStackTrace();
        }
    }

    /**
     * Pause, discontinue ....
     */
    public void pauseApp() {

    }

    /**
     * Destroy must cleanup everything.
     */
    public void destroyApp(boolean unconditional) {
    }

    /**
     * read url via stream connection
     */
    void getViaStreamConnection(String url) throws IOException {
        StreamConnection c = null;
```

Example 7-1. Fetching a page referenced by a URL (continued)

```
    InputStream s = null;
    StringBuffer b = new StringBuffer( );
    TextBox t = null;
    try {
        c = (StreamConnection)Connector.open(url);
        s = c.openInputStream( );
        int ch;
        while((ch = s.read( )) != -1) {
            b.append((char) ch);
        }
        System.out.println(b.toString( ));
        t = new TextBox("Fetch Page", b.toString( ), 1024, 0);
    } finally {
        if(s != null) {
            s.close( );
        }
        if(c != null) {
            c.close( );
        }
    }
    // display the contents of the file in a text box.
    display.setCurrent(t);
    }
}
```

When you run and activate FetchPageMidlet, you should see a screen similar to Figure 7-4.

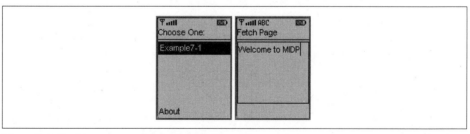

Figure 7-4. Fetching a page reference by a URL

Invoking a CGI Script (GET)

The following example shows how to invoke a CGI script from an HTTP server, capturing and displaying the results on the handheld device screen. This example uses an HttpConnection object, which is returned by the call to the Connector.open( ) method. The call to setRequestMethod( ) sets the request method to GET, followed by two calls to setRequestProperty( ), which in turn set the HTTP request header properties User-Agent and Content-Language. In this example, a script is invoked with a student ID number encoded as part of the URL. The script searches a database file and returns the final grade for the student corresponding to the ID number.

The URL has the form *http://www.javacourses.com/cgi-bin/get-grade?idnum=182016*. Alternatively, you can do this with the commented-out code shown below in bold. The latter technique can also be used if the student ID number is to be entered by the user, as you will see in the next example.

This example's source code is shown in Example 7-2.

Example 7-2. Invoking a CGI script (GET method)

```
import java.io.*;
import javax.microedition.io.*;
import javax.microedition.lcdui.*;
import javax.microedition.midlet.*;

/**
 * An example MIDlet to invoke a CGI script (GET method).
 */

public class InvokeCgiMidlet1 extends MIDlet {

    private Display display;

    String url = "http://www.javacourses.com/cgibin/getgrade.cgi?idnum=182016";

    public InvokeCgiMidlet1( ) {
        display = Display.getDisplay(this);
    }

    /**
     * Initialization. Invoked when we activate the MIDlet.
     */
    public void startApp( ) {
        try {
            getGrade(url);
        } catch (IOException e) {
            System.out.println("IOException " + e);
            e.printStackTrace( );
        }
    }

    /**
     * Pause, discontinue ....
     */
    public void pauseApp( ) {
    }

    /**
     * Destroy must cleanup everything.
     */
    public void destroyApp(boolean unconditional) {
    }
```

Example 7-2. Invoking a CGI script (GET method) (continued)

```
/**
 * Retrieve a grade....
 */

void getGrade(String url) throws IOException {
   HttpConnection c = null;
   InputStream is = null;
   OutputStream os = null;
   StringBuffer b = new StringBuffer();
   TextBox t = null;
   try {
      c = (HttpConnection)Connector.open(url);
      // set the request method to GET
      c.setRequestMethod(HttpConnection.GET);
      // set some HTTP request headers
      c.setRequestProperty("User-Agent","Profile/MIDP-1.0 Configuration/CLDC-1.0");
      c.setRequestProperty("Content-Language", "en-CA");
      os = c.openOutputStream();
      /*
      //Retrieve info for ID number 182016
       String str = "?idnum=182016";
       byte postmsg[] = str.getBytes();
       for(int i=0;i<postmsg.length;i++) {
         os.writeByte(postmsg[i]);
       }
       os.flush();
       */
      is = c.openDataInputStream();
      int ch;
      while ((ch = is.read()) != -1) {
         b.append((char) ch);
         System.out.println((char)ch);
      }
      t = new TextBox("Final Grades", b.toString(), 1024, 0);
   } finally {
      if(is!= null) {
         is.close();
      }
      if(os != null) {
         os.close();
      }
      if(c != null) {
         c.close();
      }
   }
   display.setCurrent(t);
  }
}
```

When you run and activate InvokeCgiMidlet1, you should see a screen similar to Figure 7-5.

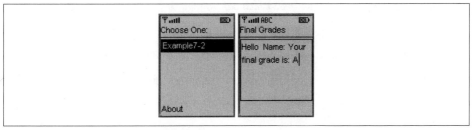

Figure 7-5. Invoking a CGI script (GET method)

Invoking a CGI Script (POST)

Now let's talk about making HTTP requests using POST. In this example, the input is sent to the CGI script, called *pgrade.cgi*, in a message.

The URL variable, defined in Example 7-3, specifies the location of the *pgrade.cgi* CGI script. In this example, an HTTP connection is opened to the CGI script, followed by opening input and output streams on the connection. Data for the script is sent through the output stream, and the response is received through the input stream. The CGI script in this example, which is written in Perl, takes a student number input value. If the student number is found in the database file, the script retrieves the corresponding final grade and returns the grade to the calling client. In the case of MIDlets, however, there are no HTML forms, so here the message name=182016 is sent to the CGI script. The source code for this example is shown in Example 7-3. Note that when using the POST method, the CONTENT_TYPE header must be set to application/x-www-form-urlencoded, because this content type:

- Specifies normal data encoding.
- Converts blanks to plus (+) signs.
- Converts non-alphanumeric characters to hexadecimal numbers preceded by a percent sign (%).
- Places an ampersand (&) between each name=value pair.

In short, this content type prevents data corruption during the transmission of form data from the browser to the server.

Example 7-3. Invoking a CGI script (POST method)

```
import java.io.*;
import javax.microedition.io.*;
import javax.microedition.lcdui.*;
import javax.microedition.midlet.*;

/**
 * An example MIDlet to invoke a CGI script (POST method is used).
 */
```

Example 7-3. Invoking a CGI script (POST method) (continued)

```
public class InvokeCgiMidlet2 extends MIDlet {

    private Display display;

    String url = "http://www.javacourses.com/cgi-bin/pgrade.cgi";

    public InvokeCgiMidlet2( ) {
        display = Display.getDisplay(this);
    }

    /**
     * Initialization. Invoked when we activate the MIDlet.
     */
    public void startApp( ) {
        try {
            getGrade(url);
        } catch (IOException e) {
            System.out.println("IOException " + e);
            e.printStackTrace( );
        }
    }

    /**
     * Pause, discontinue ....
     */
    public void pauseApp( ) {
    }

    /**
     * Destroy must cleanup everything.
     */
    public void destroyApp(boolean unconditional) {
    }

    /**
     * Retrieve a grade....
     */

    void getGrade(String url) throws IOException {
        HttpConnection c = null;
        InputStream is = null;
        OutputStream os = null;
        StringBuffer b = new StringBuffer( );
        TextBox t = null;
        try {
            c = (HttpConnection)Connector.open(url);
            c.setRequestMethod(HttpConnection.POST);
```

Example 7-3. Invoking a CGI script (POST method) (continued)

```
        c.setRequestProperty("CONTENT-TYPE",
            "application/x-www-form-urlencoded");
        c.setRequestProperty("User-Agent",
            "Profile/MIDP-1.0 Configuration/CLDC-1.0");
        c.setRequestProperty("Content-Language", "en-CA");
        os = c.openOutputStream();

        // send input
        String str = "name=182016";
        byte postmsg[] = str.getBytes();
        for(int i=0;i<postmsg.length;i++) {
            os.write(postmsg[i]);
        }
        os.flush();
        is = c.openDataInputStream();
        int ch;
        // receive output
        while ((ch = is.read()) != -1) {
            b.append((char) ch);
            System.out.println((char)ch);
        }
        t = new TextBox("Final Grades", b.toString(), 1024, 0);
    } finally {
        if(is!= null) {
            is.close();
        }
        if(os != null) {
            os.close();
        }
        if(c != null) {
            c.close();
        }
    }
    display.setCurrent(t);
  }
}
```

When you run and activate the InvokeCgiMidlet2, you should see output similar to Figure 7-6.

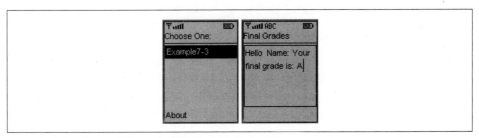

Figure 7-6. Invoking a CGI script (POST method)

Invoking a Servlet

You can invoke a servlet from a MIDlet the same way you would invoke a CGI script: by opening an HTTP connection and obtaining input/output streams on that connection. This section presents two examples.

- The first example invokes a servlet using the GET operation and collects and displays the results.
- In the second example, the servlet accepts input obtained from the user of the handset and invoked with the POST method.

FirstMidletServlet

In this example, InvokeServletMidlet1 is invoked with the GET method and the response is received and displayed on the handset. No input is sent to the servlet. When invoked, the servlet sends the "Servlet Invoked!" string and the date back to the client. The source code for the InvokeServletMidlet1 is in Example 7-4.

Example 7-4. Invoking a servlet with no input values

```java
import java.io.*;
import javax.microedition.io.*;
import javax.microedition.lcdui.*;
import javax.microedition.midlet.*;

/**
 * An example MIDlet to invoke a servlet.
 */

public class InvokeServletMidlet1 extends MIDlet {

    private Display display;

    String url = "http://127.0.0.1:8080/examples/servlet/HelloServlet";


    public InvokeServletMidlet1() {
        display = Display.getDisplay(this);
    }

    /**
     * Initialization. Invoked when we activate the MIDlet.
     */
    public void startApp() {
        try {
            invokeServlet(url);
        } catch (IOException e) {
            System.out.println("IOException " + e);
            e.printStackTrace();
        }
    }
```

Example 7-4. Invoking a servlet with no input values (continued)

```
/**
 * Pause, discontinue ....
 */
public void pauseApp( ) {
}

/**
 * Destroy must cleanup everything.
 */
public void destroyApp(boolean unconditional) {
}

/**
 * Retrieve a grade....
 */
void invokeServlet(String url) throws IOException {
    HttpConnection c = null;
    InputStream is = null;
    StringBuffer b = new StringBuffer( );
    TextBox t = null;
    try {
        c = (HttpConnection)Connector.open(url);
        c.setRequestMethod(HttpConnection.GET);
        c.setRequestProperty("User-Agent","Profile/MIDP-1.0 Configuration/CLDC-1.0");
        c.setRequestProperty("Content-Language", "en-CA");
        is = c.openDataInputStream( );
        int ch;
        while ((ch = is.read( )) != -1) {
            b.append((char) ch);
        }
        t = new TextBox("First Servlet", b.toString( ), 1024, 0);
    } finally {
        if(is!= null) {
            is.close( );
        }
        if(c != null) {
            c.close( );
        }
    }
    display.setCurrent(t);
}
}
```

The source code for the HelloServlet, which sends the message "Servlet Invoked!" and the date back to the client, is shown in Example 7-5. You will need a web server that is capable of running servlets to make this work, such as the freely distributed Apache Tomcat.

Example 7-5. HelloServlet

```
import java.io.*;
import java.util.*;
import javax.servlet.*;
import javax.servlet.http.*;

/**
 * The simplest possible servlet.
 */

public class HelloServlet extends HttpServlet {
    public void doGet(HttpServletRequest request,  HttpServletResponse response)
            throws IOException, ServletException {
        response.setContentType("text/plain");
        PrintWriter out = response.getWriter();
        out.println("Servlet Invoked!");
        out.println(new Date());
    }
}
```

When you run and activate the InvokeServletMidlet1, you should see something similar to Figure 7-7.

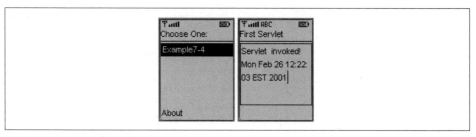

Figure 7-7. FirstServletMidlet output

SecondMidletServlet

Now let's see how to invoke a servlet that expects input with the POST method. This is a more sophisticated example than the previous one. In this example, the InvokeServletMidlet2 prompts the user to enter a value (the first name). When the user presses the key that corresponds to the Submit command, the RequestServlet is invoked. RequestServlet then retrieves the input values of the request from the buffer and returns them back to the client, showing that the servlet received the POST request. Note that the servlet and the MIDlet in this example run on the same machine. The source code for the InvokeServletMidlet2 is shown in Example 7-6.

Example 7-6. Invoking a servlet with an input value

```
import javax.microedition.rms.*;
import javax.microedition.lcdui.*;
import javax.microedition.midlet.*;
```

Example 7-6. Invoking a servlet with an input value (continued)

```java
import javax.microedition.io.*;
import java.io.*;
import java.util.Vector;

public class InvokeServletMidlet2 extends MIDlet implements CommandListener {
    Display display = null;
    List menu = null;
    TextBox input = null;
    String user = null;

    // note that the servlet and MIDlet run on the same machine
    String url =
        "http://127.0.0.1:8080/examples/servlet/RequestServlet2";
    static final Command backCommand = new Command("Back",
        Command.BACK, 0);
    static final Command submitCommand = new Command("Submit",
        Command.OK, 2);
    static final Command exitCommand = new Command("Exit",
        Command.STOP, 3);
    String currentMenu = null;

    public InvokeServletMidlet2() {
    }

    public void startApp() throws MIDletStateChangeException {
        display = Display.getDisplay(this);
        menu = new List("Invoke Servlet", Choice.IMPLICIT);
        menu.append("Add a user", null);
        menu.addCommand(exitCommand);
        menu.setCommandListener(this);
        mainMenu();
    }

    public void pauseApp() {
    }

    public void destroyApp(boolean unconditional) {
        notifyDestroyed();
    }

    void mainMenu() {
        display.setCurrent(menu);
    }

    public void addName() {
        input = new TextBox("Enter first name:", "", 5,
            TextField.ANY);
        input.addCommand(submitCommand);
        input.addCommand(backCommand);
        input.setCommandListener(this);
        input.setString("");
        display.setCurrent(input);
    }
```

Example 7-6. Invoking a servlet with an input value (continued)

```java
void invokeServlet(String url) throws IOException {
    HttpConnection c = null;
    InputStream is = null;
    OutputStream os = null;
    StringBuffer b = new StringBuffer( );
    TextBox t = null;
    try {
        c = (HttpConnection)Connector.open(url);
        c.setRequestMethod(HttpConnection.POST);
        c.setRequestProperty("CONTENT-TYPE",
            "application/x-www-form-urlencoded");
        c.setRequestProperty("User-Agent",
            "Profile/MIDP-1.0 Configuration/CLDC-1.0");
        c.setRequestProperty("Content-Language", "en-CA");

        os = c.openOutputStream( );
        String str = "name="+user;
        byte postmsg[] = str.getBytes( );
        System.out.println("Length: "+str.getBytes( ));
        for(int i=0;i<postmsg.length;i++) {
            os.write(postmsg[i]);
        }
        // or you can easily do:
        //os.write(("name="+user).getBytes( ));
        os.flush( );

        is = c.openDataInputStream( );
        int ch;
        while ((ch = is.read( )) != -1) {
            b.append((char) ch);
            System.out.print((char)ch);
        }
        t = new TextBox("Second Servlet", b.toString( ), 1024, 0);
        t.addCommand(backCommand);
        t.setCommandListener(this);
    } finally {
        if(is!= null) {
            is.close( );
        }
        if(os != null) {
            os.close( );
        }
        if(c != null) {
            c.close( );
        }
    }
    display.setCurrent(t);
}

public void commandAction(Command c, Displayable d) {
    String label = c.getLabel( );
```

Example 7-6. Invoking a servlet with an input value (continued)

```
        if (label.equals("Exit")) {
            destroyApp(true);
        } else if (label.equals("Back")) {
            mainMenu( );
        } else if (label.equals("Submit")) {
            user = input.getString( );
            try {
                invokeServlet(url);
            }catch(IOException e) {}
        } else {
            addName( );
        }
    }
}
```

The source code for the RequestServlet, which retrieves the POST request from the buffer and sends the input values back to the client, is shown in Example 7-7.

Example 7-7. RequestServlet

```
import java.io.*;
import java.text.*;
import java.util.*;
import javax.servlet.*;
import javax.servlet.http.*;
/**
 * Example servlet showing request headers
 */

public class RequestServlet extends HttpServlet {
    public void doPost(HttpServletRequest request, HttpServletResponse response)
                throws IOException, ServletException {
        response.setContentType("text/plain");
        PrintWriter out = response.getWriter( );
        BufferedReader br = request.getReader( );
        String buf = br.readLine( );
        out.print("Rec: "+buf);
    }
}
```

> In order to use ServletRequest.getParameter(String) to retrieve the input values from the MIDlet in Example 7-6, the CONTENT_TYPE header must be set to application/x-www-form-urlencoded, as discussed earlier in this chapter.

When you run InvokeServletMidlet2 and invoke it by entering your name, you should see something similar to Figure 7-8.

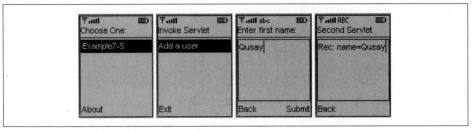

Figure 7-8. SecondMidletServlet output

Wireless Session Tracking

The term *session tracking* means maintaining state information about a series of requests from the same client. Maintaining such information for clients that use HTTP is a problem. Why? Because HTTP is a request-response protocol, which means the connection between the client and the server is not maintained for the duration of the conversation. In other words, HTTP is a *stateless* protocol. This means you cannot depend on the underlying connection protocol to maintain state information; you must find other ways to perform session tracking.

The two most widely used techniques for session tracking are *cookies* and *URL rewriting*. A cookie is a piece of data that a Web server sends to the client. This piece of data is stored by the client and used the next time the client makes a request from that server. However, if cookies are disabled by the browser or, more importantly, if the browser itself does not support them (as is the case with most current wireless devices), then cookies are not of much use. However, you can send and receive cookies through the use of the `HttpConnection.setRequestProperty( )` and `HttpConnection.getHeaderField( )` methods. To send a cookie to a server, simply set the value of the cookie request property before sending the message.

```
String myLocalCookieVariable;

HttpConnection connection = (HttpConnection)Connection.open(someURL);
Connection.setRequestProperty("cookie", myLocalCookieVariable);
```

When you receive a response back from the server, you can parse the resulting Set-cookie header field as follows:

```
is = c.openInputStream( );
String cookie = connection.getHeaderField("Set-cookie");
If (cookie != null)
    myLocalCookieVariable = cookie.substring(0, cookie.indexOf(";"));
```

The other technique for session tracking is URL rewriting. This technique is ideal for clients that do not support cookies or have cookies disabled. With this technique, the session information is encoded into URLs that the server generates. This means that instead of returning this URL (*http://www.somesite.com/servlet/shop/catalog.html*), the server generates the following URL, or something similar, instead (*http://www. somesite.com/servlet/shop/catalog.html;jsessionid=cl98373673At*).

The information that would otherwise be stored in a cookie is appended to the URL. You can parse this information out into a `String` after it arrives, using a technique similar the one we used with cookies in the previous section. The server will look for this information when a request is made from the client. The exact syntax of the encoded URL depends on the underlying server environment. However, the Java Servlet API provides facilities such as the `response.encodeURL(String)` and `response. encodeRedirectURL(String)` methods, which you can use for session tracking.

MIDlet Networking Security

Over the past few years, concerns about security on the Internet have heated up immensely. It's common in this day and age to hear of companies whose data has been hacked and from whom valuable credit card information has been stolen. It probably won't be long before people can "sniff" the data going through cell phones just as easily as data traveling across the Internet. What can you do? Fortunately, computers these days are capable of using *encryption* techniques to scramble data as it travels through the unsafe corridors of the Internet. In fact, one of the most popular forms of encryption uses a wide variety of cryptographic techniques to protect your data. It's called Secure Sockets Layer (SSL) and is built into practically every web browser.

Will you need encryption for your MIDlet programs? That's a hard question to answer. Many wireless protocols already use a sophisticated level of scrambling—far more than an average "sniffer" can decode. And while cryptographic software can be relatively small and easy to use on a desktop, using it on a cell phone can quickly expend both your processing power and program space. Understanding cryptography can take a bit of time as well.* However, if you absolutely must have security on your cell phone to protect data traveling on the Internet, we recommend checking out the open source lightweight API software from "The Legion of the Bouncy Castle" (*http://www.bouncycastle.org*).

* A great place to start, however, is Bruce Schneier's *Applied Cryptography*, Second Edition (Wiley).

CHAPTER 8
Database Programming

A database is a non-volatile place for storing the state of objects. For some applications, you might need objects to exist even after the application that created them closes. Without a storage mechanism, objects and their states are destroyed when an application closes. However, if you save objects to a *persistent storage facility*, such as a database, they can be read in later by the same application or even other applications.

The persistent storage facilities provided in the J2SE platform, such as the JDBC and Object Serialization APIs, are too large for handheld devices with a small memory footprint. Storage requirements vary significantly from one resource-constrained device to another. J2ME and the MIDP solve this problem by using the Record Management System (RMS).

This chapter introduces the details of the MIDP RMS, a persistent storage facility for MIDlets, and shows you how to develop MIDP database applications, using an example involving stocks. Throughout this chapter, the terms *record store* and *database* are used interchangeably.

The Record Management System

An RMS database (or record store) consists of a collection of records that remain persistent after the MIDlet closes. When you invoke the MIDlet again, it can retrieve data from the persistent record store. However, to use the RMS, we need to get familiar with some of the classes and concepts provided by the javax.microedition. rms package.

Record Stores

Record stores, which are binary files, are actually platform-dependent because they are created in platform-unique locations. MIDlets within a single application (a

MIDlet suite) can create multiple record stores with different names. The RMS APIs provide the following types of functionality.

- They allow MIDlets to manipulate (add and remove) records within a record store.
- They allow MIDlets in the same application or suite to share records (access each other's record store directly).

Note that no mechanism, however, is provided for sharing records between MIDlets in different MIDlet suites.

Record stores have names that are case-sensitive and cannot be more than 32 characters in length. A MIDlet cannot create two record stores with the same name in the same application. However, it can create a record store with the same name in another application. When you create a new record store in an emulator, it is typically stored under a directory called *NOJAM*. For example, let's assume you are using the Wireless Toolkit and it is installed under *C:\J2MEWTK*. If your project name is *StockQuotes* and your record store is *mystocks*, the record store is created under *C:\J2MEWTK\NOJAM* and has the name *mystocks.db*.

The MIDP RMS implementation ensures that all individual record store operations are atomic, synchronous, and serialized, so no corruption occurs with multiple access. However, if your MIDlets use multiple threads to access a record store, it is your responsibility to synchronize this access. Otherwise, some of your records might accidentally be overwritten if your application is not thread-safe.

The javax.microedition.rms Package

The javax.microedition.rms package consists of four interfaces, one class, and five exception classes.

Interfaces

Table 8-1 lists the four interfaces in the javax.microedition.rms package.

Table 8-1. The interfaces in javax.microedition.rms

Interface	Description
RecordComparator	This interface defines a comparator to compare two records.
RecordEnumeration	This interface represents a bidirectional record enumerator.
RecordFilter	This interface defines a filter to examine a record and check if it matches, based on a criteria defined by the application.
RecordListener	This interface receives records that were added, changed, or deleted from a record store.

Classes

There is one class in this package, as shown in Table 8-2.

Table 8-2. The class in javax.microedition.rms

Class	Description
RecordStore	This class represents a record store.

Exceptions

There are five exceptions in the package, as shown in Table 8-3.

Table 8-3. The exceptions in javax.microedition.rms

Exception	Description
InvalidRecordIDException	This exception is thrown to indicate that the RecordID is invalid.
RecordStoreException	This exception is thrown when a general exception is thrown by the RecordStore class.
RecordStoreFullException	This exception is thrown when the record store filesystem is full.
RecordStoreNotFoundException	This exception is thrown when the record store could not be found.
RecordStoreNotOpenException	This exception is thrown to indicate an operation on a closed record store.

Programming with the RMS

Database programming with the RMS is relatively straightforward. A record store consists of a collection of records that is uniquely identified by its record ID, which is an integer value. The record ID is the primary key for the records. The first record has an ID of 1, and each additional record is assigned an ID that is the previous value plus 1. The record ID is stored as an integer value, which gives the theoretical limit of 2,147,483,647 records.[*]

Opening, Closing, and Deleting a Record Store

To open a record store, you need to be familiar with the static openRecordStore( ) method of the RecordStore class:

```
public static RecordStore openRecordStore(String recordStoreName,
    Boolean createIfNecessary) throws RecordStoreException,
    RecordStoreFullException, RecordStoreNotFoundException
```

Here is an example of using this method:

```
RecordStore db = null;

try {
    db = RecordStore.openRecordStore("myDBfile", true);
```

---

[*] But if your devices had at least 2.1 gig of memory, you probably wouldn't need to use the J2ME!

```
    } catch (RecordStoreNotFoundException rsnfe) {
        // Handle exception
    } catch (RecordStoreFullException fsfe) {
        // Handle exception
    } catch (RecordStoreException rse) {
        // Handle exception
    }
```

Assuming that everything works right, this line of code creates a new database file named *myDBfile*. The second parameter, a boolean which is set to true, says that if the record store does not exist, then you should create it.

 If the openRecordStore( ) method is called by a MIDlet when the record store is already open by another MIDlet in the same MIDlet suite, the method returns a reference to the same RecordStore object.

Once we've opened a record store, we will eventually need to close it. We can do this with the following RecordStore method:

```
public void closeRecordStore( ) throws RecordStoreNotOpenException,
    RecordStoreException
```

It is important to note that the record store will not actually be closed until closeRecordStore() is called as many times as openRecordStore( ) was called. Therefore, the programmer must balance the number of close calls and open calls before the record store is actually closed. Keeping a record store open can take up a great deal of memory. Consider closing a record store even when a MIDlet is placed in the paused state.

Sometimes it's necessary to locate a particular record store among several that are currently on the device. If you want to find out the names of all the record stores currently on the device, use the following static method:

```
public static String[] listRecordStores( )
```

You can delete an entire record store from the database, using the following static RecordStore method:

```
public static void deleteRecordStore(String recordStoreName) throws
    RecordStoreException, RecordStoreNotFoundException
```

You can find out the size of the currently opened record store in bytes, using the getSize( ) method:

```
public int getSize( ) throws RecordStoreNotOpenException
```

In addition, if you want to find out how many bytes the current record store can still grow, use the following:

```
public int getSizeAvailable( ) throws RecordStoreNotOpenException
```

Finally, you can use the getVersion( ) method of the RecordStore to find out the "version" of the current record store. Here, the version does not have anything to do with the version of software that the database is using. Instead, the version is actually an integer stored with the record store that increments each time a record is added, modified, or deleted.

```
public int getVersion( ) throws RecordStoreNotOpenException
```

Creating and Modifying Records

A record is simply an array of bytes. You can use the DataInputStream, DataOutputStream, ByteArrayInputStream, and ByteArrayOutputStream classes to pack and unpack data in and out of byte arrays. For example, suppose you have the following record, represented by a single string: "Firstname, LastName, Age". To add this record to the record store, you can use the addRecord( ) method:

```
public int addRecord(byte[] data, int offset, int numBytes) throws
    RecordStoreNotOpenException, RecordStoreException,
    RecordStoreFullException
```

This method adds all or part of the contents of a byte array of data, starting at the offset specified and continuing the numBytes, and places it in the record store. The method then returns the index assigned to that record in the database. Continuing from the previous example:

```
try {
    ByteArrayOutputStream baos = new ByteArrayOutputstream( );
    DataOutputStream dos = new DataOutputStream(baos);
    dos.writeUTF(record);
    Byte b[] = baos.toByteArray( );
    recordNumber = db.addRecord(b, 0, b.length);
} catch (Exception e) {
    // Handle exceptions
}
```

Here, we construct a DataOutputStream for writing the record to the record store, then convert the ByteArrayOutputStream to a byte array. Finally, we invoke addRecord( ) to add the record to the record store. This is not the only way to construct and add a new record to a record store, however. Instead of creating a series of linked streams, it is easier to convert a string into a series of bytes using the getBytes( ) method of String:

```
try {
    String record = "Firstname, Lastname, Age";
    Byte b[] = record.getBytes( );
    recordNumber = db.adRecord(b, 0, b.length);
} catch (Exception e) {
    // Handle Exceptions
}
```

You can also use the setRecord( ) method if you want to explicitly reset an indexed record in the record store. This works the same as addRecord( ), except that the first parameter is the specific record ID that you wish to set:

```
public void setRecord(int recordId, byte[] newData, int offset,
    int numBytes) throws RecordStoreNotOpenException,
    InvalidRecordIDException, RecordStoreException,
    RecordStoreFullException
```

To read a record from the record store, you can use one of two getRecord( ) methods:

```
public byte[] getRecord(int recordID) throws
    RecordStoreNotOpenException, InvalidRecordIDException,
    RecordStoreException
public int getRecord(int recordID, byte[] buffer, int offset)
    throws RecordStoreNotOpenException, InvalidRecordIDException,
    RecordStoreException
```

The first method returns a byte array containing the entire record that was stored at the specified record ID. The second method will attempt to fill the byte array passed in starting at the specified offset with the contents of the specified record ID. The second method will return the amount of bytes actually copied as an integer. Be sure that there is enough room in the byte array to handle the data from the record, or an exception will be thrown.

To extract the data from a byte array, we can do the opposite of what we did before: construct input streams instead of output streams. Here is an example:

```
String in = null;

try {
    byte[] record = new byte[db.getRecordSize(recordNumber)];
    db.getRecord(recordNumber, record, 0);
    ByteArrayInputStream bais = new ByteArrayInputStream(record);
    DataInputStream dis = new DataInputStream(bais);
    in = dis.readUTF( );
} catch (Exception e) {
    // Handle exceptions
}
```

Or, if we don't want to filter the data through any sort of stream, we can take the easy route and simply pass the byte array directly into the String constructor:

```
String in = null;

try {
    byte[] record = new byte[db.getRecordSize(recordNumber)];
    db.getRecord(recordNumber, record, 0);
    in = new String(record);
} catch (Exception e) {
    // Handle exceptions
}
```

To delete a record from the record store, you have to know the record ID of the record to be deleted. To delete the record, use the deleteRecord( ) method.

```
public void deleteRecord(int recordID) throws
    RecordStoreNotOpenException, InvalidRecordIDException,
    RecordStoreException
```

Note that the other records will not change their ID. In fact, the record store will not reuse the ID of a record once it is deleted.

There are a number of other methods that you can use in the RecordStore class. If you want to find out when the record store was last modified, you can use the following method:

```
public long getLastModified() throws RecordStoreNotOpenException
```

This method returns a date in the form of a long, which is equivalent to the format used by System.currentTimeMillis( ). This can be passed into the constructor of the java.util.Date object, which can in turn be used by the java.util.Calendar object, as well as the javax.microedition.lcdui.DateField component.

If you want to know the name of the current record store, use the getName( ) method:

```
public String getName() throws RecordStoreNotOpenException
```

If you want to find out the next ID that the database will use when storing a record, you can use the getNextRecordID( ) method:

```
public int getNextRecordID() throws RecordStoreNotOpenException,
    RecordStoreException
```

To get a tally of the number of records currently in the record store, use the following method:

```
public int getNumRecords() throws RecordStoreNotOpenException
```

If you wish to find out the number of bytes in a currently stored record, use the getRecordSize( ) method (as we did in one of the previous examples to initialize the receiving byte array):

```
public int getRecordSize(int recordId) throws
    RecordStoreNotOpenException, InvalidRecordIDException,
    RecordStoreException
```

Finally, there is one other method that RecordStore includes that allows us to enumerate all the records located in the current record store. It looks like the following:

```
public RecordEnumeration enumerateRecords(RecordFilter filter,
    RecordComparator comparator, boolean keepUpdated) throws
    RecordStoreNotOpenException
```

This method will list all the records in the record store, first using the appropriate filter to select those records, then sorting them using the record comparator, and finally returning the results inside a specially designed enumeration object. However, there are several interfaces that we need to go over first before we can grasp the broad picture of what this method does.

Filtering Records

First, the enumerateRecords() method must determine which records will be included in the enumeration that you are requesting. The method determines this by passing in an object that implements the javax.microedition.rms.RecordFilter interface. Luckily, only one method in this interface needs to be implemented:

```
public boolean matches(byte[] candidate);
```

This method takes in a byte array that represents a candidate record from a record store. The implementation must return a boolean that indicates whether the record should be included in the enumeration. If the method returns true, the record will be included; if it's false, it will not be. If you want all records to be included in the enumeration, simply pass in null to that parameter of the enumerateRecords() method.

Here is a sample implementation for the RecordFilter interface that only accepts String-based records that start with the letters "JULY":

```
import javax.microedition.rms.*;

public class MyFilter implements RecordFilter {

    public boolean matches(byte[] candidate) {
        String c = new String(candidate);
        if (c.startsWith("JULY"))
            return true;
        else
            return false;
    }
}
```

Comparing Records

The enumerateRecords() method has the ability to sort the records that it is returning. If you would like it to do so, you must give it the ability to compare records in the record store. For this, your application must provide an object that implements the javax.microedition.rms.RecordComparator interface. Again, this is relatively simple, as you must implement only one method in this interface:

```
public int compare(byte[] record1, byte[] record2)
```

The return value of this method indicates how the two records compare, and it can be one of three constants. For example, suppose you want to lexigraphically compare two strings that you retrieved from two records. Here is a sample implementation:

```
import javax.microedition.rms.*;

public class MyComparator implements RecordComparator {

    public int compare(byte record1[], byte record2[]) {
```

```
            String name1 = new String(record1);
            String name2 = new String(record2);

            int num = name1.compareTo(name2);

            if(num > 0) {
                return RecordComparator.FOLLOWS;
            } else if (num < 0) {
                return RecordComparator.PRECEDES;
            } else {
                return RecordComparator.EQUIVALENT;
            }
        }
    }
}
```

The constants that the object should return, `RecordComparator.FOLLOWS`, `RecordComparator.PRECEDES`, and `RecordComparator.EQUIVALENT`, are declared in the `RecordComparator` interface and have the following meanings:

`RecordComparator.FOLLOWS`
> The first record follows the second record in terms of search or sort order.

`RecordComparator.PRECEDES`
> The first record precedes the second record in terms of search or sort order.

`RecordComparator.EQUIVALENT`
> The two records are the same.

If the ID of each of the records is acceptable as an order, then you can pass in `null` to that parameter of the enumerateRecords( ) method.

Enumerating Records

Finally, the enumerateRecords( ) method will return to you an object that implements the `javax.microedition.rms.RecordEnumeration` interface. This interface is used to provide a standard set of methods to access the enumeration, and acts like a more sophisticated version of the `java.util.Enumeration` class. It looks like the following:

```
public interface RecordEnumeration {

    public void destroy( );
    public boolean hasNextElement( );
    public boolean hasPreviousElement( );
    public boolean isKeptUpdated( );
    public void keepUpdated(boolean keepUpdated);
    public byte[] nextRecord( ) throws InvalidRecordIDException,
        RecordStoreNotOpenException, RecordStoreException;
    public int nextRecordId( ) throws InvalidRecordIDException;
    public int numRecords( );
    public byte[] previousRecord( ) throws InvalidRecordIDException,
        RecordStoreNotOpenException, RecordStoreException;
```

```
public int previousRecordID( ) throws InvalidRecordIDException;
public void rebuild( );
public void reset( );
```

    }

If you recall the signature of the enumerateRecords( ) method, you'll remember that it had a third parameter, which was a boolean, called keepUpdated. The function of this boolean is to have the enumeration monitor the current record store. If there are several threads updating the record store at any given time, the enumeration may not have the correct values inside it.

However, if the boolean parameter to enumerateRecords( ) is set to true, the RecordEnumeration becomes a listener to the record store. If there are any changes to the records, the RecordEnumeration will update itself automatically. However, if the boolean value is set to false, the RecordEnumeration will not update itself until the rebuild( ) method is called. Which method to use is entirely your choice. However, keep in mind that each call to enumerateRecords( ) can take quite a bit of time to complete. If you have a large data store, it may be better to implement another strategy.

The following methods of RecordEnumeration will also set and retrieve the boolean property to keep the enumeration updated with any changes to the record store:

```
public void keepUpdated(boolean keepUpdated);
public boolean isKeptUpdated( );
```

To find out how many records have been filtered into the enumeration itself, use the following method. (Note the number of filtered records may not be the same as the total amount of records in the record store.)

```
public int numRecords( );
```

If you wish to find out if the enumeration has an element before or after the current position, you can use the following methods. Note that the enumeration will loop around in the event that it travels before the first element or after the final element.

```
public boolean hasPreviousElement( );
public boolean hasNextElement( );
```

If you wish to find the record ID that the previous methods refer to, use these methods:

```
public int nextRecordId( ) throws InvalidRecordIDException;
public int previousRecordID( ) throws InvalidRecordIDException;
```

You can obtain the next and previous records themselves using the following methods:

```
public byte[] nextRecord( ) throws InvalidRecordIDException,
    RecordStoreNotOpenException, RecordStoreException;
public byte[] previousRecord( ) throws InvalidRecordIDException,
    RecordStoreNotOpenException, RecordStoreException;
```

This method returns the current position of the enumeration to the state it was at when the enumeration was first created:

```
public void reset();
```

And finally, if you want to release all the data that has been stored in the enumeration in order to gain back the memory used, utilize the following method:

```
public void destroy();
```

Listening to Record Stores

If you wish to monitor any changes that take place in a record store, you can create an object that implements the javax.microedition.rms.RecordListener interface. This interface contains only three methods:

```
public interface RecordListener {
    public void recordAdded(RecordStore recordStore, int recordID);
    public void recordRemoved(RecordStore recordStore, int recordID);
    public void recordModified(RecordStore recordStore, int recordID);
}
```

As you probably guessed, the first method will be called if a record is added, the second will be called if a record is removed, and the third method will be called if a record is modified. All three methods have the same two parameters. The first is a reference to the RecordStore object, and the second parameter is an integer that refers to the actual record store ID that was changed.

Once you've created an object that implements the RecordListener interface, you can add or remove it from the list of listeners of a record store by using the following two methods of the RecordStore class:

```
public void addRecordListener(RecordListener listener);
public void removeRecordListener(RecordListener listener);
```

A Stock Database

Now let's see how we would use the RMS package to build a stock database. This example demonstrates how to work with the RMS to build a real MIDlet application. The application builds on the network programming experience we gained in Chapter 7 and is similar to the StockMIDlet demo that comes with the MIDP. The MIDlet for this example does the following:

- Creates a record store (database).
- Adds new records (stocks) to the record store.
- Views the stocks in the database.

To add a stock to the database, the user enters the stock symbol (such as SUNW, IBM, IT, MS, GM, or Ford). The MIDlet retrieves the corresponding stock quote from Yahoo! Finance (*http://quote.yahoo.com*), constructs a record, and adds it to the database. To view the stocks in the database, the MIDlet iterates through the records in the record store and prints them on the display in a nice format. The implementation of this MIDlet consists of the following three classes: Stock.java, StockDB.java, and QuotesMIDlet.java.

The Stock.java Class

This class parses a string obtained from Yahoo! Finance or from the record store into fields that represent, for example, the name of the stock or its price. The string returned from Yahoo! Finance has the following format:

```
NAME TIME PRICE CHANGELOWHIGHOPENPREV
    "SUNW","2:1PM - <b>79.75</b>",+3.6875,"64.1875 - 129.3125",78,76.0625
```

In the MIDlet shown in Example 8-1, the fields retrieved are the name of the stock, the time, and the price.

Example 8-1. Parses a string obtained from Yahoo! Finance or from a database

```java
public class Stock {

    private static String name, time, price;

    // Given a quote from the server,
    // retrieve the name,
    // price, and date of the stock

    public static void parse(String data) {
        int index = data.indexOf('"');
        name = data.substring(++index,(index = data.
            indexOf('"', index)));
        index +=3;
        time = data.substring(index, (index = data.
            indexOf('-', index))-1);
        index +=5;
        price = data.substring(index, (index = data.
            indexOf('<', index)));
    }

    // Get the name of the stock from
    // the record store
    public static String getName(String record) {
        parse(record);
        return(name);
    }

    // Get the price of the stock from
    // the record store
    public static String getPrice(String record) {
        parse(record);
        return(price);
    }
}
```

The StockDB.java Class

This class provides methods that perform the following operations:

- Opens a new record store.
- Adds a new record to the record store.
- Closes the record store.
- Enumerates through the records.

Once you understand how to open a record store, add a new record, and close the record store, the code in Example 8-2 is easy to follow.

Example 8-2. Provide methods for record store operations

```java
import javax.microedition.rms.*;
import java.util.Enumeration;
import java.util.Vector;
import java.io.*;

public class StockDB {
    RecordStore recordStore = null;
    public StockDB( ) {}

    // Open a record store with the given name
    public StockDB(String fileName) {
        try {
            recordStore = RecordStore.openRecordStore(fileName, true);
        } catch(RecordStoreException rse) {
            rse.printStackTrace( );
        }
    }

    // Close the record store
    public void close( ) throws RecordStoreNotOpenException,
      RecordStoreException {
        if (recordStore.getNumRecords( ) == 0) {
            String fileName = recordStore.getName( );
            recordStore.closeRecordStore( );
            recordStore.deleteRecordStore(fileName);
        } else {
            recordStore.closeRecordStore( );
        }
    }

    // Add a new record (stock)
    // to the record store

    public synchronized void addNewStock(String record) {
        ByteArrayOutputStream baos = new ByteArrayOutputStream( );
        DataOutputStream outputStream = new DataOutputStream(baos);
        try {
            outputStream.writeUTF(record);
        } catch (IOException ioe) {
            System.out.println(ioe);
```

Example 8-2. Provide methods for record store operations (continued)

```
        ioe.printStackTrace( );
    }
    byte[] b = baos.toByteArray( );
    try {
        recordStore.addRecord(b, 0, b.length);
    } catch (RecordStoreException rse) {
        System.out.println(rse);
        rse.printStackTrace( );
    }
}

// Enumerate through the records.
public synchronized RecordEnumeration enumerate( ) throws
                    RecordStoreNotOpenException {
    return recordStore.enumerateRecords(null, null, false);
}
}
```

The QuotesMIDlet.java Class

Finally, the QuotesMIDlet class is the actual MIDlet that performs the following tasks:

- Create commands (List Stocks, Add a New Stock, Back, Save, Exit)
- Handle command events
- Connect to Yahoo! Finance and retrieve quotes
- Invoke methods from Stock and StockDB to parse quotes and add new stocks to the record store

The source for this file is listed in Example 8-3.

Example 8-3. A MIDlet for the stock database

```
import javax.microedition.rms.*;
import javax.microedition.lcdui.*;
import javax.microedition.midlet.*;
import javax.microedition.io.*;
import java.io.*;
import java.util.Vector;

public class QuotesMIDlet extends MIDlet implements CommandListener {
    Display display = null;
    List menu = null; // main menu
    List choose = null;
    TextBox input = null;
    Ticker ticker = new Ticker("Database Application");
    String quoteServer =
        "http://quote.yahoo.com/d/quotes.csv?s=";
    String quoteFormat = "&f=slc1wop"; // The only format supported

    static final Command backCommand = new Command("Back",
        Command.BACK, 0);
```

Example 8-3. A MIDlet for the stock database (continued)

```
static final Command mainMenuCommand = new Command("Main",
    Command.SCREEN, 1);
static final Command saveCommand = new Command("Save",
    Command.OK, 2);
static final Command exitCommand = new Command("Exit",
    Command.STOP, 3);
String currentMenu = null;

// Stock data
String name, date, price;

// record store
StockDB db = null;

public QuotesMIDlet( ) { // constructor
}

// start the MIDlet
public void startApp( ) throws MIDletStateChangeException {
    display = Display.getDisplay(this);
    // open a db stock file
    try {
        db = new StockDB("mystocks");
    } catch(Exception e) {}
        menu = new List("Stocks Database", Choice.IMPLICIT);
        menu.append("List Stocks", null);
        menu.append("Add A New Stock", null);
        menu.addCommand(exitCommand);
        menu.setCommandListener(this);
        menu.setTicker(ticker);

        mainMenu( );
}

public void pauseApp( ) {
    display = null;
    choose = null;
    menu = null;
    ticker = null;

    try {
        db.close( );
        db = null;
    } catch(Exception e) {}
}

public void destroyApp(boolean unconditional) {
    try {
        db.close( );
    } catch(Exception e) {}
    notifyDestroyed( );
}
```

Example 8-3. A MIDlet for the stock database (continued)

```
void mainMenu( ) {
    display.setCurrent(menu);
    currentMenu = "Main";
}

// Construct a running ticker
// with stock names and prices
public String tickerString( ) {
    StringBuffer ticks = null;
    try {
        RecordEnumeration enum = db.enumerate( );
        ticks = new StringBuffer( );
        while(enum.hasNextElement( )) {
            String stock1 = new String(enum.nextRecord( ));
            ticks.append(Stock.getName(stock1));
            ticks.append(" @ ");
            ticks.append(Stock.getPrice(stock1));
            ticks.append("    ");
        }
    } catch(Exception ex) {}
        return (ticks.toString( ));
}

// Add a new stock to the record store
// by calling StockDB.addNewStock( )
public void addStock( ) {
    input = new TextBox("Enter a Stock Name:", "", 5,
        TextField.ANY);
    input.setTicker(ticker);
    input.addCommand(saveCommand);
    input.addCommand(backCommand);
    input.setCommandListener(this);
    input.setString("");
    display.setCurrent(input);
    currentMenu = "Add";
}

// Connect to quote.yahoo.com and
// retrieve the data for a given
// stock symbol.
public String getQuote(String input) throws IOException,
  NumberFormatException {
    String url = quoteServer + input + quoteFormat;
    StreamConnection c = (StreamConnection)Connector.open(
                         url, Connector.READ_WRITE);
    InputStream is = c.openInputStream( );
    StringBuffer sb = new StringBuffer( );
    int ch;
    while((ch = is.read( )) != -1) {
      sb.append((char)ch);
    }
    return(sb.toString( ));
}
```

Example 8-3. A MIDlet for the stock database (continued)

```java
// List the stocks in the record store
public void listStocks( ) {
    choose = new List("Choose Stocks", Choice.MULTIPLE);
    choose.setTicker(new Ticker(tickerString( )));
    choose.addCommand(backCommand);
    choose.setCommandListener(this);
    try {
        RecordEnumeration re = db.enumerate( );
        while(re.hasNextElement( )) {
            String theStock = new String(re.nextRecord( ));
            choose.append(Stock.getName(theStock)+" @ " +
                            Stock.getPrice(theStock),null);
        }
    } catch(Exception ex) {}
    display.setCurrent(choose);
    currentMenu = "List";
}


// Handle command events
public void commandAction(Command c, Displayable d) {
    String label = c.getLabel( );
    if (label.equals("Exit")) {
        destroyApp(true);
    } else if (label.equals("Save")) {
        if(currentMenu.equals("Add")) {
            // add it to database
            try {
                String userInput = input.getString( );
                String pr = getQuote(userInput);
                db.addNewStock(pr);
                ticker.setString(tickerString( ));
            } catch(IOException e) {
            } catch(NumberFormatException se) {
            }
            mainMenu( );
        }
    } else if (label.equals("Back")) {
        if(currentMenu.equals("List")) {
            // go back to menu
            mainMenu( );
        } else if(currentMenu.equals("Add")) {
            // go back to menu
            mainMenu( );
        }
    } else {
        List down = (List)display.getCurrent( );
        switch(down.getSelectedIndex( )) {
            case 0: listStocks( );break;
            case 1: addStock( );break;
        }
    }
}
}
```

Testing QuotesMIDlet

To test `QuotesMIDlet`, use the J2ME Wireless Toolkit as we have throughout the book:

1. Create a new project and compile the code.
2. Run the MIDlet in the emulator. You should see `QuotesMIDlet` running in the emulator, as shown in Figure 8-1.

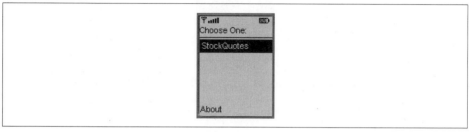

Figure 8-1. QuotesMIDlet

3. Activate `QuotesMIDlet`. You should see a menu with the following two options: List Stocks, and Add a New Stock, as shown in Figure 8-2.

Figure 8-2. QuotesMIDlet stock database

4. Choose the Add a New Stock option and add a few stocks. Figure 8-3 shows that the stocks IBM, GM, and NOR were added in this example.

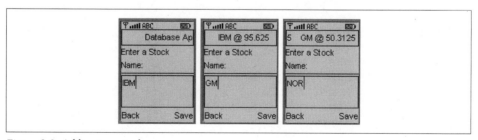

Figure 8-3. Adding new stocks

5. Go back and choose the View Stocks option. Figure 8-4 shows that this option reads the record store and retrieves all the records (stocks) that have been added.

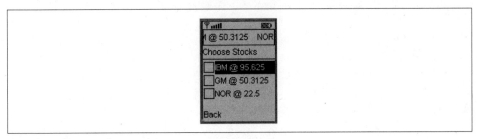

Figure 8-4. Viewing the record store

Have fun keeping track of your stocks! In the next chapter, we will discuss how to install MIDlets such as this on Palm computing platforms.

CHAPTER 9

The MIDP for Palm OS

An early access release of the MIDP for Palm OS was released just before JavaOne 2001, in early June, and the First Customer Shipping (FCS) of the MIDP for Palm OS 1.0 was released in mid-October, 2001. The MIDP for Palm OS is a J2ME application runtime environment based on the CLDC 1.0 and MIDP 1.0 specifications. It is targeted at handheld devices (such as Palm Pilot, Handspring Visor, and so on) running Palm OS version 3.5 or higher.

This chapter explains how to install the MIDP for Palm OS on your handheld device, and then how to convert existing MIDlets, developed in earlier chapters, into Palm Resource Code (PRC) files (executable Palm OS applications). The J2ME Wireless Toolkit 1.0.3 supports the MIDP for Palm OS. Hence, it is possible to test MIDlets using a Palm OS device, as shown in Chapter 4.

Installing the MIDP for Palm OS on the Windows Platform

To install the MIDP for Palm OS, you need to perform the following steps:

1. Download the MIDP for Palm OS. This package (*midp4palm-1_0.zip*), which is less than one megabyte, is the early access release of the MIDP for Palm OS implementation. You can download it from the Java web site at *http://java.sun.com/products/midp4palm*.

2. Unzip the package. Do this in the root directory *C:*. This gives you a new folder called *midp4palm1.0* that contains tools and sample applications. Check to make sure you have a file called *MIDP.prc* in the *PRCfiles* directory, which is the application runtime environment that supports the MIDP for Palm OS.

At this point, you are ready to install the MIDP for Palm OS on your Palm device.

Installing the MIDP for Palm OS on the Device

Use the HotSync application that came with the PalmPilot to install the *MIDP.prc* on your Palm OS device.

1. Place your Palm device in the cradle.

2. Using your Palm Desktop software on the PC (or a similar program), click the Install icon and browse to *C:\midp4palm1.0\PRCfiles* to select *MIDP.prc*, as shown in Figure 9-1. Press the HotSync button on the cradle to install the file.

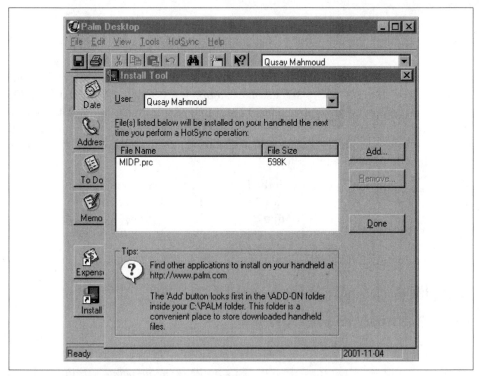

Figure 9-1. Using Palm Desktop to install MIDP.prc

3. Go to the application directory on your Palm and check to see if the Java HQ is there. The Java HQ is the application runtime environment that supports the MIDP for Palm OS. Note that the Java Manager environment takes up roughly 600K of your Palm OS device's storage.

You should see the Java HQ icon, as shown in Figure 9-2. If you do not see it, click on another application (e.g., Calculator) and then go back to the application directory to reset the display.

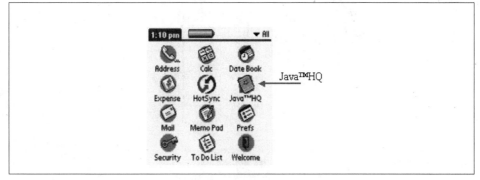

Figure 9-2. Java HQ special icon on Palm

If you tap the Java HQ icon, you'll see the About screen, as shown in Figure 9-3. This contains the copyright notice and gives you the option to change the Java HQ preferences that apply to every Java application running on the device. More information on the Java HQ preference settings is presented later in this chapter.

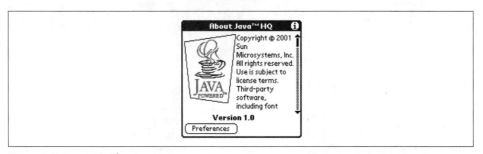

Figure 9-3. Java HQ About screen

Now you are ready to install other Java applications on your Palm.

Running Sample Applications

There are several applications for the Palm that are written in Java and that come with the software you just installed. All the files with the *.prc* extension in the directory *C:\midp4palm1.0\PRCfiles* are MIDP-based Java applications for the Palm. You can use the HotSync to install them.

As an example, use the HotSync and install the files *Games.prc* and *Demos.prc*. Once you have installed these two files, you will see two new icons, as shown in Figure 9-4.

A MIDP-based Java application for the Palm runs just like any other Palm application. Simply tap the corresponding icon. Note that the Java HQ must already be installed. When you launch a Java application on the Palm, the Java HQ (which is

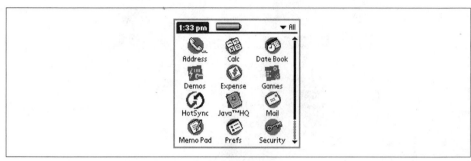

Figure 9-4. Installing sample MIDP-based Java applications

equivalent to the application manager) runs automatically. Also, it is important to note that the first time you launch an application, you are asked to read and accept the MIDP license; the application starts automatically once you tap Accept, as shown in Figure 9-5.

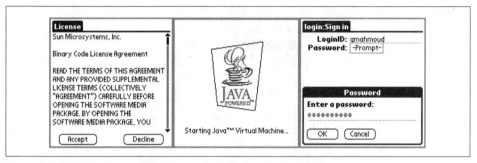

Figure 9-5. Running Java applications on the Palm for the first time

If you open an application suite (such as Demos), you are prompted to choose which application you want to run, as shown in Figure 9-6. Select an application to run by tapping on its arrow.

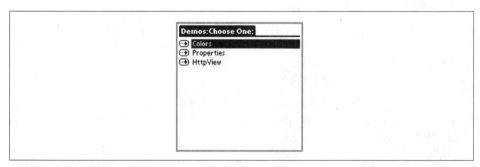

Figure 9-6. Selecting an application to run from a suite

Developing New Applications

You can easily develop new Java applications for the Palm if you are familiar with the MIDlet programming model. If you have run the MIDlets in earlier chapters, or have developed new ones, you can easily turn them into Palm applications by using a converter tool, which we will describe later in this chapter. The development life cycle of a Palm application can be summarized in the following three steps:

1. Develop a MIDlet or a MIDlet suite.
2. Convert the JAR/JAD file pair into a PRC file (executable Palm application).
3. Install the PRC file on the Palm and test the application.

Develop a MIDlet

As always, you can use either the Sun Microsystems Wireless Toolkit or your favorite development environment to develop a MIDlet. Example 9-1 lists the MIDlet that was developed in Chapter 6, which shows how to create various GUI components. The MIDlet for this example allows you to test lists, forms, choices, gauges, text fields, and text boxes.

Example 9-1. GuiTests.java

```java
import javax.microedition.lcdui.*;
import javax.microedition.midlet.*;

public class GuiTests extends MIDlet implements CommandListener {

    // display manager
    Display display = null;

    // a menu with items
    List menu = null; // main menu

    // list of choices
    List choose = null;

    // textbox
    TextBox input = null;

    // ticker
    Ticker ticker = new Ticker("Test GUI Components");

    // alerts
    final Alert soundAlert = new Alert("sound Alert");

    // date
    DateField date = new DateField("Today's date: ",
        DateField.DATE);

    // form
```

Example 9-1. GuiTests.java (continued)

```java
Form form = new Form("Form for Stuff");

// gauge
Gauge gauge = new Gauge("Progress Bar", false, 20, 9);

// text field
TextField textfield = new TextField("TextField Label", "abc",
    50, 0);

// command
static final Command backCommand = new Command("Back",
    Command.BACK, 0);
static final Command mainMenuCommand = new Command("Main",
    Command.SCREEN, 1);
static final Command exitCommand = new Command("Exit",
    Command.STOP, 2);
String currentMenu = null;

// constructor.
public GuiTests() {
}

/**
 * Start the MIDlet by creating a list of items and associating
 * the exit command with it.
 */

public void startApp() throws MIDletStateChangeException {
  display = Display.getDisplay(this);
  // open a db stock file

  menu = new List("Test Components", Choice.IMPLICIT);
  menu.append("Test TextBox", null);
  menu.append("Test List", null);
  menu.append("Test Alert", null);
  menu.append("Test Date", null);
  menu.append("Test Form", null);
  menu.addCommand(exitCommand);
  menu.setCommandListener(this);
  menu.setTicker(ticker);

  mainMenu();
}

public void pauseApp() {
  display = null;
  choose = null;
  menu = null;
  ticker = null;
  form = null;
  input = null;
  gauge = null;
  textfield = null;
```

Example 9-1. GuiTests.java (continued)

```java
    }

    public void destroyApp(boolean unconditional) {
        notifyDestroyed();
    }

    // main menu
    void mainMenu() {
        display.setCurrent(menu);
        currentMenu = "Main";
    }

    /**
     * Test the TextBox component.
     */
    public void testTextBox() {
        input = new TextBox("Enter Some Text:", "", 10,
            TextField.ANY);
        input.setTicker(new Ticker("Testing TextBox"));
        input.addCommand(backCommand);
        input.setCommandListener(this);
        input.setString("");
        display.setCurrent(input);
        currentMenu = "input";
    }

    /**
     * Test the List component.
     */
    public void testList() {
        choose = new List("Choose Items", Choice.MULTIPLE);
        choose.setTicker(new Ticker("Testing List"));
        choose.addCommand(backCommand);
        choose.setCommandListener(this);
        choose.append("Item 1", null);
        choose.append("Item 2", null);
        choose.append("Item 3", null);
        display.setCurrent(choose);
        currentMenu = "list";
    }

    /**
     * Test the Alert component.
     */

    public void testAlert() {
        soundAlert.setType(AlertType.ERROR);
        //soundAlert.setTimeout(20);
        soundAlert.setString("** ERROR **");
        display.setCurrent(soundAlert);
    }

    /**
```

Example 9-1. GuiTests.java (continued)

```java
     * Test the DateField component.
     */
    public void testDate( ) {
        java.util.Date now = new java.util.Date( );
        date.setDate(now);
        Form f = new Form("Today's date");
        f.append(date);
        f.addCommand(backCommand);
        f.setCommandListener(this);
        display.setCurrent(f);
        currentMenu = "date";
    }

    /**
     * Test the Form component.
     */
    public void testForm( ) {
        form.append(gauge);
        form.append(textfield);
        form.addCommand(backCommand);
        form.setCommandListener(this);
        display.setCurrent(form);
        currentMenu = "form";
    }

    /**
     * Handle events.
     */
    public void commandAction(Command c, Displayable d) {
        String label = c.getLabel( );
        if (label.equals("Exit")) {
            destroyApp(true);
        } else if (label.equals("Back")) {
            if(currentMenu.equals("list") ||
                 currentMenu.equals("input") ||
                 currentMenu.equals("date") ||
                 currentMenu.equals("form")) {
              // go back to menu
              mainMenu( );
            }

        } else {
            List down = (List)display.getCurrent( );
            switch(down.getSelectedIndex( )) {
              case 0: testTextBox( );break;
              case 1: testList( );break;
              case 2: testAlert( );break;
              case 3: testDate( );break;
              case 4: testForm( );break;
            }

        }
    }
}
```

Convert a MIDlet into a PRC file

This section will explain how to convert a MIDlet file into a PRC file. First, build the MIDlet in Example 9-1 and make sure there are no compilation errors. Most development tools will create the JAR and JAD files for you automatically. These are the two files needed to convert a MIDlet or a MIDlet suite into a PRC file. If you are using the Wireless Toolkit, the JAR and JAD files can be found in the *bin* directory of your project.

The MIDP for Palm OS comes with a converter tool to convert a MIDlet JAR/JAD into an executable Palm application. To run the PRC converter tool, you can use the batch file distributed with the release. However, if you have set the *JAVA_HOME* environment variable on your desktop, edit the *CONVERTER.BAT* file and change all the *JAVA_PATH* references to *JAVA_HOME*. Then run the converted batch file. Alternatively, you can run the tool using the command:

```
C:\midp4palm1.0\converter> java -jar Converter.jar
```

The *converter.jar* archive contains the implementations for the PRC converter tool. If the above command runs successfully, you should see a window similar to Figure 9-7.

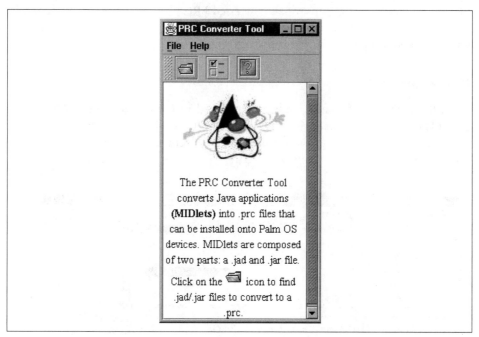

Figure 9-7. PRC converter tool

Now, select Convert from the File menu, and navigate to the directory where the JAD and JAR files are located (as with deployment on the Motorola i85s and the i50x, they must be in the same directory). Select the JAD file to be converted, then click on the Convert button to convert the file into a PRC file. If everything is okay, you will see a success message, as shown in Figure 9-8.

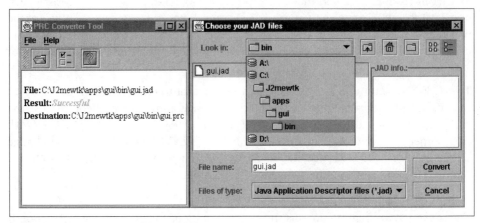

Figure 9-8. Converting JAD/JAR to PRC

By default, the converted PRC file will be saved in the same directory as the JAD/JAR file pair. If you like, you can save all converted PRC files under another directory by choosing Preferences from the Converter's File menu. Then you can select a folder of your choice for output.

Install and Test

Once the JAD/JAR file pair have been converted to a PRC file, you can install the PRC file on your Palm OS device using HotSync. Once installed, you can run it and select components to test, as shown in Figure 9-9. Here, we have tested a form with a progress bar, a text field, an alert, and a date.

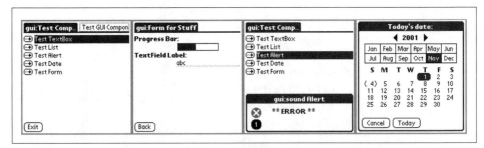

Figure 9-9. Testing a MIDP application for the Palm OS

PRC Command-Line Conversion

The PRC GUI-based converter tool is easy to use. However, this comes at the expense of functionality. For example, what if you wish to associate a new icon with your application rather than have the default icon? You can use the command-line converter to complete this and other tasks.

The MIDP for Palm OS distribution comes with a command-line tool for converting JAR files to PRC files. The tool is the *MakeMIDPApp*, which is part of the *converter.jar* archive. To run this converter, use the command:

```
C:\mid4palm1.0\converter> java -cp converter.jar com.sun.midp.palm.database.MakeMIDPApp
    [options] JARfile
```

The options for this command are shown in Table 9-1:

Table 9-1. Command-line PRC converter tool options

Option	Description
-v	Verbose output
-v -v	More information
-verbose	Same as -v
-icon <file>	File containing icon (in bmp, pbm, or bin Palm resource format) for the list view of the application
-smallicon <file>	File containing a small icon for the Palm OS device's icon view
-name <name>	Short name for the application, for the Palm OS device's icon view
-longname <name>	Long name for the application, for Palm OS device list view
-creator <crid>	Creator ID for the application
-type <type>	Type file for the application (default is appl)
-outfile <file>	Name of the PRC file to create
-o <file>	Same as -outfile
-version <string>	Change version
-help	Print help information
-jad <JADfile>	A JAD file is specified (MIDlet suite packaging)

With the command-line tool, you can produce PRC files from a single MIDlet or from a MIDlet suite. For example, the following command can be used to convert a JAR file (containing one MIDlet or a MIDlet suite) to a PRC file:

```
C:\midp4palm1.0\converter> java -cp Converter.jar com.sun.midp.database.MakeMIDPApp -type
    Data gui.jar
```

This command will produce a PRC file called *gui.prc* from the JAR file *gui.jar*. Note that the type of application being converted can be either appl ot Data (case-sensitive). If you don't provide the -type option, then MakeMIDPApp uses the default type, which is appl. It is important to note, however, that if you don't provide a creator ID with the -creator option, you must set the type to Data. The creator ID specifies the unique, four-character identifier for a Palm application. Every Palm application must have a creator ID, and if you do not provide one, then MakeMIDPApp will automatically generate a creator ID for your application. To find out the creator ID, use the -v -v option.

Any application converted using the GUI-based converter tool or the command-line tool is, by default, not beamable from the Palm launcher screen, as shown in Figure 9-10. If you use the command-line tool, however, and provide a creator ID, then the application will be beamable.

Figure 9-10. An application cannot be beamed (by default)

Advanced Java Applications

You have seen how to develop a simple Java application for the Palm that creates various GUI components. What about advanced applications that use networking and databases? Well, the MIDP for Palm OS supports all the MIDP features, including the Generic Connection Framework and the RMS. So, now let's look at a couple of sample applications developed in Chapter 7 and Chapter 8.

First, however, there are two things that need to be set if you want to test network-based applications from the Palm OS Emulator (POSE).

1. Redirect Netlib calls to host TCP/IP. To do this, right-click on the POSE window, select Setting → Properties, and check the Redirect NetLib calls to host TCP/IP, as shown in Figure 9-11.

2. Enable Networking. To do this, tap the Java HQ icon, then tap Preferences and select Networking Enabled, as shown in Figure 9-12.

The Java HQ allows you to set special preferences. For example, it allows you to set how much memory is used to run Java applications, how many colors are used, the drawing speed, how your device will connect to the Internet, and how the controls should be displayed on the screen. You can easily set all of these options using the Java HQ. However, if you are running an application and would like to set some preferences, select the Preferences item from the Options menu. You can choose whether you want to set Application preferences, Global preferences, or Java HQ

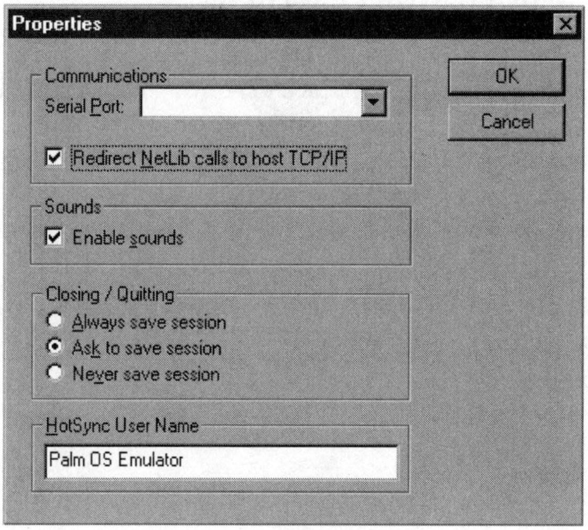

Figure 9-11. POSE property settings

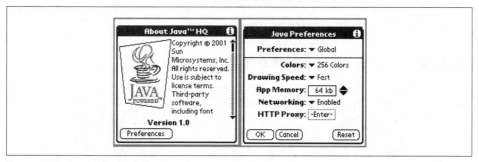

Figure 9-12. Java HQ networking preferences

preferences, as shown in Figure 9-13. Application preferences affect only the Java application you are running; Global preferences affect every Java application running in your device.

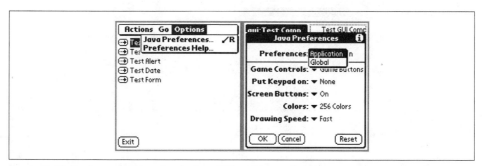

Figure 9-13. Preference settings for the Java HQ and its applications

Fetching a Page Using HttpConnection

In Chapter 7, a MIDlet was developed to retrieve the contents of a file from a remote server using the HttpConnection interface. The MIDlet that implements this functionality is *SecondExample.java*. Create a new project in the Wireless Toolkit and use *SecondExample.java* as its source file. Build it, locate the JAR and JAD files, and use the PRC converter tool to convert them into a PRC file. Install the PRC file on POSE and then run the application. If all goes well, you should see something similar to Figure 9-14.

Figure 9-14. Retrieving a file from a remote server

Retrieving Stock Quotes and Working with Databases

In Chapter 8, a MIDlet was developed that allows you to create a database, add stocks (which are retrieved from Yahoo! Finance) to the database, and view the database. Download the files *Stock.java*, *StockDB.java*, and *QuotesMIDlet.java*. Build the application and create the JAR and JAD file pair. Then use the PRC converter tool to produce a PRC file. Install the PRC file on POSE and then run it. Add a few stocks and then view the stocks from the database. If everything goes well, you should see something similar to Figure 9-15.

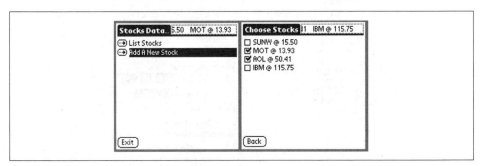

Figure 9-15. Stock quotes

A Final Thought

The Palm OS implementation of MIDP provides a runtime environment and tools that allow you to convert your MIDlets into Palm applications without writing a single line of code. I do not know of any easier way to develop fully functional Java applications for the Palm. These applications can be used just like any other Palm application; they run like any Palm program and can be removed from your Palm OS device the same way that you would remove any other application. However, it remains to be seen whether the MIDP for Palm OS is here to stay, or if it will be superseded by the PDA Profile for J2ME, which is based on the CLDC and will provide user interface and data storage APIs for handheld devices. As of this writing, the PDA profile is still in the works and no reference implementation is available.

API Quick Reference

Part III presents quick-reference material for the J2ME CLDC and MIDP APIs.

The java.io Package

java.io.ByteArrayInputStream

This class is identical to its J2SE counterpart. It is a subclass of InputStream, which reads data in as a series of bytes.

```
public class ByteArrayInputStream extends java.io.InputStream {
    // protected fields
    protected byte[] buf;
    protected int count;
    protected int mark;
    protected int pos;

    // constructors
    public ByteArrayInputStream(byte[] buf);
    public ByteArrayInputStream(byte[] buf, int offset, int length);

    // public instance methods
    public synchronized int available();
    public synchronized  void close() throws java.io.IOException;
    public void mark(int readAheadLimit);
    public boolean markSupported();
    public synchronized int read();
    public synchronized int read(byte[] b, int off, int len);
    public synchronized void reset();
    public synchronized long skip(long n);
}
```

java.io.ByteArrayOutputStream

This class is a slightly smaller version of its J2SE counterpart. It is a subclass of java.io. OutputStream, which writes data out as a series of bytes.

```
public class ByteArrayOutputStream extends java.io.OutputStream {
    // protected fields
    protected byte[] buf;
    protected int count;
```

```
// constructors
public ByteArrayOutputStream();
public ByteArrayOutputStream(int size);

// public instance methods
public synchronized void close() throws java.io.IOException;
public synchronized void reset();
public int size();
public synchronized byte[] toByteArray();
public String toString();
public synchronized void write(int b);
public synchronized void write(byte[] b, int off, int len);
}
```

java.io.DataInput

This interface is a slightly smaller version of its J2SE counterpart. It defines methods to read primitive data types from a platform-dependent binary format.

```
public interface DataInput {
    // public methods
    public boolean readBoolean() throws java.io.IOException;
    public byte readByte() throws java.io.IOException;
    public char readChar() throws java.io.IOException;
    public void readFully(byte[] b) throws java.io.IOException;
    public void readFully(byte[] b, int off, int len)
        throws java.io.IOException;
    public int readInt() throws java.io.IOException;
    public long readLong() throws java.io.IOException;
    public short readShort() throws java.io.IOException;
    public int readUnsignedByte() throws java.io.IOException;
    public int readUnsignedShort() throws java.io.IOException;
    public String readUTF() throws java.io.IOException;
    public int skipBytes(int n) throws java.io.IOException;
}
```

java.io.DataInputStream

This class is a slightly smaller version of the J2SE DataInputStream class. The class can be used to read in primitive data types from a platform-dependent source. Most of the methods of this class read from the stream and return a Java primitive data type. Other important methods include available(), which returns the number of available bytes that can be read without blocking; the generic read() methods, which read in a specified amount of data, blocking if the data is not available yet. Also, skipBytes() skips over a number of bytes in the stream, blocking if the data is not yet available. Finally, readFully() reads the specified amount of data into a byte array.

```
public class DataInputStream extends java.io.InputStream
    implements java.io.DataInput {
    // protected fields
    protected InputStream in;
```

```
    // constructor
    public DataInputStream(InputStream in);

    // static methods
    public static final String readUTF(DataInput in)
       throws java.io.IOException;

    // public instance methods
    public int available() throws java.io.IOException;
    public void close() throws java.io.IOException;
    public synchronized void mark(int readlimit);
    public boolean markSupported();
    public int read() throws java.io.IOException;
    public final int read(byte[] b) throws java.io.IOException;
    public final int read(byte[] b, int off, int len)
       throws java.io.IOException;
    public final boolean readBoolean() throws java.io.IOException;
    public final byte readByte() throws java.io.IOException;
    public final char readChar() throws java.io.IOException;
    public final void readFully(byte[] b) throws java.io.IOException;
    public final void readFully(byte[] b, int off, int len)
       throws java.io.IOException;
    public final int readInt() throws java.io.IOException;
    public final long readLong() throws java.io.IOException;
    public final short readShort() throws java.io.IOException;
    public final int readUnsignedByte() throws java.io.IOException;
    public final int readUnsignedShort() throws java.io.IOException;
    public final String readUTF() throws java.io.IOException;
    public synchronized void reset() throws java.io.IOException;
    public long skip(long n) throws java.io.IOException;
    public final int skipBytes(int n) throws java.io.IOException;
}
```

java.io.DataOutput

This interface is a slightly smaller version of its J2SE counterpart. It defines methods to write primitive data types to a platform-dependent binary format.

```
public interface DataOutput {
    // public methods
    public void write(int b) throws java.io.IOException;
    public void write(byte[] b) throws java.io.IOException;
    public void write(byte[] b, int off, int len) throws java.io.IOException;
    public void writeBoolean(boolean v) throws java.io.IOException;
    public void writeByte(int v) throws java.io.IOException;
    public void writeChar(int v) throws java.io.IOException;
    public void writeChars(String s) throws java.io.IOException;
    public void writeInt(int v) throws java.io.IOException;
    public void writeLong(long v) throws java.io.IOException;
    public void writeShort(int v) throws java.io.IOException;
    public void writeUTF(String str) throws java.io.IOException;
}
```

java.io.DataOutputStream

This class is a slightly smaller version of the J2SE DataOutputStream class. The class can be used to write out primitive data types to a platform-dependent source. Most of the methods of this class write a Java primitive data type to a stream. The write() methods write out a single byte or a byte array (or portion thereof) to the output stream. flush() flushes out the I/O buffer, and close() closes the output stream.

```java
public class DataOutputStream extends java.io.OutputStream
    implements java.io.DataOutput {
    // protected fields
    protected OutputStream out;

    // constructor
    public DataOutputStream(OutputStream out);

    // public instance methods
    public void close() throws java.io.IOException;
    public void flush() throws java.ioIOException;
    public void write(int b) throws java.io.IOException;
    public void write(byte[] b, int off, int len) throws java.io.IOException;
    public final void writeBoolean(boolean v) throws java.io.IOException;
    public final void writeByte(int v) throws java.io.IOException;
    public final void writeChar(int v) throws java.io.IOException;
    public final void writeChars(String s) throws java.io.IOException;
    public final void writeInt(int v) throws java.io.IOException;
    public final void writeLong(long v) throws java.io.IOException;
    public final void writeShort(int v) throws java.io.IOException;
    public final void writeUTF(String str) throws java.io.IOException;
}
```

java.io.EOFException

This exception is identical to its J2SE counterpart. It signifies that the end of the file has been reached.

```java
public class EOFException extends java.io.IOException {
    // constructors
    public EOFException();
    public EOFException(String s);
}
```

java.io.InputStream

This abstract class is identical to the J2SE InputStream class. All input streams must extend this class. Applications that define a subclass of InputStream must always implement the abstract read() method, which reads in a single byte of data or –1 if there is no more data to be read. Other important methods include available(), which returns the number of available bytes that can be read without blocking, as well as skip(), which skips over the specified number of bytes. Finally, close() will close the input stream, releasing any resources associated with it.

```
public abstract class InputStream {
    // constructor
    public InputStream();

    // public instance methods
    public int available() throws java.io.IOException;
    public void close();
    public synchronized void mark(int readlimit);
    public boolean markSupported();
    public abstract int read() throws java.io.IOException;
    public int read(byte[] b) throws java.io.IOException;
    public int read(byte[] b, int off, int len) throws java.io.IOException;
    public synchronized void reset() throws java.io.IOException;
    public long skip(long n) throws java.io.IOException;
}
```

java.io.InputStreamReader

This class is a slightly modified version of the InputStreamReader class used in J2SE. The class creates a character input stream, which translates data coming from a byte input stream, based on a specific encoding. The read() method reads in a single character value or an array of characters. The skip() method skips over the specified number of characters. The ready() method returns a Boolean, indicating whether the stream is ready to be read.

```
public class InputStreamReader extends java.io.Reader {
    // constructors
    public InputStreamReader(InputStream is);
    public InputStreamReader(InputStream is, String enc)
        throws java.io.UnsupportedEncodingException;

    // public instance methods
    public void close() throws java.io.IOException;
    public void mark(int readAheadLimit) throws java.io.IOException;
    public boolean markSupported();
    public int read() throws java.io.IOException;
    public int read(char[] cbuf, int off, int len)
        throws java.io.IOException;
    public boolean ready() throws java.io.IOException;
    public void reset() throws java.io.IOException;
    public long skip(long n) throws java.io.IOException;
}
```

java.io.InterruptedIOException

This exception is identical to its J2SE counterpart. It signifies that an input or output operation was interrupted. The bytesTransferred field indicates the number of bytes that were successfully transferred before the interruption took place.

```
public class InterruptedIOException extends java.io.IOException {
    // public fields
    public int bytesTransferred;

    // constructors
    public InterruptedIOException();
    public InterruptedIOException(String s);
}
```

java.io.IOException

This exception is identical to its J2SE counterpart. It signifies that an error occurred during data input or output. Many exceptions in this package extend IOException.

```
public class IOException extends java.lang.Exception {
    // constructors
    public IOException();
    public IOException(String s);
}
```

java.io.OutputStream

This abstract class is the superclass of all types of output streams. Classes that extend OutputStream must provide an implementation for the abstract write() method. Other methods include flush(), which flushes the output buffer, and close(), which closes the output stream and releases any resources associated with it.

```
public abstract class OutputStream {
    // constructor
    public OutputStream();

    // public instance methods
    public abstract void write(int b) throws java.io.IOException;
    public void write(byte[] b) throws java.io.IOException;
    public void write(byte[] b, int off, int len)
        throws java.io.IOException;
    public void flush() throws java.io.IOException;
    public void close() throws java.io.IOException;
}
```

java.io.OutputStreamWriter

This class is a slightly modified version of the OutputStreamReader class used in J2SE. The class outputs data from a character input stream, based on a specific encoding, to a byte input stream. The write() methods output a single character, an array (or sub-array) of characters, or a string (or sub-string) to the output stream. Other methods include flush(), which flushes the output buffer, and close(), which closes the output stream and releases any resources associated with it.

```
public class OutputStreamWriter extends java.io.Writer {
    // constructors
    public OutputStreamWriter(OutputStream os);
    public OutputStreamWriter(OutputStream os, String enc)
        throws java.io.UnsupportedEncodingException;

    // public instance methods
    public void write(int c) throws java.io.IOException;
    public void write(char[] cbuf, int off, int len)
        throws java.io.IOException;
    public void write(String str, int off, int len)
        throws java.io.IOException;
    public void flush() throws java.io.IOException;
    public void close() throws java.io.IOException;
}
```

java.io.PrintStream

This class is slightly modified from the J2SE class of the same name. The PrintStream class outputs textual representations of various data. Note that the PrintStream never throws an IOException, unlike other streams. Instead, you should use the checkError() method to determine if an exceptional condition has occurred.

```
public class PrintStream {

    // constructor
    public PrintStream(OutputStream out);
    // protected instance methods
    protected void setError();

    // public instance methods
    public boolean checkError();
    public void close();
    public void flush();
    public void print(boolean b);
    public void print(char c);
    public void print(char[] s);
    public void print(int i);
    public void print(long l);
    public void print(Object obj);
    public void print(String s);
```

```
    public void println();
    public void println(boolean x);
    public void println(char x);
    public void println(char[] x);
    public void println(int x);
    public void println(long x);
    public void println(Object x);
    public void println(String x);
    public void write(int b);
    public void write(byte[] buf, int off, int len);
}
```

java.io.Reader

This abstract class is identical to the J2SE Reader class. It is the superclass for all classes that read character streams. The only methods that a Reader subclass must implement are the abstract read() and close() methods, although many implementations override other methods. Other important methods include skip(), which skips over the specified number of characters, and close(), which closes the input stream and releases any resources associated with it. Finally, the ready() method returns a Boolean, indicating if the stream can have more data read from it.

```
    public abstract class Reader {
        // protected fields
        protected Object lock;

        // constructors
        protected Reader();
        protected Reader(Object lock);

        // public instance methods
        public abstract void close() throws java.io.IOException;
        public void mark(int readAheadLimit) throws java.io.IOException;
        public boolean markSupported();
        public int read() throws java.io.IOException;
        public int read(char[] cbuf) throws java.io.IOException;
        public abstract int read(char[] cbuf, int off, int len)
            throws java.io.IOException;
        public boolean ready() throws java.io.IOException;
        public void reset() throws java.io.IOException;
        public long skip(long n) throws java.io.IOException;
    }
```

java.io.UnsupportedEncodingException

This exception is identical to its J2SE counterpart. It is thrown when the requested character encoding is not supported by the current operation.

```
    public class UnsupportedEncodingException extends java.io.IOException {
        // public constructors
        public UnsupportedEncodingException();
        public UnsupportedEncodingException(String s);
    }
```

java.io.UTFDataFormatException

This exception is identical to its J2SE counterpart. It is thrown when a malformed UTF-8 string has been detected.

```
public class UTFDataFormatException extends java.io.IOException {
    // constructors
    public UTFDataFormatException();
    public UTFDataFormatException(String s);
}
```

java.io.Writer

This abstract class is identical to the J2SE Writer class. It is the superclass for all classes that write character streams. The only methods that a Writer subclass must implement are the abstract write(), flush(), and close() methods, although many implementations override other methods. Several write() methods are provided to output single characters, arrays (or sub-arrays), or characters, strings, and substrings.

```
public abstract class Writer {
    // protected fields
    protected Object lock;

    // constructors
    protected Writer();
    protected Writer(Object lock);

    // public instance methods
    public abstract void close() throws java.io.IOException;
    public abstract void flush() throws java.io.IOException;
    public void write(int c) throws java.io.IOException;
    public void write(char[] cbuf) throws java.io.IOException;
    public abstract void write(char[] cbuf, int off, int len)
        throws java.io.IOException;
    public void write(String str) throws java.io.IOException;
    public void write(String str, int off, int len)
        throws java.io.IOException;
}
```

The java.lang Package

java.lang.ArithmeticException

This exception is identical to its J2SE counterpart. It signifies an illegal arithmetic condition, the most common of which is a division by zero.

```
public class ArithmeticException extends java.lang.RuntimeException {
    // constructors
    public ArithmeticException();
    public ArithmeticException(String s);
}
```

java.lang.ArrayIndexOutOfBoundsException

This exception is identical to its J2SE counterpart. It signifies that an attempt was made to access an array with either a negative index value or an index value greater than or equal to the array size.

```
public class ArrayIndexOutOfBoundsException extends
    java.lang.IndexOutOfBoundsException {
    // constructors
    public ArrayIndexOutOfBoundsException();
    public ArrayIndexOutOfBoundsException(int index);
    public ArrayIndexOutOfBoundsException(String s);
}
```

java.lang.ArrayStoreException

This exception is identical to its J2SE counterpart. It signifies that an attempt was made to store the wrong type of object into an array.

```
public class ArrayStoreException extends java.lang.RuntimeException {
    // constructors
    public ArrayStoreException();
    public ArrayStoreException(String s);
}
```

java.lang.Boolean

This class is a smaller counterpart to the J2SE Boolean class. It provides an object wrapper around the boolean primitive data type. The boolean is the object's only field, which is set by the constructor and accessed using the booleanValue() method.

```
public final class Boolean {
    // public constructor
    public Boolean(boolean value);

    // public instance methods
    public boolean booleanValue();
    public boolean equals(Object obj);
    public int hashCode();
    public String toString();

}
```

java.lang.Byte

This class is a smaller counterpart to the J2SE Byte class. It provides an object wrapper around the byte primitive data type. The class provides minimum and maximum constant values that can be used to test the legal size of the byte. The value of the object's byte is accessed using the byteValue() method. In addition, the two parseByte() methods can take a number from a specified string or an optionally specified radix and return it as a byte.

```
public final class Byte {
    // constants
    public static final byte MIN_VALUE;
    public static final byte MAX_VALUE;

    // public constructor
    public Byte(byte value);

    //  static methods
    public static byte parseByte(String s) throws NumberFormatException;
    public static byte parseByte(String s, int radix) throws NumberFormatException;

    //  public instance methods
    public byte byteValue();
    public boolean equals(Object obj);
    public int hashCode();
    public String toString();
}
```

java.lang.Character

This class is a smaller counterpart to the J2SE Character class. It provides an object wrapper around a single char primitive data type. The class contains several static methods for testing the type of character stored, as well as for converting between uppercase and lowercase letters. Use the static `digit()` method to convert the character to a decimal value, using the specified radix (e.g., radix 8 for octal). To dump the stored character back into a primitive char data type, use the `charValue()` method.

```java
public final class Character {
    // constants
    public static final int MIN_RADIX;
    public static final int MAX_RADIX;
    public static final char MIN_VALUE;
    public static final char MAX_VALUE;

    // static methods
    public static int digit(char ch, int radix);
    public static boolean isDigit(char ch);
    public static boolean isLowerCase(char ch);
    public static boolean isUpperCase(char ch);
    public static char toLowerCase(char ch);
    public static char toUpperCase(char ch);

    // public constructor
    public Character(char value);

    // public instance methods
    public char charValue();
    public boolean equals(Object obj);
    public int hashCode();
    public String toString();

}
```

java.lang.Class

This class is a much smaller counterpart to the J2SE Class class. It represents a Java class, array, or interface. A class can be dynamically loaded using the static `forName()` method, which takes the fully qualified name of the class and returns a `Class` object. The `isArray()` and `isInterface()` methods test whether the class is an array or interface, respectively. To test if a specific object is an instance of this class, pass the object into the `isInstance()` method. Use the `newInstance()` method to create an object by invoking its zero-argument constructor. Finally, `getResourceAsStream()` can be used to load external resources (such as bitmap images) into an input stream.

```java
public final class Class {

    // static methods
    public static native Class forName(String className)
        throws java.lang.ClassNotFoundException;

    // public instance methods
    public String getName();
    public InputStream getResourceAsStream(String name);
    public boolean isArray();
    public boolean isAssignableFrom(Class cls);
```

```
    public boolean isInstance(Object obj);
    public boolean isInterface();
    public Object newInstance() throws java.lang.InstantiationException,
        java.lang.IllegalAccessException;
    public String toString();
}
```

java.lang.ClassCastException

This exception is identical to its J2SE counterpart. It signifies an illegal attempt to cast an object to a class of which the object is not an instance.

```
public class ClassCastException extends java.lang.RuntimeException {
    // constructors
    public ClassCastException();
    public ClassCaseException(String s);
}
```

java.lang.ClassNotFoundException

This exception is identical to its J2SE counterpart. It signifies that a requested class could not be found by the class loader.

```
public class ClassNotFoundException extends java.lang.Exception {
    // constructors
    public ClassNotFoundException();
    public ClassNotFoundException(String s);
}
```

java.lang.Error

This class is identical to its J2SE counterpart. It forms the base of the J2ME error hierarchy. Errors in Java typically mean that a severe condition has occurred and therefore should not be caught.

```
public class Error extends java.lang.Throwable {
    // constructors
    public Error();
    public Error(String s);
}
```

java.lang.Exception

This class is identical to its J2SE counterpart. It forms the base of the J2ME exception hierarchy.

```
public class Exception extends java.lang.Throwable {
    // constructors
    public Exception();
    public Exception(String s);
}
```

java.lang.IllegalAccessException

This exception is identical to its J2SE counterpart. It signifies that a class or initializer is not accessible to the caller.

```
public class IllegalAccessException extends java.lang.Exception {
    // constructors
    public IllegalAccessException();
    public IllegalAccessException(String s);
}
```

java.lang.IllegalArgumentException

This exception is identical to its J2SE counterpart. It signifies that an illegal argument has been passed to a method.

```
public class IllegalArgumentException extends java.lang.RuntimeException {
    // constructors
    public IllegalArgumentException();
    public IllegalArgumentException(String s);
}
```

java.lang.IllegalMonitorStateException

This exception is identical to its J2SE counterpart. It indicates that an illegal monitor state has occurred in a thread that is itself either waiting or attempting to notify a waiting thread.

```
public class IllegalMonitorStateException extends java.lang.RuntimeException {
    // constructors
    public IllegalMonitorStateException();
    public IllegalMonitorStateException(String s);
}
```

java.lang.IllegalStateException

This exception is identical to its J2SE counterpart. It is thrown when an illegal transition is requested, such as invoking a method at an illegal or inappropriate time.

```
public class IllegalStateException extends java.lang.RuntimeException {
    // public constructors
    public IllegalStateException();
    public IllegalStateException(String s);
}
```

java.lang.IllegalThreadStateException

This exception is identical to its J2SE counterpart. It is thrown when illegal transitions are requested on a thread that is not in the appropriate state.

```
public class IllegalThreadStateException extends
    java.lang.IllegalArgumentException {
```

```
// constructors
public IllegalThreadStateException();
public IllegalThreadStateException(String s);
}
```

java.lang.IndexOutOfBoundsException

This exception is identical to its J2SE counterpart. It is thrown when an index has exceeded the bounds placed on it.

```
public class IndexOutOfBoundsException extends java.lang.RuntimeException {
    // constructors
    public IndexOutOfBoundsException();
    public IndexOutOfBoundsException(String s);
}
```

java.lang.InstantiationException

This exception is identical to its J2SE counterpart. It is thrown when an attempt is made to instantiate an interface or an abstract class.

```
public class InstantiationException extends java.lang.Exception {
    // constructors
    public InstantiationException();
    public InstantiationException(String s);
}
```

java.lang.Integer

This class is a smaller counterpart to the J2SE Integer class. It provides an object wrapper around a single int primitive data type. The class contains several static methods for converting an int to various formats, as well as two valueOf() methods to convert a string with an optionally specified radix back into an Integer. To dump the stored character back into a primitive int, long, or short data type, use the intValue(), longValue(), or shortValue() methods, respectively.

```
public final class Integer {
    // public constants
    public static final int MIN_VALUE;
    public static final int MAX_VALUE;

    // static methods
    public static int parseInt(String s, int radix) throws
        java.lang.NumberFormatException;
    public static int parseInt(String s) throws java.lang.NumberFormatException;
    public static String toBinaryString(int i);
    public static String toHexString(int i);
    public static String toOctalString(int i);
    public static String toString(int i);
    public static String toString(int i, int radix);
```

```
public static Integer valueOf(String s, int radix) throws
    java.lang.NumberFormatException;
public static Integer.valueOf(String s) throws java.lang.NumberFormatException;

// public constructor
public Integer(int value);

// public instance methods
public byte byteValue();
public boolean equals(Object obj);
public int hashCode();
public int intValue();
public long longValue();
public short shortValue();
public String toString();

}
```

java.lang.InterruptedException

This exception is identical to its J2SE counterpart. It is thrown when a thread has been interrupted.

```
public class InterruptedException extends java.lang.Exception {
    // constructors
    public InterruptedException();
    public InterruptedException(String s);
}
```

java.lang.Long

This class is a smaller counterpart to the J2SE Long class. It provides an object wrapper around a single long primitive data type. The class provides minimum and maximum constant values that can be used to test the legal size of a long. The value of the object's long is accessed using the longValue() method. In addition, the parseByte()and toString() methods can convert a number from a String to a long, and vice versa, with an optionally specified radix.

```
public final class Long {

    // public constants
    public static final long MIN_VALUE;
    public static final long MAX_VALUE;

    // static methods
    public static long parseLong(String s) throws java.lang.NumberFormatException;
    public static long parseLong(String s, int radix) throws
        java.lang.NumberFormatException;
    public static String toString(long i);
    public static String toString(long i, int radix);
```

```
    // public constructor
    public Long(long value);

    // public instance methods
    public boolean equals(Object obj);
    public int hashCode();
    public long longValue();
    public String toString();
}
```

java.lang.Math

This class is a much smaller counterpart to the J2SE Math class. Because J2ME does not support floating-point variables, the class only provides six static methods for determining the absolute value of an int or a long, as well as the smaller (minimum) and larger (maximum) of two int or long variables.

```
public final class Math {
    // static methods
public static int abs(int a);
public static long abs(long a);
public static int max(int a, int b);
public static long max(long a, long b);
public static int min(int a, int b);
public static long min(long a, long b);
}
```

java.lang.NegativeArraySizeException

This exception is identical to its J2SE counterpart. It signifies an attempt to instantiate an array with a negative number of elements.

```
public class NegativeArraySizeException extends java.lang.RuntimeException {
    // constructors
    public NegativeArraySizeException();
    public NegativeArraySizeException(String s);
}
```

java.lang.NullPointerException

This exception is identical to its J2SE counterpart. It signifies an attempt to reference an object that has not yet been instantiated.

```
public class NullPointerException extends java.lang.RuntimeException {
    // constructors
    public NullPointerException();
    public NullPointerException(String s);
}
```

java.lang.NumberFormatException

This exception is identical to its J2SE counterpart. It signifies that the format of a number is illegal for the invoked operation.

```
public class NumberFormatException extends
    java.lang.IllegalArgumentException {
    // constructors
    public NumberFormatException();
    public NumberFormatException(String s);
}
```

java.lang.Object

This class is a slightly smaller counterpart to the J2SE Object class. It forms the base of the object hierarchy in Java; in other words, all classes are subclasses of Object. The equals() method tests for a byte-for-byte equivalence between the data of two objects. (Be sure not to confuse this with the == operator, which simply tests if two references point to the same object.) getClass() returns a Class object associated with this object. The three wait() methods, as well as notify() and notifyAll(), are used for thread synchronization on an object. As with any J2SE object, subclasses should override toString() and hashCode() if appropriate (e.g., creating an object that acts as a key in a Hashtable). Finally, note that the finalize() method has been eliminated in the J2ME version of Object.

```
public class Object {
    // public constructor
    public Object();

    // public instance methods
    public boolean equals(Object obj);
    public final Class getClass();
    public int hashCode();
    public final void notify();
    public final void notifyAll();
    public String toString();
    public final void wait() throws java.lang.InterruptedException;
    public final void wait(long timeout) throws java.lang.InterruptedException;
    public final void wait(long timeout, int nanos) throws
        java.lang.InterruptedException;
}
```

java.lang.OutOfMemoryError

This error is identical to its J2SE counterpart. It signifies that the virtual machine has run out of memory.

```
public class OutOfMemoryError extends java.lang.VirtualMachineError {
    // constructors
    public OutOfMemoryError();
    public OutOfMemoryError(String s);
}
```

java.lang.Runnable

This interface is identical to the Runnable interface in J2SE. It consists of only one method, run(), which is often used in conjunction with threads.

```
public interface Runnable {
    // methods
    public void run();
}
```

java.lang.Runtime

This class is a stripped-down version of the J2SE Runtime class. Aside from the static getRuntime() method, which ensures a single Runtime object for the system, this class consists of only four methods to encapsulate platform-dependent system functions: two for monitoring total and currently used memory, one for garbage collection, and one to exit the program.

```
public class Runtime {
    // static methods
    public static Runtime getRuntime();

    // public instance methods
    public void exit(int status);
    public native long freeMemory();
    public native void gc();
    public native long totalMemory();
}
```

java.lang.RuntimeException

This exception is identical to its J2SE counterpart. It is a superclass of a number of exceptions that signify that an unexpected condition has occurred at runtime. Applications are not required to catch runtime exceptions, as they can be thrown at any time.

```
public class RuntimeException extends java.lang.Exception {
    // constructors
    public RuntimeException();
    public RuntimeException(String s);
}
```

java.lang.SecurityException

This exception is identical to its J2SE counterpart. It signifies that an operation is not allowed due to security reasons.

```
public class SecurityException extends java.lang.RuntimeException {
    // constructors
    public SecurityException();
    public SecurityException(String s);
}
```

java.lang.Short

This class is a smaller counterpart to the J2SE Short class. It provides an object wrapper around a single short primitive data type. The class provides minimum and maximum constant values that can be used to test the legal size of a short. The value of the object's short is accessed using the shortValue() method. In addition, the parseShort() methods can convert a number from a String to a short, and vice versa, with an optionally specified radix.

```java
public final class Short {
    // public constants
    public static final short MIN_VALUE;
    public static final short MAX_VALUE;

    // static methods
    public static short parseShort(String s) throws
        java.lang.NumberFormatException;
    public static short parseShort(String s, int radix) throws
        java.lang.NumberFormatException;

    // constructor
    public Short(short value);

    // public instance methods
    public boolean equals(Object obj);
    public int hashCode();
    public short shortValue();
    public String toString();
}
```

java.lang.String

This class represents a scaled-down version of the J2SE String object. The String object holds a concatenation of characters in an immutable format. The static valueOf() methods are used to convert the value of a primitive data type into a String. compareTo() performs a lexicographical comparison between two strings. startsWith() and endsWith() test whether the string begins or ends with the specified characters. indexOf() and lastIndexOf() specify the offset from the beginning of the first or last occurrence of a string. substring() creates a smaller string from the specified character offsets. trim() removes white spaces from both ends of the string.

```java
public final class String {

    // static methods
    public static String valueOf(boolean b);
    public static String valueOf(char c);
    public static String valueOf(char[] data);
    public static String valueOf(char[] data, int offset, int count);
    public static String valueOf(int i);
    public static String valueOf(long l);
    public static String valueOf(Object obj);
```

```
    // public constructors
    public String();
    public String(String value);
    public String(char[] value);
    public String(char[] value, int offset, int count);
    public String(byte[] bytes, int off, int len, String enc)
        throws java.io.UnsupportedEncodingException;
    public String(byte[] bytes, String enc) throws
        java.io.UnsupportedEncodingException;
    public String(byte[] bytes, int off, int len);
    public String(byte[] bytes);
    public String(StringBuffer buffer);

    // public instance methods
    public char charAt(int index);
    public int compareTo(String anotherString);
    public String concat(String str);
    public boolean endsWith(String suffix);
    public boolean equals(Object anObject);
    public byte[] getBytes();
    public byte[] getBytes(String enc) throws
        java.io.UnsupportedEncodingException;
    public void getChars(int srcBegin, int srcEnd, char[] dst, int dstBegin);
    public int hashCode();
    public int indexOf(int ch);
    public int indexOf(int ch, int fromIndex);
    public int indexOf(String str);
    public int indexOf(String str, int fromIndex);
    public int lastIndexOf(int ch);
    public int lastIndexOf(int ch, int fromIndex);
    public int length();
    public boolean regionMatches(boolean ignoreCase, int toffset, String other,
        int ooffset, int len);
    public String replace(char oldChar, char newChar);
    public boolean startsWith(String prefix, int toffset);
    public boolean startsWith(String prefix);
    public String substring(int beginIndex);
    public String substring(int beginIndex, int endIndex);
    public char[] toCharArray();
    public String toLowerCase();
    public String toString();
    public String toUpperCase();
    public String trim();
}
```

java.lang.StringBuffer

This class is a scaled-down version of the J2SE StringBuffer class. It creates an editable concatenation of characters. Use the append() and insert() methods to add characters to the middle or end of the StringBuffer. Utilize the capacity() and ensureCapacity() methods to ensure that the size requirements of the buffer are sufficient. The delete() and

deleteCharAt() methods can be used to remove portions of the buffer. The reverse()
method will replace the current string with a backward copy of itself.

```
public final class StringBuffer {
    // public constructors
    public StringBuffer();
    public StringBuffer(int length);
    public StringBuffer(String str);

    // public instance methods
    public StringBuffer append(boolean b);
    public synchronized StringBuffer append(char c);
    public synchronized StringBuffer append(char[] str);
    public synchronized StringBuffer append(char[] str, int offset, int len);
    public StringBuffer append(int i);
    public StringBuffer append(long l);
    public synchronized StringBuffer append(Object obj);
    public synchronized StringBuffer append(String str);
    public int capacity();
    public synchronized char charAt(int index);
    public synchronized StringBuffer delete(int start, int end);
    public synchronized StringBuffer deleteCharAt(int index);
    public synchronized void ensureCapacity(int minimumCapacity);
    public synchronized void getChars(int srcBegin, int srcEnd,
        char[] dst, int dstBegin);
    public StringBuffer insert(int offset, boolean b);
    public synchronized StringBuffer insert(int offset, char[] str);
    public synchronized StringBuffer insert(int offset, char c);
    public StringBuffer insert(int offset, int i);
    public StringBuffer insert(int offset, long l);
    public synchronized StringBuffer insert(int offset, Object obj);
    public synchronized StringBuffer insert(int offset, String str);
    public int length();
    public synchronized StringBuffer reverse();
    public synchronized void setCharAt(int index, char ch);
    public synchronized void setLength(int newLength);
    public String toString();
}
```

java.lang.StringIndexOutOfBoundsException

This exception is identical to its J2SE counterpart. It signifies that an index into a String or
StringBuffer is either negative or too large.

```
public class StringIndexOutOfBoundsException extends
    java.lang.IndexOutOfBoundsException {
    // constructors
    public StringIndexOutOfBoundsException();
    public StringIndexOutOfBoundsException(int index);
    public StringIndexOutOfBoundsException(String s);
}
```

java.lang.System

This class is a much smaller version of the J2SE System class, which provides static methods to access system functionality. The err and out streams represent their standard I/O equivalents. The getProperty() method returns a named property from the system properties list. (Note that the MIDP APIs redefine the microedition.locale property to include at least "MIDP-1.0".)

The following list describes the characteristics of several properties.

microedition.platform
> Name of the host platform/device (CLDC)

microedition.encoding
> Default character encoding (CLDC)

microedition.configuration
> Name/version of the configuration (CLDC)

microedition.profiles
> Names of the supported profiles (CLDC)

microedition.locale
> Current locale (MIDP)

The arraycopy() method is preserved from the J2SE System class; it copies a section of an array from a source to a destination. currentTimeMillis() returns the current time in milliseconds from the epoch, midnight GMT, January 1, 1970. The exit() method terminates the application with a status code. gc() performs a system-wide garbage collection.

```
public final class System {
    // public instance fields
    public static final PrintStream err;
    public static final PrintStream out;

    // static methods
    public static native void arraycopy(Object src, int src_position, Object dst,
        int dst_position, int length);
    public static native long currentTimeMillis()
    public static void exit(int status);
    public static void gc();
    public static String getProperty(String key);
    public static native int identityHashCode(Object x);
}
```

java.lang.Thread

This class is a scaled-down version of the J2SE Thread class, which represents a system thread in the Java virtual machine. Classes can create threads by either extending the Thread class and providing a run() method, or passing a Runnable object into the Thread constructor. Threads execute when the start() method is called, and will continue until the end of the run() method, unless run() is interrupted. The isAlive() method returns a boolean that indicates if the current thread is executing.

activeCount() returns the total number of threads active. The getPriority() and setPriority() methods can access the integer priority level of the thread, which can be used in conjunction with the three constants, MIN_PRIORITY, NORM_PRIORITY, and MAX_PRIORITY. currentThread() returns a reference to the thread that is currently active. sleep() will cause the current thread to halt execution for the specified amount of time, while yield() gives up control to other threads of equal priority that are waiting to run. Finally, join() will suspend execution until the target thread has completed or is interrupted.

```java
public class Thread implements Runnable {
    // public constants
    public static final int MIN_PRIORITY;
    public static final int NORM_PRIORITY;
    public static final int MAX_PRIORITY;

    // static methods
    public static native int activeCount();
    public static native Thread currentThread();
    public static native void sleep(long millis) throws
        java.lang.InterruptedException;
    public static native void yield();


    // constructors
    public Thread();
    public Thread(Runnable target);

    // public instance methods
    public final int getPriority();
    public final native boolean isAlive();
    public final void join();
    public void run();
    public final void setPriority(int newPriority);
    public native synchronized void start();
    public String toString();
}
```

java.lang.Throwable

This class is a scaled-down version of the J2SE Throwable class. It is the superclass of all errors and exceptions in the Java language, and only objects that extend this class can be thrown or caught in the Java virtual machine. The getMessage() method returns any error messages that are set in the constructor. printStackTrace() creates a stack trace that shows precisely where a specific error occurred in an application.

```java
public class Throwable {
    // constructors
    public Throwable();
    public Throwable(String message);
```

```
    // public instance methods
    public String getMessage();
    public void printStackTrace();
    public String toString();
}
```

java.lang.VirtualMachineError

This error is identical to its J2SE counterpart. It signifies that the virtual machine does not
have the required resources to complete an operation.

```
public abstract class VirtualMachineError extends java.lang.Error {
    // constructors
    public VirtualMachineError();
    public VirtualMachineError(String s);
}
```

The java.util Package

java.util.Calendar

This abstract class is a scaled-down version of the J2SE Calendar class. Subclasses can use the functionality provided to calculate and compare dates. Calendar defines a number of constants for time-related items such as the days of the week and the months of the year. Other constants, such as DAY_OF_MONTH and HOUR_OF_DAY, are used with the various get and set methods to indicate which fields are desired. The getInstance() methods are used to create an instance of the Calendar; note that the constructor is not public.

```java
public abstract class Calendar {
    // constants
    public static final int YEAR;
    public static final int MONTH;
    public static final int DATE;
    public static final int DAY_OF_MONTH;
    public static final int DAY_OF_WEEK;
    public static final int AM_PM;
    public static final int HOUR;
    public static final int HOUR_OF_DAY;
    public static final int MINUTE;
    public static final int SECOND;
    public static final int MILLISECOND;
    public static final int SUNDAY;
    public static final int MONDAY;
    public static final int TUESDAY;
    public static final int WEDNESDAY;
    public static final int THURSDAY;
    public static final int FRIDAY;
    public static final int SATURDAY;
    public static final int JANUARY;
    public static final int FEBRUARY;
    public static final int MARCH;
    public static final int APRIL;
    public static final int MAY;
    public static final int JUNE;
    public static final int JULY;
    public static final int AUGUST;
```

```
      public static final int SEPTEMBER;
      public static final int OCTOBER;
      public static final int NOVEMBER;
      public static final int DECEMBER;
      public static final int AM;
      public static final int PM;

      // constructor
      protected Calendar();

      // static methods
      public static synchronized Calendar getInstance();
      public static synchronized Calendar getInstance(TimeZone zone);

      // protected instance methods
      protected long getTimeInMillis();
      protected void setTimeInMillis(long millis);

      // public instance methods
      public boolean after(Object when);
      public boolean before(Object when);
      public boolean equals(Object obj);
      public final int get(int field);
      public final Date getTime();
      public TimeZone getTimeZone();
      public final void set(int field, int value);
      public final void setTime(Date date);
      public void setTimeZone(TimeZone value);
}
```

java.util.Date

The Date class is a smaller version of its J2SE counterpart. It represents an instance in time, specified as the number of milliseconds since the epoch (midnight GMT, January 1, 1970). To create a Date object that represents the current system time, do the following:

```
Date currentDate = new Date();
```

This is equivalent to:

```
Date currentDate = new Date(System.currentTimeMillis());
```

You can also access the date and time represented by this object with the getTime() and setTime() methods.

```
public class Date {
    public Date();
    public Date(long date);

    public long getTime();
    public void setTime(long time);
    public boolean equals(Object obj);
    public int hashCode();
}
```

java.util.Enumeration

This interface is identical to the Enumeration interface of the J2SE. Classes that implement this interface allow the programmer to iterate through a series of values, such as the keys or elements in a hashtable.

```
public interface Enumeration {
    public boolean hasMoreElements();
    public Object nextElement();
}
```

java.util.EmptyStackException

This exception is identical to its J2SE counterpart. It signifies that an operation was performed on a stack that was empty.

```
public class EmptyStackException extends java.lang.RuntimeException {
    // constructors
    public EmptyStackException();
}
```

java.util.Hashtable

This class is a scaled-down version of the J2SE Hashtable class. It provides a thread-safe implementation of a hashtable, which allows for efficient storage and lookup of a target element based on the hash code of another object that serves as its "key." Objects are placed in the hashtable with the put() method, retrieved with the get() method, and deleted with the remove() method. The contains() and containsKey() methods indicate whether the specified element or key is present in the hashtable. clear() removes all entries from the hashtable, at which point isEmpty() will return true. The elements() and keys() methods return an Enumeration object that you can use to iterate through the hashtable elements or key objects.

```
public interface Hashtable {
    // constructors
    public Hashtable(int initialCapacity);
    public Hashtable();

    // protected instance methods
    protected void rehash();

    // public instance methods
    public synchronized void clear();
    public synchronized boolean contains(Object value);
    public synchronized boolean containsKey(Object key);
    public synchronized Enumeration elements();
    public synchronized Object get(Object key);
    public boolean isEmpty();
    public synchronized Enumeration keys();
    public synchronized Object put(Object key, Object value);
    public synchronized Object remove(Object key);
```

```
    public int size();
    public String toString();
}
```

java.util.NoSuchElementException

This exception is identical to its J2SE counterpart. It signifies that there are no elements available for the requested operation.

```
public class NoSuchElementException extends java.lang.RuntimeException {
    // constructors
    public NoSuchElementException();
    public NoSuchElementException(String s);
}
```

java.util.Random

This class is a smaller version of the J2SE Random class and is used as a pseudo-random number generator. The constructor takes a long integer seed, which it uses to initialize the random number generator. The nextInt() and nextLong() methods can then be used to create random numbers of the appropriate data type. The seed can be reset using the setSeed() method.

```
public class Random {
    // constructors
    public Random();
    public Random(long seed);

    // protected instance methods
    protected int next(int bits);

    // public instance methods
    public int nextInt();
    public long nextLong();
    public void setSeed(long seed);
}
```

java.util.Stack

This class is identical to the J2SE Stack class. It extends the Vector class to allow a simple Last-In-First-Out (LIFO) stack, where elements are placed on the top of the stack using the push() method and removed from the top using the pop() method. peek() returns the object at the top of the stack without actually removing it. search() will search the stack for the specified object, returning the index of the element if found or −1 if it is not found.

```
public class Stack extends java.util.Vector {
    // constructor
    public Stack();

    // public instance methods
    public boolean empty();
```

```
    public Object peek();
    public Object pop();
    public Object push(Object item);
    public int search(Object o);
}
```

java.util.Timer

This class defines a facility for threads to schedule tasks for future execution in a background thread. There are four versions of the schedule() method; each schedules tasks to execute at a specific time using a Date object or after a specific delay in milliseconds. The scheduleAtFixedrate() method can be used to schedule tasks for repeated execution in intervals relative to the scheduled execution time of the first execution. If an execution is delayed for any reason (such as garbage collection or other background activity), two or more subsequent executions are scheduled at shorter intervals to catch up.

```
    public class Timer {
        // public constructors
        public Timer();
        // public instance methods
        public void cancel();
        public void schedule(TimerTask task, Date time);
        public void schedule(TimerTask task, long delay);
        public void schedule(TimerTask task, Date firstTime, long period);
        public void schedule(TimerTask task, long delay, long period);
        public void scheduleAtFixedRate(TimerTask task, Date firstTime, long period);
        public void scheduleAtFixedRate(TimerTask task, long delay, long period);
    }
```

java.util.TimerTask

TimerTask is an abstract class that acts as the base class for all scheduled tasks. A task can be scheduled for one-time or repeated execution by a Timer. To define a task, create a subclass of TimerTask and implement the run() method. For example:

```
    import java.util.*;
    public class MyTask extends TimerTask {
        public void run() {
            System.out.println("Run Task");
        }
    }
```

The run() method is being implemented simply because the TimerTask implements the Runnable interface. The run() method is invoked by the Timer class to run the task.

After you define a task, you schedule it for execution by creating a Timer object and invoking the schedule() method, as shown here:

```
    Timer timer = new Timer();
    TimerTask task = new MyTask();
```

```
// wait five seconds before executing
timer.schedule(task, 5000);
// wait two seconds before executing then execute every five seconds
timer.schedule(task, 2000, 5000);
```

Here we are using two of the four versions of the schedule() method of the Timer class.

```
public abstract class TimerTask implements java.lang.Runnable {
    // protected constructors
    protected TimerTask();
    // public instance methods
    public boolean cancel();
    public abstract void run();
    public long scheduledExecutionTime();
}
```

java.util.TimeZone

This class is a scaled-down version of the J2SE TimeZone class. It represents a geographic time zone and can be used in conjunction with the Calendar object. Time zones can be created by passing in an ID, such as "America/Chicago" or "GMT," to the static getTimeZone() method. To check the available IDs recognized by this class, call the getAvailableIDs() method. An object representing the current time zone of the device can be obtained with the static getDefault() method. getOffset() returns an integer milliseconds offset, which you add to the GMT time in order to get the current time, taking into account daylight savings, while getRawOffset() simply returns the geographic offset in milliseconds. To test whether the TimeZone object is currently using daylight savings in its calculations, call useDaylightTime().

```
public abstract class TimeZone {
    // constructor
    public TimeZone();

    // static methods
    public static TimeZone getTimeZone(String ID);
    public static TimeZone getDefault();
    public static String[] getAvailableIDs();

    // public instance methods methods
    public abstract int getOffset(int era, int year, int month, int day,
        int dayOfWeek, int millis);
    public abstract int getRawOffset();
    public abstract boolean useDaylightTime();
}
```

java.util.Vector

This class is a scaled-down version of the J2SE Vector class. The class represents a dynamic array that can grow and shrink as necessary. A vector starts with an array of a preset capacity, set either through the constructor or the ensureCapacity() method, and increases the size if needed. Elements can be added to the vector using the addElement() method. The indexOf() method can be used to obtain the index of a desired element in the array, which can be removed using the elementAt() method. Note that the object returned is simply an Object; be sure to recast it to the appropriate type. You can remove elements using the removeElement() and removeElementAt() methods. size() returns the size of the element array. trimToSize() reduces the size of the vector's array to match the current number of elements.

```java
public class Vector {
    // protected fields
    protected int capacityIncrement;
    protected int elementCount;
    protected Object[] elementData;

    // constructors
    public Vector();
    public Vector(int initialCapacity);
    public Vector(int initialCapacity, int capacityIncrement);

    // public instance methods
    public synchronized void addElement(Object obj);
    public int capacity();
    public boolean contains(Object elem);
    public synchronized void copyInto(Object[] anArray);
    public synchronized Object elementAt(int index);
    public synchronized Enumeration elements();
    public synchronized void ensureCapacity(int minCapacity);
    public synchronized Object firstElement();
    public int indexOf(Object elem);
    public synchronized int indexOf(Object elem, int index);
    public synchronized void insertElementAt(Object obj, int index);
    public boolean isEmpty();
    public synchronized Object lastElement();
    public int lastIndexOf(Object elem);
    public synchronized int lastIndexOf(Object elem, int index);
    public synchronized void removeAllElements();
    public synchronized boolean removeElement(Object obj);
    public synchronized void removeElementAt(int index);
    public synchronized void setElementAt(Object obj, int index);
    public synchronized void setSize(int newSize);
    public int size();
    public synchronized String toString();
    public synchronized void trimToSize();
}
```

The javax.microedition.io Package

This package provides all the I/O mechanisms in the CLDC. The package consists of eight interfaces, one class, and one exception class.

javax.microedition.io.Connection

This interface defines the basic type of generic connection. The close( ) method is used to close a connection. Closing an already closed connection has no effect.

```
public interface Connection {
    // public instance methods
    public void close( ) throws IOException;
}
```

javax.microedition.io.ContentConnection

This interface defines the stream connection over which content is passed. The getEncoding() method returns a string describing the encoding of the content, and getType( ) returns the type of content provided.

```
public interface ContentConnection extends StreamConnection {
    // public instance methods
    public String getEncoding( );
    public String getLength( );
    public long getType( );
}
```

javax.microedition.io.Datagram

This interface represents the generic datagram interface. It acts as a holder for data to be sent to or received from a datagram connection.

```
public interface Datagram extends DataInput, DataOutput {
    // public instance methods
    public String getAddress( );
    public byte[] getData( );
```

```
    public int getLength( );
    public int getOffset( );
    public void reset( );
    public void setAddress(Datagram reference);
    public void setAddress(String address) throws IOException;
    public void setData(byte[] buffer, int offset, int len);
    public void setLength(int len);
}
```

javax.microedition.io.DatagramConnection

This interface defines the methods that a datagram connection must have. A datagram connection can be established in a client mode or a server mode. For example, in a server mode (client initiates communication and server accepts connections), there is no need to specify the hostname: *datagram://2233*. And, in client mode, the hostname must be specified so that the client knows with whom to initiate communication: *datagram://134.15.13.1:2233*. Note that the port number in both modes is the same. In server mode, the same port number is used for both sending and receiving, and in client mode, the reply-to port is always dynamically allocated.

```
    public interface DatagramConnection extends Connection {
        // public instance methods
        public int getMaximumLength( ) throws IOException;
        public int getNominalLength( ) throws IOException;
        public Datagram newData(byte[] buf, int size) throws IOException;
        public Datagram newData(byte[] buf, int size, String addr) throws IOException;
        public Datagram newDatagram(int size) throws IOException;
        public Datagram newDatagram(int size, String addr) throws IOException;
        public void receive(Datagram dgram) throws IOException;
        public void send(Datagram dgram) throws IOException;
    }
```

javax.microedition.io.HttpConnection

This interface defines the necessary constants and methods for an HTTP connection. For some usage examples, see Chapter 7.

```
    public interface HttpConnection extends javax.microedition.io.ContentConnection {
        // public class fields
        public static final String GET = "GET";
        public static final String HEAD = "HEAD";
        public static final String POST = "POST";
        public static final int HTTP_ACCEPTED = 202;
        public static final int HTTP_BAD_GATEWAY = 502;
        public static final int HTTP_BAD_METHOD = 405;
        public static final int HTTP_BAD_REQUEST = 400;
        public static final int HTTP_CLIENT_TIMEOUT = 408;
        public static final int HTTP_CONFLICT = 409;
        public static final int HTTP_CREATED = 201;
        public static final int HTTP_ENTITY_TOO_LARGE = 413;
        public static final int HTTP_EXPECT_FAILED = 417;
```

```
      public static final int HTTP_FORBIDDEN = 403;
      public static final int HTTP_GATEWAY_TIMEOUT = 504;
      public static final int HTTP_GONE = 410;
      public static final int HTTP_INTERNAL_ERROR = 500;
      public static final int HTTP_LENGTH_REQUIRED = 411;
      public static final int HTTP_MOVED_PERM = 301;
      public static final int HTTP_MOVED_TEMP = 302;
      public static final int HTTP_MULT_CHOICE = 300;
      public static final int HTTP_NO_CONTENT = 204;
      public static final int HTTP_NOT_ACCEPTABLE = 406;
      public static final int HTTP_NOT_AUTHORITATIVE = 203;
      public static final int HTTP_NOT_FOUND = 404;
      public static final int HTTP_NOT_IMPLEMENTED = 501;
      public static final int HTTP_NOT_MODIFIED = 304;
      public static final int HTTP_OK = 200;
      public static final int HTTP_PARTIAL = 206;
      public static final int HTTP_PAYMENT_REQUIRED = 402;
      public static final int HTTP_PRECON_FAILED = 412;
      public static final int HTTP_PROXY_AUTH = 407;
      public static final int HTTP_REQ_TOO_LONG = 414;
      public static final int HTTP_RESET = 205;
      public static final int HTTP_SEE_OTHER = 303;
      public static final int HTTP_TEMP_REDIRECT = 307;
      public static final int HTTP_UNAUTHORIZED = 401;
      public static final int HTTP_UNAVAILABLE = 503;
      public static final int HTTP_UNSUPPORTED_RANGE = 416;
      public static final int HTTP_UNSUPPORTED_TYPE = 415;
      public static final int HTTP_USE_PROXY = 305;
      public static final int HTTP_VERSION = 505;
      // public instance methods
      public long getDate( ) throws IOException;
      public long getExpiration( ) throws IOException;
      public String getFile( );
      public String getHeaderField(int n) throws IOException;
      public String getHeaderField(String name) throws IOException;
      public long getHeaderFieldDate(String name, long def) throws IOException;
      public int getHeaderFieldInt(String name, int def) throws IOException;
      public String getHeaderFieldKey(int n) throws IOException;
      public String getHost( );
      public long getLastModified( ) throws IOException;
      public int getPort( );
      public String getProtocol( );
      public String getQuery( );
      public String getRef( );
      public String getRequestMethod( );
      public String getRequestProperty(String key);
      public int getResponseCode( ) throws IOException;
      public String getResponseMessage( ) throws IOException;
      public String getURL( );
      public void setRequestMethod(String method) throws IOException;
      public void setRequestProperty(String key, String value) throws IOException;
}
```

javax.microedition.io.InputConnection

This interface defines the capabilities that an input stream connection must have. The openInputStream( ) method opens and returns an input stream for a connection, and openDataInputStream( ) opens and returns a data input stream for a connection.

```
public interface InputConnection extends Connection {
    // public instance methods
    public DataInputStream openDataInputStream( ) throws IOException;
    public InputStream openInputStream( ) throws IOException;
}
```

javax.microedition.io.OutputConnection

This interface defines the capabilities that an output stream connection must have. The openOutputStream( ) opens and returns an output stream for a connection, and openDataOutputStream( ) opens and returns a data output stream for a connection.

```
public interface OutputConnection extends Connection {
    // public instance methods
    public DataOutputStream openDataOutputStream( ) throws IOException;
    public OutputStream openOutputStream( ) throws IOException;
}
```

javax.microedition.io.StreamConnection

This interface defines the capabilities that a stream connection must have. It does not define any methods of its own, but it inherits all methods from InputConnection and OutputConnection.

```
public interface StreamConnection extends InputConnection, OutputConnection {
    // all methods inherited from InputConnection and OutputConnection
}
```

javax.microedition.io.StreamConnectionNotifier

This interface defines the capabilities that a connection notifier must have. The acceptAndOpen( ) method returns a StreamConnection that represents a server-side socket connection.

```
public interface StreamConnectionNotifier extends Connection {
    // public instance methods
    public StreamConnection acceptAndOpen( ) throws IOException;
}
```

javax.microedition.io.Connector

This class acts as a placeholder for the class methods that are used to create all the connection objects. When opening a connection, an access mode can be specified as READ, WRITE, or READ_WRITE. This means that a connection can be used for reading, writing, or both. This, however, is protocol-dependent, as some protocol connections may not allow READ access (a connection to a printer, for example). In this case an IllegalArgumentException will be thrown. If no access mode is specified, then the default READ_WRITE will be used.

```
public class Connector {
    // public class fields
    public static final int READ = 1;
    public static final int WRITE = 2;
    public static final int READ_WRITE = (READ|WRITE);
    // public class methods
    public static Connection open(String name) throws IOException;
    public static Connection open(String name, int mode) throws IOException;
    public static Connection open(String name, int mode, boolean timeouts) throws
                    IOException;
    public static DataInputStream openDataInputStream(String name) throws
                    IOException;
    public static DataOutputStream openDataOutputStream(String name) throws
                    IOException;
    public static InputStream openInputStream(String name) throws IOException;
    public static OutputStream openOutputStream(String name) throws IOException;
}
```

javax.microedition.io.ConnectionNotFoundException

This exception is thrown to signal that a connection target could not be found.

```
public class ConnectionNotFoundException extends IOException {
    // public contructors
    public ConnectionNotFoundException();
    public ConnectionNotFoundException(String s);
}
```

The javax.microedition.lcdui Package

This package provides a set of features for the implementation of user interfaces for MIDP applications. This package consists of three interfaces and twenty-one classes. The MIDP User Interface API consists of two APIs: high-level and low-level. The classes implementing the high-level API are the subclasses of Screen. The classes Canvas and Graphics implement the low-level API.

javax.microedition.lcdui.Choice

This interface defines an API for user interface components, such as List and ChoiceGroup, implementing selection from a predefined number of choices. Each element of a choice is composed of a text string and an optional image. If you do not want the element to have an image, pass in null.

There are three types of choices:

EXCLUSIVE

Presents a series of elements and interacts with the user. When the user selects an element, it is shown to be selected using a distinct visual representation. Exactly one element must be selected at any given time.

IMPLICIT

Serves as an EXCLUSIVE choice where the focused element is implicitly selected when a command is initiated.

MULTIPLE

Presents a series of elements and allows the user to select multiple elements.

```
public interface Choice {
    // public class fields
    public static final int EXCLUSIVE = 1;
    public static final int IMPLICIT = 2;
    public static final int MULTIPLE = 3;
    // public instance methods
    public int append(String stringPart, Image imagePart);
    public void delete(int elementNum);
    public Image getImage(int elementNum);
    public int getSelectedFlags(boolean[] selectedArray);
```

```
    public int getSelectedIndex( );
    public String getString(int elementNum);
    public void insert(int elementNum, String stringPart, Image imagePart);
    public boolean isSelected(int elementNum);
    public void set(int elementNum, String stringPart, Image imagePart);
    public void setSelectedFlags(boolean[] selectedArray);
    public void setSelectedIndex(int elementNum, boolean selected);
    public int size( );
}
```

javax.microedition.lcdui.CommandListener

This interface should be implemented by MIDlets that need to receive high-level events from the implementation. The commandAction( ) method indicates that a command event has occurred on Displayable.

```
public interface CommandListener {
    // public instance methods
    public void commandAction(Command c, Displayable d);
}
```

javax.microedition.lcdui.ItemStateListener

This interface is implemented by MIDlets that need to receive events that indicate changes in the internal state of the interactive items within a Form screen. The itemStateChanged( ) method is called when the internal state of an item has been changed by the user. This happens when the user changes the set of selected values in a ChoiceGroup, adjusts the value of an interactive Gauge, enters or modifies the value in a TextField, or enters a new date or time in a DateField.

```
public interface ItemStateListener {
    // public static methods
    public void itemStateChanged(Item item);
}
```

javax.microedition.lcdui.Alert

This class implements an alert, which is an ordinary screen that can contain text and images and that handles events like other screens. The purpose of an alert is to inform the user about errors and other exceptional conditions.

The alert screen usually waits for a certain period of time before proceeding to the next screen. Alternatively, the alert timer can be set to infinity, using setTimeout(Alert. FOREVER). In this case, the implementation allows the user to dismiss the alert.

An alert may have a type (see the AlertType class) that the implementation may use to play an appropriate sound when the alert is presented to the user. To set the alert type, use setType( ).

```
public class Alert extends Screen {
    // public class fields
    public static final int FOREVER = -2;
    // public constructors
    public Alert(String title);
    public Alert(String title, String alertText, Image image, AlertType alertType);
    // public instance methods
    public void addCommand(Command cmd);
    public int getDefaultTimeout();
    public Image getImage();
    public String getString();
    public int getTimeOut();
    public AlertType getType();
    public void setCommandListener(CommandListener l);
    public void setImage(Image image);
    public void setString(String str);
    public void setTimeout(int time);
    public void setType(AlertType type);
}
```

javax.microedition.lcdui.AlertType

This class provides an indication of the nature of alerts. The alert type allows the implementation to directly signal the user without changing the current Displayable. The playSound() method can be used to generate a sound to alert the user. The predefined types of alerts are:

INFO

Provides non-threatening information to the user.

WARNING

Warns the user of a potentially dangerous operation.

ERROR

Alerts the user of a dangerous operation.

ALARM

Lets the user know of an event of which he previously requested to be notified.

CONFIRMATION

Confirms user action.

```
public class AlertType {
    // public class fields
    public static final AlertType ALARM;
    public static final AlertType CONFIRMATION;
    public static final AlertType ERROR;
    public static final AlertType INFO;
    public static final AlertType WARNING;
    // protected constructors
    protected AlertType();
    // public instance methods
    public boolean playSound(Display display);
}
```

javax.microedition.lcdui.Canvas

Canvas is an abstract class, which is the base class for writing MIDlets that need to implement low-level events and to issue graphics calls for drawing on the display. Since this class will be used heavily for game applications, it provides ways to handle game actions, key events, and pointer events.

```java
public abstract class Canvas extends Displayable {
    // public class fields
    public static final int DOWN = 6;
    public static final int FIRE = 8;
    public static final int GAME_A = 9;
    public static final int GAME_B = 10;
    public static final int GAME_C = 11;
    public static final int GAME_D = 12;
    public static final int KEY_NUM0 = 48;
    public static final int KEY_NUM1 = 49;
    public static final int KEY_NUM2 = 50;
    public static final int KEY_NUM3 = 51;
    public static final int KEY_NUM4 = 52;
    public static final int KEY_NUM5 = 53;
    public static final int KEY_NUM6 = 54;
    public static final int KEY_NUM7 = 55;
    public static final int KEY_NUM8 = 56;
    public static final int KEY_NUM9 = 57;
    public static final int KEY_POUND = 35;
    public static final int KEY_STAR = 42;
    public static final int LEFT = 2;
    public static final int RIGHT = 5;
    public static final int UP = 1;
    // protected constructors
    protected Canvas( );
    // protected instance methods
    protected void hideNotify( );
    protected void keyPressed(int keyCode);
    protected void keyReleased(int keyCode);
    protected void keyRepeated(int keyCode);
    protected abstract void paint(Graphics g);
    protected void pointerDragged(int x, int y);
    protected void pointerPressed(int x, int y);
    protected void pointerReleased(int x, int y);
    protected void showNotify( );
    // public instance methods
    public int getGameAction(int keyCode);
    public int getHeight( );
    public int getKeyCode(int gameAction);
    public String getKeyName(int keyCode);
    public int getWidth( );
    public boolean hasPointerEvents( );
    public boolean hasPointerMotionEvents( );
    public boolean hasRepeatEvents( );
    public boolean isDoubleBuffered( );
```

```
    public final void repaint();
    public final void repaint(int x, int y, int width, int height);
    public final void serviceRepaints();
}
```

javax.microedition.lcdui.ChoiceGroup

This class implements a group of selectable elements intended to be placed within a Form. The group may have a mode that requires a single choice to be made or that allows multiple choices. It is up to the implementation to decide on the graphical representation of these modes, but it must provide visually different graphics for different modes—for example, radio buttons for single-choice mode and checkboxes for multiple-choice mode.

```
    public class ChoiceGroup extends Item implements Choice {
        // public constructors
        public ChoiceGroup(String label, int choiceType);
        public ChoiceGroup(String label, int choiceType, String[] stringElements,
            Image[] imgElements);
        // public instance methods
        public int append(String stringPart, Image imagePart);
        public void delete(int elementNum);
        public Image getImage(int elementNum);
        public int getSelectedFlags(boolean[] selectedArray);
        public int getSelectedIndex();
        public String getString(int elementNum);
        public void insert(int elementNum, String stringElement, Image imageElement);
        public boolean isSelected(int elementNum);
        public void set(int elementNum, String stringPart, Image imagePart);
        public void setsSelectedFlags(boolean[] selectedArray);
        public void setSelectedIndex(int elementNum, boolean selected);
        public int size();
    }
```

javax.microedition.lcdui.Command

This class encapsulates the semantic information of an action. The command itself contains only information about a command, but not the actual action that happens when a command is activated. The action is defined in a CommandListener object associated with the screen. The Command class constructor takes three parameters, and therefore contains the following three pieces of information: *label*, *command type*, and *priority*.

Label

> A string used for the visual representation of the command. For example, the label may appear next to a soft button on the device or as an element in a menu.

Command Type

> An integer that specifies the command intent. The defined types are: BACK, CANCEL, EXIT, HELP, ITEM, OK, SCREEN, and STOP. The meaning of these types is explained in Table E-1.

Table E-1. Command types

Command Type	Description
BACK	A navigation command that returns the user to the logically previous screen.
CANCEL	A command that is a standard negative answer to a dialog implemented by the current screen. With this command type, the application hints to the implementation that the user wants to dismiss the current screen without taking any action, and usually that the user wants to go back to the prior screen. Hence, CANCEL is often interchangeable with BACK.
EXIT	A command used for exiting from the application.
HELP	A command that specifies a request for online help.
ITEM	An application with this command type hints to the implementation that the command is specific to a particular item on the screen.
OK	A command that is a standard positive answer to a dialog implemented by the current screen. With this command type, the application hints to the implementation that the user will use this command to ask the application to confirm the data that has been entered in the current screen and to proceed to the next logical screen.
SCREEN	A command of this type specifies a command that pertains to the current screen.
STOP	A command that will stop some currently running process or operation. Examples of such processes might include downloading or sending data. Note that using the STOP command does not necessarily lead to a switch to another screen.

Priority

An integer value that describes the importance of the command relative to other commands on the screen. A priority value of 1 indicates the most important command, and higher priority values indicate commands of lesser importance.

A typical implementation first chooses the placement of a command based on the type of command and then places similar commands based on a priority order. This means that the command with the highest priority (lowest integer) is placed so that the user can trigger it directly, and that commands with lower priority are placed on a menu.

```
public class Command {
    // public class fields
    public static final int BACK = 2;
    public static final int CANCEL = 3;
    public static final int EXIT = 7;
    public static final int HELP = 5;
    public static final int ITEM = 8;
    public static final int OK = 4;
    public static final int SCREEN = 1;
    public static final int STOP = 6;
    // public constructors
    public Command(String label, int commandType, int priority);
    // public instance methods
    public int getCommandType( );
    public String getLabel( );
    public int getPriority( );
}
```

javax.microedition.lcdui.DateField

This class implements an editable component for presenting calendar (date and time) information that may be placed in a form.

```
public class DateField extends Item {
    // public class fields
    public static final int DATE = 1;
    public static final int DATE_TIME = 3;
    public static final int TIME = 2;
    // public constructors
    public DateField(String label, int mode);
    public DateField(String label, int  mode, TimeZone timeZone);
    // public instance methods
    public Date getDate( );
    public int getInputMode( );
    public void setDate(Date date);
    public void setInputMode(int mode) throws IllegalArgumentException;
}
```

javax.microedition.lcdui.Display

This class implements the manager of the display and input devices of the system. It includes methods for requesting that objects be displayed on the devices, and for retrieving properties of the devices. The setCurrent( ) method is used for setting the current Displayable and the getCurrent() method for retrieving the current Displayable. The callSerially( ) method causes the Runnable object to have its run( ) method called later. This method can be used by applications to run an animation that is properly synchronized with the repaint cycle.

```
public class Display {
    //  public class methods
    public static Display getDisplay(MIDlet m);
    // public instance methods
    public void callSerially(Runnable r);
    public Displayable getCurrent( );
    public boolean isColor( );
    public int numColors( );
    public void setCurrent(Alert alert, Displayable display);
    public void setCurrent(Displayable display);
}
```

javax.microedition.lcdui.Displayable

This class is an object that has the capability of being placed on the display, and it may have commands and listeners associated with it. Subclasses define the contents and their interactions with the user. Both Canvas and Screen are direct subclasses of Displayable.

```
public abstract class Displayable {
    // public instance methods
    public void addCommand(Command cmd);
```

```
    public boolean isShown( );
    public void removeCommand(Command cmd);
    public void setCommandListener(CommandListener l);
}
```

javax.microedition.lcdui.Font

This class represents fonts and font metrics. Applications query for fonts based on font attributes and the system will attempt to provide a font that matches the requested attributes as closely as possible. Some of these attributes are style, size, and face. Values for the style attribute may be combined using the logical OR operator (e.g., STYLE_BOLD | STYLE_ITALIC), whereas values for the other attributes may not be combined (e.g., SIZE_LARGE | SIZE_SMALL is illegal).

```
public final class Font {
    // public class fields
    public static final int FACE_MONOSPACE = 32;
    public static final int FACE_PROPORTIONAL = 64;
    public static final int FACE_SYSTEM = 0;
    public static final int SIZE_LARGE = 16;
    public static final int SIZE_MEDIUM = 0;
    public static final int SIZE_SMALL = 8;
    public static final int STYLE_BOLD = 1;
    public static final int STYLE_ITALIC = 2;
    public static final int STYLE_PLAIN = 0;
    public static final int STYLE_UNDERLINED = 4;
    // public class methods
    public static Font getDefaultFont( );
    public static Font getFont(int face, int style, int size);
    // public instance methods
    public int charsWidth(char[] ch, int offset, int length);
    public int charWidth(char ch);
    public int getBaselinePosition( );
    public int getFace( );
    public int getHeight( );
    public int getSize( );
    public int getStyle( );
    public boolean isBold( );
    public boolean isItalic( );
    public boolean isPlain( );
    public boolean isUnderlined( );
    public int stringWidth(String str);
    public int substringWidth(String str, int offset, int len);
}
```

javax.microedition.lcdui.Form

This class extends the Screen class, and therefore a form is a screen that contains an arbitrary mixture of items (e.g., images, text, date fields, etc). As a general rule, any subclass of the Item class may be contained within a form.

```
public class Form extends Screen {
    // public constructors
    public Form(String title);
    public Form(String title, Item[] items);
    // public instance methods
    public int append(Image img);
    public int append(Item item);
    public int append(String str);
    public void delete(int itemNum);
    public Item get(int itemnum);
    public void insert(int itemNum, Item item);
    public void set(int itemNum, Item item);
    public void setItemStateListener(ItemStateListener listener)
    public int size();
}
```

javax.microedition.lcdui.Gauge

This class implements a bar graph, optionally interactive, that displays values intended for use in a form.

```
public class Gauge extends Item {
    // public constructors
    public Gauge(String label, boolean interactive, int max, int initial);
    // public instance methods
    public int getMaxValue();
    public int getValue();
    public boolean isInteractive();
    public void setMaxValue(int maxValue);
    public void setValue(int value);
}
```

javax.microedition.lcdui.Graphics

This class provides a simple two-dimensional geometric rendering capability. It provides drawing primitives for text, images, lines, rectangles, and arcs. Pixel replacement is the only drawing operation provided.

```
public class Graphics {
    // public class fields
    public static final int BASELINE = 64;
    public static final int BOTTOM = 32;
    public static final int DOTTED = 1;
    public static final int HCENTER = 1;
    public static final int LEFT = 4;
    public static final int RIGHT = 8;
    public static final int SOLID = 0;
    public static final int TOP = 16;
    public static final int VCENTER = 2;
    // public instance methods
    public void clipRect(int x, int y, int width, int height);
```

```java
    public void drawArc(int x, int y, int width, int height, int startAngle, int
            arcAngle);
    public void drawChar(char character, int x, int y, int anchor);
    public void drawChars(char[] data, int offset, int length, int x, int y, int
            anchor);
    public void drawImage(Image img, int x, int y, int anchor);
    public void drawLine(int x1, int y1, int x2, int y2);
    public void drawRect(int x, int y, int width, int height);
    public void drawRoundRect(int x, int y, int width, int height, int arcWidth, int
            arcHeight);
    public void drawString(String str, int x, int y, int anchor);
    public void drawSubString(String str, int offset, int len, int x, int y, int
            anchor);
    public void fillArc(int x, int y, int width, int height, int startAngle, int
            arcAngle);
    public void fillRect(int x, int y, int width, int height);
    public void fillRoundRect(int x, int y, int width, int height, int arcWidth, int
            arcHeight);
    public int getBlueComponent();
    public int getClipHeight();
    public int getClipWidth();
    public int getClipX();
    public int getClipY();
    public int getColor();
    public Font getFont();
    public int getGrayScale();
    public int getGreenComponent();
    public int getRedComponent();
    public int getStrokeStyle();
    public int getTranslateX();
    public int getTranslateY();
    public void setClip(int x, int y, int width, int height);
    public void setColor(int RGB);
    public void setColor(int red, int green, int blue);
    public void setFont(Font font);
    public void setGrayScale(int value);
    public void getStrokeStyle(int value);
    public void translate(int style);
}
```

javax.microedition.lcdui.Image

This class is used to hold graphical image data. Images are either *mutable* or *immutable*, depending upon how they are created. Mutable images are created in offscreen memory and immutable images are generally created by loading images from resource bundles, files, or the network.

All the MIDP implementations are required to support images stored in PNG format.

```java
    public class Image {
        // public class methods
        public static Image createImage(byte[] imageData, int imgOffset, int imgLength);
        public static Image createImage(Image source);
```

```
    public static Image createImage(int width, int height);
    public static Image createImage(String name);
    // public instance methods
    public Graphics getGraphics();
    public int getHeight();
    public int getWidth();
    public boolean isMutable();
}
```

javax.microedition.lcdui.ImageItem

This class provides layout control when Image objects are added to a form or to an alert.

```
public class ImageItem extends Item {
    // public class fields
    public static final int LAYOUT_CENTER = 3;
    public static final int LAYOUT_DEFAULT = 0;
    public static final int LAYOUT_LEFT = 1;
    public static final int LAYOUT_NEWLINE_AFTER = 0x100;
    public static final int LAYOUT_NEWLINE_BEFORE = 0x200;
    public static final int LAYOUT_RIGHT = 2;
    // public constructors
    public ImageItem(String label, Image img, int layout, String altText);
    // public instance methods
    public String getAltText();
    public Image getImage();
    public int getLayout();
    public void setAltTest(String text);
    public void setImage(Image img);
    public void setLayout(int layout);
}
```

javax.microedition.lcdui.Item

This abstract class is the base class for any component that can be added to a form or an alert. All item objects have a label field (a string that is attached to the item). Direct subclasses are: ChoiceGroup, DateField, Gauge, ImageItem, StringItem, and TextField.

```
public abstract class Item {
    // public instance methods
    public String getLabel();
    public void setLabel(String label);
}
```

javax.microedition.lcdui.List

This class is a screen containing a list of choices. A user can interact with a list either by traversing from element to element, or by scrolling.

```
public class List extends Screen implements Choice {
    // public class fields
    public static final Command SELECT_COMMAND;
```

```
    // public constructors
    public List(String title, int listType);
    public List(String title, int listType, String[] stringElements, Image[]
        imageElements);
    // public instance methods
    public int append(String stringPart, Image imagePart);
    public void delete(int elementNum);
    public Image getImage(int elementNum);
    public int getSelectedFlags(boolean[] selectedArray);
    public int getSelectedIndex();
    public String getString(int elementNum);
    public void insert(int elementNum, String stringPart, Image imagePart);
    public boolean isSelected(int elementNum);
    public void set(int elementNum, String stringPart, Image imagePart);
    public void setSelectedFlags(boolean[] selectedArray);
    public void setSelectedIndex(int elementNum, boolean selected);
    public int size();
}
```

javax.microedition.lcdui.Screen

This abstract class is the common superclass of all high-level user interface classes. It provides methods to add an optional title and a tickertape to the Displayable class.

```
    public abstract class Screen extends Displayable {
        // public instance methods
        public Ticker getTicker();
        public String getTitle();
        public void setTicker(Ticker ticker);
        public setTitle(String s);
    }
```

javax.microedition.lcdui.StringItem

This class, which extends the Item class, is an item that can contain a string.

```
    public class StringItem extends Item {
        // public constructors
        public StringItem(String label, String text);
        // public instance methods
        public String getText();
        public void setText(String text);
    }
```

javax.microedition.lcdui.TextBox

This class, which extends the Screen class, is a screen that allows the user to enter and edit text. A TextBox object has a title, a default string, a maximum size, and a constraint.

```
    public class TextBox extends Screen {
        // public constructors
        public TextBox(String title, String text, int maxSize, int constraints);
```

```
    // public instance methods
    public void delete(int offset, int length);
    public int getCaretPosition();
    public int getChars(char[] data);
    public int getConstraints();
    public int getMaxSize();
    public String getString();
    public void insert(char[] data, int offset, int length, int position);
    public void insert(String src, int position);
    public void setChars(char[] data, int offset, int length);
    public void setConstraints(int constraints);
    public int setMaxSize(int maxsize);
    public void setString(String text);
    public int size();
}
```

javax.microedition.lcdui.TextField

This class, which extends the Item class, is an editable text component that may be placed into a form. A TextField object has a label, a default string, a maximum size, and some constraints. The constraints, which are shared with TextBox, are:

ANY

> The user is allowed to enter any text.

EMAILADDR

> The user is allowed to enter an email address.

NUMERIC

> The user is allowed to enter only an integer value.

PASSWORD

> The text entered must be masked (replaced with '*'), so that the characters typed are not visible.

PHONENUMBER

> The user is allowed to enter a phone number.

URL

> The user is allowed to enter a URL.

```
    public class TextField extends Item {
        // public class fields
        public static final int ANY = 0
        public static final int CONSTRAINT_MASK = 0xFFFF;
        public static final int EMAILADDR = 1
        public static final int NUMERIC = 2
        public static final int PASSWORD = 0x10000
        public static final int PHONENUMBER = 3
        public static final int URL = 4
        // public constructors
        public TextField(String label, String text, int maxSize, int constraints);
        // public instance methods
        public void delete(int offset, int length);
        public int getCaretPosition();
        public int getChars(char[] data);
```

```
    public int getConstraints();
    public int getMaxSize();
    public String getString();
    public void insert(char[] data, int offset, int length, int position);
    public void insert(String src, int position);
    public void setChars(char[] data, int offset, int length);
    public void setConstraints(int constraints);
    public int setMaxSize(int maxSize);
    public void setString(String text);
    public int size();
}
```

javax.microedition.lcdui.Ticker

This class implements a tickertape, which is a piece of text that runs continuously across the display. The direction and speed of scrolling are determined by the implementation.

```
public class Ticker {
    // public constructors
    public Ticker(String str);
    // public instance methods
    public String getString();
    public void setString(String str);
}
```

APPENDIX F

The javax.microedition.midlet Package

This package defines MIDP applications and the interactions with their environment. It consists of one class and one exception class.

javax.microedition.midlet.MIDlet

This abstract class is the base class of all MIDlet applications. The methods specified in this class allow MIDlet management software to create, start, pause, and destroy a MIDlet. Hence, a MIDlet can be in one of three states: *paused*, *active*, or *destroyed*.

A MIDlet becomes active when the startApp( ) method is called. In this state, the MIDlet may hold resources. To change the MIDlet's state to pause, the pauseApp( ) method is used. The destroyApp( ) method is used to terminate and enter the destroyed state. In the destroyed state, the MIDlet must release all resources and save any persistent data. This method can be called from the active and paused states. If destroyApp( ) is passed true, the MIDlet must clean up and release all resources. If false, the MIDlet *may* throw MIDletStateChangeException, indicating it does not want to be destroyed.

```
public abstract class MIDlet {
    // protected constructors
    protected MIDlet( );
    // protected instance methods
    protected abstract void destroyApp(boolean unconditional) throws
                        MIDletStateChangeException;
    protected abstract void pauseApp( );
    protected abstract void startApp( ) throws MIDletStateChangeException;
    // public instance methods
    public final String getAppProperty(String key);
    public final void notifyDestroyed( );
    public final void notifyPaused( );
    public final void resumeRequest( );
}
```

javax.microedition.midlet.MIDletStateChangeException

This exception is thrown to signal that a request MIDlet state change failed.

```
public class MIDletStateChangeException extends java.lang.Exception {
    // public constructors
    public MIDletStateChangeException( );
    public MIDletStateChangeException(String s);
}
```

APPENDIX G
The javax.microedition.rms Package

This package provides a mechanism for MIDlets to persistently store and retrieve data. This mechanism is modeled after a simple record-oriented database and it is called the Record Management System (RMS). This package consists of four interfaces, one class, and five exception classes.

javax.microedition.rms.RecordComparator

This interface defines several constants and the compare( ) method that can be used to compare two records to check if they match, or what their relative sort order is. A class that needs to compare two candidate records should implement this interface by providing an implementation for the compare( ) method. The constants defined in this interface have the following meaning in terms of sort order:

EQUIVALENT
    The two records are the same but not necessarily identical.

FOLLOWS
    Rec1 follows rec2.

PRECEDES
    Rec1 precedes rec2.

The compare( ) method returns EQUIVALENT if rec1 and rec2 are equivalent in terms of sort order, PRECEDES if rec1 precedes rec2, or FOLLOWS if rec1 follows rec2.

```
public interface RecordComparator {
    // public class fields
    public static final int EQUIVALENT = 0;
    public static final int FOLLOWS = 1;
    public static final int PRECEDES = -1;
    // public instance methods
    public int compare(byte rec1[], byte rec2[]);
}
```

javax.microedition.rms.RecordEnumeration

This interface maintains a sequence of the record IDs of the records in a record store. The enumerator iterates over all the records in an order determined by an optional record comparator. In order to iterate over a subset of the records, a filter can be supplied.

```
public interface RecordEnumeration {
    // public instance methods
    public void destroy() throws IllegalStateException;
    public boolean hasNextElement();
    public boolean hasPreviousElement();
    public boolean isKeptUpdated();
    public void keepUpdated(boolean keepUpdated);
    public byte[] nextRecord() throws InvalidRecordIDException,
            RecordStoreNotOpenException, RecordStoreException;
    public int nextRecordId() InvalidRecordIDException;
    public int numRecords();
    public byte[] previousRecord() throws InvalidRecordIDException,
            RecordStoreNotOpenException, RecordStoreException;
    public int previousRecordId() InvalidRecordIDException;
    public void rebuild();
    public void reset();
}
```

javax.microedition.rms.RecordFilter

This interface defines a filter that examines a record to check if it matches an application-defined criteria. It can be used for searching or subsetting records. The matches() method returns true if the candidate record is selected by the RecordFilter.

```
public interface RecordFilter {
    // public static methods
    boolean public boolean matches(byte candidate[]);
}
```

javax.microedition.rms.RecordListener

This interface provides a listener for receiving record events (such as change, add, delete) from a record store. The recordAdded() method is called when a record has been added to a record store, recordChanged() is called after a record in a store has been changed, and recordDeleted() is called after a record has been deleted from a record store.

```
public interface RecordListener {
    public void recordAdded(RecordStore recordStore, int recordId);
    public void recordChanged(RecordStore recordStore, int recordId);
    public void recordDeleted(RecordStore recordStore, int recordId);
}
```

javax.microedition.rms.RecordStore

This class represents a record store, which is a collection of records that remains persistent across multiple invocations of the MIDlet. To open a new record store, use openRecordStore( ) where the name of the record store is case-sensitive and may consist of any combination of up to 32 Unicode characters. This class provides several self-explanatory methods for adding and deleting records, enumerating through records, and so on.

```
public class RecordStore extends Object {
    // public class methods
    public static void deleteRecordStore(String recordStoreName) throws
                    RecordStoreException, RecordStoreNotFoundException;
    public static String[] listRecordStores( );
    public static RecordStore openRecordStore(String recordStoreName, boolean
                createIfNecessary) throws RecordStoreException,
                RecordStoreFullException, RecordStoreNotFoundException;
    // public instance methods
    public int addRecord(byte data[], int offset, int numBytes) throws
                RecordStoreNotOpenException, RecordStoreException,
                RecordStoreFullException;
    public void addRecordListener(RecordListener listener);
    public void closeRecordStore( ) throws RecordStoreNotOpenException,
                RecordStoreException;
    public void deleteRecord(int recordId) throws RecordStoreNotOpenException,
                InvalidRecordIDException, RecordStoreException;
    public RecordEnumeration enumerateRecords(RecordFilter filter,
                        RecordComparator comparator, boolean keepUpdated)
                        throws RecordStoreNotOpenException;
    public long getLastModified( ) throws RecordStoreNotOpenException;
    public String getName( ) throws RecordStoreNotOpenException;
    public int getNextRecordID( ) throws RecordStoreNotOpenException,
                RecordStoreException;
    public int getNumRecords( ) throws RecordStoreNotOpenException;
    public byte[] getRecord(int recordId) throws RecordStoreNotOpenException,
                InvalidRecordIDException, RecordStoreException;
    public int getRecord(int recordId, byte buffer[], int offset) throws
                RecordStoreNotOpenException, InvalidRecordIDException,
                RecordStoreException;
    public int getRecordSize(int recordId) throws RecordStoreNotOpenException,
                InvalidRecordIDException, RecordStoreException;
    public int getSize( ) throws RecordStoreNotOpenException;
    public int getSizeAvailable( ) throws RecordStoreNotOpenException;
    public int getVersion( ) throws RecordStoreNotOpenException;
    public void removeRecordListener(RecordListener listener);
    public void setRecord(int recordId, byte[] newData, int offset, int numBytes)
                throws RecordStoreNotOpenException, InvalidRecordIDException,
                RecordStoreException, RecordStoreFullException;
}
```

javax.microedition.rms.RecordStoreException

This exception is thrown when a general exception occurred in a record store operation.

```
public class RecordStoreException extends Exception {
    // public constructors
    public RecordStoreException( );
    public RecordStoreException(String message);
}
```

javax.microedition.rms.InvalidRecordIDException

This exception is thrown when an operation could not be completed because the record ID was invalid.

```
public class InvalidRecordIDException extends RecordStoreException {
    // public constructors
    public InvalidRecordIDException( );
    public InvalidRecordIDException(String message);
}
```

javax.microedition.rms.RecordStoreFullException

This exception is thrown when an operation could not be completed because the record store file storage is full.

```
public class RecordStoreFullException extends RecordStoreException {
    // public constructors
    public RecordStoreFullException( );
    public RecordStoreFullException(String message);
}
```

javax.microedition.rms.RecordStoreNotFoundException

This exception is thrown when an operation could not be completed because the record store could not be found.

```
public class RecordStoreNotFoundException extends RecordStoreException {
    // public constructors
    public RecordStoreNotFoundException( );
    public RecordStoreNotFoundException(String message);
}
```

javax.microedition.rms.RecordStoreNotOpenException

This exception is thrown when an operation was attempted on a closed record store.

```
public class RecordStoreNotOpenException extends RecordStoreException {
    // public constructors
    public RecordStoreNotOpenException( );
    public RecordStoreNotOpenException(String message);
}
```

Resources

Additional Resources

All Java specifications are developed using the Java Community Process, which is the program that Sun Microsystems is using for revising existing specifications and developing new ones. The Java Community Process Web site is *http://www.jcp.org*. Each specification is known as a Java Specification Request (JSR) and is assigned a unique number.

Unlike J2SE or J2EE, there is no J2ME specification, per se. All the specifications below comprise the J2ME specification. Note, however, that JSR068 is the next-generation J2ME specification and will introduce building blocks, to make the creation of profiles an easier task.

CLDC Specification (JSR-30)
    http://www.jcp.org/jsr/detail/30.jsp

CLDC Next Generation (JSR-139)
    http://www.jcp.org/jsr/detail/139.jsp

MIDP Specification (JSR-37)
    http://www.jcp.org/jsr/detail/37.jsp

Mobile Information Device Next Generation (JSR-118)
    http://www.jcp.org/jsr/detail/132.jsp

PDA Profile Specification (JSR-75)
    http://www.jcp.org/details/jsr/75.jsp

CDC Specification (JSR-36)
    http://www.jcp.org/jsr/detail/36.jsp

Foundation Profile Specification (JSR-46)
    http://www.jcp.org/jsr/detail/46.jsp

Personal Profile Specification (JSR-62)
    http://www.jcp.org/jsr/detail/62.jsp

RMI Profile Specification (JSR-66)
http://www.jcp.org/jsr/detail/66.jsp

Java Game Profile (JSR-134)
http://www.jcp.org/jsr/detail/134.jsp

J2ME Multimedia API Specification (JSR-135)
http://www.jcp.org/jsr/detaill/135.jsp

J2ME White Papers

KVM
http://java.sun.com/products/cldc/wp

Applications for Mobile Devices
http://java.sun.com/j2me/docs/pdf/midpwp.pdf

J2ME Technologies

J2ME
http://java.sun.com/j2me

CLDC and KVM
http://java.sun.com/products/cldc

MIDP
http://java.sun.com/products/midp

MIDP for Palm OS
http://java.sun.com/

CDC and CVM
http://java.sun.com/products/cdc

J2ME Development Kits

J2ME Wireless Toolkit
http://java.sun.com/products/j2mewtoolkit

Metrowerks CodeWarrior for J2ME
http://www.metrowerks.com/desktop/java

Zucotto WHITEboard SDK
http://www.zucotto.com/whiteboard

RIM BlackBerry Java IDE
http://www.developers.rim.net/handhelds/software/jde

J2ME Developer Resources

Java Developer Connection
   http://developer.java.sun.com/developer

Java Wireless Developer Initiative
   http://java.sun.com/wireless

Wireless Developer Network
   http://www.wirelessdevnet.com

Micro Java Network
   http://www.microjava.com

Java Mobile Community
   http://www.javamobile.org

Java Enabled Phones and PDAs
   http://www.javamobiles.com

KVM World
   http://www.kvmworld.com

KVM-Interest Mailing List Archive
   http://archives.java.sun.com/archives/kvm-interest.html

XML Parsers for J2ME

TinyXML Parser
   http://gibaradunn.srac.org/tiny

NanoXML Parser
   http://nanoxml.sourceforge.net

Index

We'd like to hear your suggestions for improving our indexes. Send email to *index@oreilly.com*.

About the Author

Qusay H. Mahmoud is an independent contractor for Sun Microsystems. He has written several articles for the Java Developer Connection that cover J2ME, including the MIDP and the CLDC APIs. He has also presented tutorials on developing wireless applications at a number of international conferences. He is the author of *Distributed Programming with Java* (Manning Publications).

Colophon

Our look is the result of reader comments, our own experimentation, and feedback from distribution channels. Distinctive covers complement our distinctive approach to technical topics, breathing personality and life into potentially dry subjects.

The animal on the cover of *Learning Wireless Java* is a Senegal galago. Galagos, also called bush babies, are native to forest and bush regions of sub-Saharan Africa, including the island of Zanzibar. Galagos have lightly built bodies with long hind legs for leaping. The flattened tips of their toes are padded with thick skin for gripping tree trunks and branches, and on each of their back feet, the index toe has an extended claw for grasping. Galagos leap from branch to branch, tree to tree, sometimes jumping as far as 15 feet.

The galago has soft, woolly fur, either brown or gray in color. Its face is small and pointy, with large eyes that allow it to see well in the dark. Its large, mobile ears can move either independently or simultaneously. The combination of the galago's huge eyes and mobile ears not only give the animal its trademark quizzical expression, but also aid the nocturnal galago after dark. At night, families of up to 20 galagos defend territories 15 to 20 acres in size. When a predator approaches, the galago emits a rasping shout that sounds much like an excited child. During the day, each family crowds into an enclosed space, such as a hollowed tree trunk, to sleep.

Galagos eat mostly insects, such as grasshoppers, dung beetles, and caterpillars, but they are also quick enough to catch mice, lizards, and small birds. In addition, they eat fruit, seeds, and flowers, sometimes aiding in pollination. In some parts of Africa, the *Galago senegalensis*, or "lesser bush baby," is kept as a pet.

Claire Cloutier was the production editor and copyeditor for *Learning Wireless Java*. Sue Willing was the proofreader. Ann Schirmer and Jeff Holcomb provided quality control. Judy Hoer wrote the index. Edie Shapiro, Derek Di Matteo, and Phil Dangler provided composition assistance.

Ellie Volckhausen designed the cover of this book, based on a series design by Edie Freedman. The cover image is a 19th-century engraving from *The Royal Natural History*. Emma Colby produced the cover layout with QuarkXPress 4.1, using Adobe's ITC Garamond font.

Melanie Wang designed the interior layout, based on a series design by David Futato. Mihaela Maier converted the files from Microsoft Word to FrameMaker 5.5.6, using tools created by Mike Sierra. The text font is Linotype Birka; the heading font is Adobe Myriad Condensed; and the code font is LucasFont's TheSans Mono Condensed. The illustrations that appear in the book were produced by Robert Romano and Jessamyn Read using Macromedia FreeHand 9 and Adobe Photoshop 6. The tip and warning icons were drawn by Christopher Bing. Linley Dolby and Rachel Wheeler wrote this colophon.

Whenever possible, our books use a durable and flexible lay-flat binding.

How to stay in touch with O'Reilly

1. Visit Our Award-Winning Web Site

http://www.oreilly.com/

★ "Top 100 Sites on the Web" —PC Magazine
★ "Top 5% Web sites" —Point Communications
★ "3-Star site" —The McKinley Group

Our web site contains a library of comprehensive product information (including book excerpts and tables of contents), downloadable software, background articles, interviews with technology leaders, links to relevant sites, book cover art, and more. File us in your Bookmarks or Hotlist!

2. Join Our Email Mailing Lists

New Product Releases
To receive automatic email with brief descriptions of all new O'Reilly products as they are released, send email to:
ora-news-subscribe@lists.oreilly.com
Put the following information in the first line of your message (not in the Subject field):
subscribe ora-news

O'Reilly Events
If you'd also like us to send information about trade show events, special promotions, and other O'Reilly events, send email to:
ora-news-subscribe@lists.oreilly.com
Put the following information in the first line of your message (not in the Subject field):
subscribe ora-events

3. Get Examples from Our Books via FTP

There are two ways to access an archive of example files from our books:

Regular FTP
• ftp to:
  ftp.oreilly.com
  (login: anonymous
  password: your email address)
• Point your web browser to:
  ftp://ftp.oreilly.com/

FTPMAIL
• Send an email message to:
  ftpmail@online.oreilly.com
  (Write "help" in the message body)

4. Contact Us via Email

order@oreilly.com
To place a book or software order online. Good for North American and international customers.

subscriptions@oreilly.com
To place an order for any of our newsletters or periodicals.

books@oreilly.com
General questions about any of our books.

cs@oreilly.com
For answers to problems regarding your order or our products.

booktech@oreilly.com
For book content technical questions or corrections.

proposals@oreilly.com
To submit new book or software proposals to our editors and product managers.

international@oreilly.com
For information about our international distributors or translation queries. For a list of our distributors outside of North America check out:
http://www.oreilly.com/distributors.html

5. Work with Us

Check out our website for current employment opportunites:
http://jobs.oreilly.com/

O'Reilly & Associates, Inc.
1005 Gravenstein Hwy North
Sebastopol, CA 95472 USA
TEL   707-829-0515 or 800-998-9938
        (6am to 5pm PST)
FAX   707-829-0104

O'REILLY®

TO ORDER: **800-998-9938** • **order@oreilly.com** • **www.oreilly.com**
ONLINE EDITIONS OF MOST O'REILLY TITLES ARE AVAILABLE BY SUBSCRIPTION AT **safari.oreilly.com**
ALSO AVAILABLE AT MOST RETAIL AND ONLINE BOOKSTORES

International Distributors

http://international.oreilly.com/distributors.html • international@oreilly.com

UK, EUROPE, MIDDLE EAST, AND AFRICA (EXCEPT FRANCE, GERMANY, AUSTRIA, SWITZERLAND, LUXEMBOURG, AND LIECHTENSTEIN)

INQUIRIES
O'Reilly UK Limited
4 Castle Street
Farnham
Surrey, GU9 7HS
United Kingdom
Telephone: 44-1252-711776
Fax: 44-1252-734211
Email: information@oreilly.co.uk

ORDERS
Wiley Distribution Services Ltd.
1 Oldlands Way
Bognor Regis
West Sussex PO22 9SA
United Kingdom
Telephone: 44-1243-843294
UK Freephone: 0800-243207
Fax: 44-1243-843302 (Europe/EU orders)
or 44-1243-843274 (Middle East/Africa)
Email: cs-books@wiley.co.uk

FRANCE

INQUIRIES & ORDERS
Éditions O'Reilly
18 rue Séguier
75006 Paris, France
Tel: 33-1-40-51-71-89
Fax: 33-1-40-51-72-26
Email: france@oreilly.fr

GERMANY, SWITZERLAND, AUSTRIA, LUXEMBOURG, AND LIECHTENSTEIN

INQUIRIES & ORDERS
O'Reilly Verlag
Balthasarstr. 81
D-50670 Köln, Germany
Telephone: 49-221-973160-91
Fax: 49-221-973160-8
Email: anfragen@oreilly.de (inquiries)
Email: order@oreilly.de (orders)

CANADA

(FRENCH LANGUAGE BOOKS)
Les Éditions Flammarion ltée
375, Avenue Laurier Ouest
Montréal (Québec) H2V 2K3
Tel: 1-514-277-8807
Fax: 1-514-278-2085
Email: info@flammarion.qc.ca

HONG KONG

City Discount Subscription Service, Ltd.
Unit A, 6th Floor, Yan's Tower
27 Wong Chuk Hang Road
Aberdeen, Hong Kong
Tel: 852-2580-3539
Fax: 852-2580-6463
Email: citydis@ppn.com.hk

KOREA

Hanbit Media, Inc.
Chungmu Bldg. 210
Yonnam-dong 568-33
Mapo-gu
Seoul, Korea
Tel: 822-325-0397
Fax: 822-325-9697
Email: hant93@chollian.dacom.co.kr

PHILIPPINES

Global Publishing
G/F Benavides Garden
1186 Benavides Street
Manila, Philippines
Tel: 632-254-8949/632-252-2582
Fax: 632-734-5060/632-252-2733
Email: globalp@pacific.net.ph

TAIWAN

O'Reilly Taiwan
1st Floor, No. 21, Lane 295
Section 1, Fu-Shing South Road
Taipei, 106 Taiwan
Tel: 886-2-27099669
Fax: 886-2-27038802
Email: mori@oreilly.com

INDIA

Shroff Publishers & Distributors Pvt. Ltd.
12, "Roseland", 2nd Floor
180, Waterfield Road, Bandra (West)
Mumbai 400 050
Tel: 91-22-641-1800/643-9910
Fax: 91-22-643-2422
Email: spd@vsnl.com

CHINA

O'Reilly Beijing
SIGMA Building, Suite B809
No. 49 Zhichun Road
Haidian District
Beijing, China PR 100080
Tel: 86-10-8809-7475
Fax: 86-10-8809-7463
Email: beijing@oreilly.com

JAPAN

O'Reilly Japan, Inc.
Yotsuya Y's Building
7 Banch 6, Honshio-cho
Shinjuku-ku
Tokyo 160-0003 Japan
Tel: 81-3-3356-5227
Fax: 81-3-3356-5261
Email: japan@oreilly.com

SINGAPORE, INDONESIA, MALAYSIA, AND THAILAND

TransQuest Publishers Pte Ltd
30 Old Toh Tuck Road #05-02
Sembawang Kimtrans Logistics Centre
Singapore 597654
Tel: 65-4623112
Fax: 65-4625761
Email: wendiw@transquest.com.sg

AUSTRALIA

Woodslane Pty., Ltd.
7/5 Vuko Place
Warriewood NSW 2102
Australia
Tel: 61-2-9970-5111
Fax: 61-2-9970-5002
Email: info@woodslane.com.au

NEW ZEALAND

Woodslane New Zealand, Ltd.
21 Cooks Street (P.O. Box 575)
Waganui, New Zealand
Tel: 64-6-347-6543
Fax: 64-6-345-4840
Email: info@woodslane.com.au

ARGENTINA

Distribuidora Cuspide
Suipacha 764
1008 Buenos Aires
Argentina
Phone: 54-11-4322-8868
Fax: 54-11-4322-3456
Email: libros@cuspide.com

ALL OTHER COUNTRIES

O'Reilly & Associates, Inc.
1005 Gravenstein Hwy North
Sebastopol, CA 95472 USA
Tel: 707-829-0515
Fax: 707-829-0104
Email: order@oreilly.com

O'REILLY®

TO ORDER: **800-998-9938** • *order@oreilly.com* • *www.oreilly.com*
ONLINE EDITIONS OF MOST O'REILLY TITLES ARE AVAILABLE BY SUBSCRIPTION AT **safari.oreilly.com**
ALSO AVAILABLE AT MOST RETAIL AND ONLINE BOOKSTORES